INTERNATIONAL SOCIALISM ★

A quarterly journal of socialist theory

Winter 1992
Contents

Issue 57 of INTERNATIONAL SOCIALISM, quarterly journal of the Socialist Workers Party (Britain)

Published November 1992
Copyright © International Socialism
Distribution/subscriptions: International Socialism,
PO Box 82, London E3.
American distribution: B de Boer, 113 East Center St, Nutley,
New Jersey 07110.
Subscriptions and back copies: PO Box 16085, Chicago
Illinois 60616
Editorial and production: 071-538 1626/071-538 3307
Sales and subscriptions: 071-538 5821
American sales: 312 666 7337

ISBN 0-906224-77-2

Printed by BPCC Wheatons Ltd, Exeter, England
Typeset by East End Offset, London E3

Cover design by Ian Goodyer

For details of back copies see the end pages of this book

Subscription rates for one year (four issues) are:

Britain and overseas (surface):	individual	£12.00 ($25)
	institutional	£20.00
Air speeded supplement:	North America	nil
	Europe/South America	£1.00
	elsewhere	£2.00

Note to contributors
The deadline for articles intended for issue 58 of
International Socialism is 1 January 1993

All contributions should be double-spaced with wide margins.
Please submit two copies. If you write your contribution
using a computer, please also supply a disk, together with
details of the computer and programme used.

INTERNATIONAL
SOCIALISM ★
A quarterly journal of socialist theory

BRITAIN'S TORY government and the capitalist system that it represents have plummeted from the easy certainties of the 1980s' boom into the worst slump since the 1930s. Social deprivation stares out from every street corner. The talismans of Thatcher's reign—the police, the courts and the monarchy—have rarely fallen so low in public esteem.

Yet the left and the organised working class still seems mired in its own crisis following the failures of Labourism and Stalinism. Can the working class movement recover? And, even if it does, how near will we be to fundamental change in Britain? Lindsey German challenges the pessimism of the left and recovers the genuine Marxist theory of revolution in a hard headed look at the prospects for revolution in Britain.

COLUMBUS REMAINS as controversial now as when he discovered the Americas 500 years ago. Mike Gonzalez uncovers the myths of Columbus, myths which were first formulated in the years immediately after his voyages and which have been perpetuated down to our own time. Mike Haynes looks at Columbus from another angle, tracing the effect of the discovery of the Americas on the development of European capitalism. Together these articles strike a decisive blow to the apologists for imperialism and propose a critique of Third Worldist and Green commentators who see the indigenous societies of Latin America as a model for change today.

PAUL FOOT'S 'Poetry and Revolution' examines the impact of political change on poetry from Milton and the English Revolution to contemporary Irish poetry with the help of interviews with Terry Eagleton, Tom Paullin, Christopher Hill, Marilyn Butler and Tony Harrison.

ALEX CALLINICOS replies to Ernest Mandel's article printed in our previous issue.

Editor: John Rees, Assistant Editors: Alex Callinicos, Sue Clegg, Chris Harman, John Molyneux, Lindsey German, Pete Green, Costas Lapavitsas, Colin Sparks, Mike Gonzalez, Peter Morgan, Ruth Brown, Mike Haynes and Rob Hoveman.

Can there be a revolution in Britain?

LINDSEY GERMAN

Revolution in Britain, or any advanced capitalist country, seems a pipedream. These societies appear too stable, their working classes too wedded to peaceful reform, ever to change. Those who espouse openly revolutionary politics are either regarded as outdated or utopian, not least by former left wingers. They argue that the centre of Marx's theory of revolution, the working class, is supposedly a dwindling force, its political parties and trade unions on the wane. State owner-ship and state 'socialism' have been discredited, and the best that we can hope for is the market with a human face. In Britain, the humiliat-ing defeat of Labour in the 1992 election, despite recession, unemploy-ment and dissatisfaction with the government only seems to underline the view that even reform is too much to hope for.

This situation presents a paradox: in many ways objective prospects for revolution internationally are better than they have been for decades. The settlement arrived at after the Second World War, based on an equilibrium created by the two superpowers and their respective blocs, has broken down, and we live in a world of increasing turmoil and uncertainty. The collapse of the USSR has produced a massive and still unresolved crisis within its own borders. Throughout eastern Europe the states once under Russia's influence are all also in crisis; Czechoslovakia is on the point of divorce and the Balkans have been plunged into war. The advanced Western states have escaped this degree of upheaval so far, but have been hit by severe recession matched by increasing political instability.

Disillusion with the effects of the market has increased markedly in the US, Britain and the other advanced capitalisms. No wonder at a recent G7 summit, France's President Mitterrand described the mood of the world leaders as 'morose', reflecting a 'loss of faith' among the advanced countries' populations.[1] The riots in Los Angeles and the recent public sector strikes in Germany both in their different ways reflect this disillusion. And the huge crisis developing in Europe round ratification of the Maastricht Treaty and the crisis of the ERM is likely to presage further instability. But nowhere has the discontent yet turned into the sort of challenge to governments and rulers which could begin to significantly alter the balance of class forces. So far the degree of ruling class crisis has not been translated into working class gains. It would be a mistake, however, to believe that the present situation will continue for very long. The dramatic changes taking place around the world open up even the most apparently stable societies to social upheaval of the sort that we have already seen in eastern Europe, and which can develop elsewhere.

Changed circumstances in turn can expose large numbers of workers to new ideas. Most of the time any shift in the dominant ideology seems unlikely if not impossible. Many socialists felt this throughout the 1980s, when the ideas of 'Thatcherism' permeated the consciousness of large numbers of workers, and when the ideologues of *Marxism Today* assured us that these were permanent and unshifting attitudes, reflecting an individualistic and materialistic working class which would no longer embrace collective values. This view was encapsulated by an influential article by Charlie Leadbeter written shortly after the 1987 election, when the Lawson boom was still at its height; astonishingly despite the events of the intervening five years, such views are still widely held on the left:

> [The] *affluent working class has been the agent of enormous social change in Britain over the last few years. It has been at large in the ranks of share buyers and homebuyers. It has wrought social change through Ford Escort convertibles and compact discs rather than the dour task of revolutionary struggle. Why vote for a politics with traces of the latter when you can have the former?*[2]

This was typical of an analysis which mistook the superficial attitudes of some workers for fundamental changes in the ideology of the working class as a whole, but it is also typical of the deep pessimism which pervades much of the left in periods of history when it seems that nothing will change and that the mass of workers will never fight. This has been true throughout the history of the working class. Yet even long periods where the vast majority of workers are quite committed to and satisfied with the existing system do end, often very suddenly. It then seems incredible, at least for a time, that anyone believed the stability would endure.

So, for example, in Britain the decades from the defeat of Chartism and the European revolutions of 1848 right through to the 1880s were ones of relative social calm. Most workers had no union organisation. Even the best organised supported the Liberals rather than any sort of workers' party. It was only with the development of small socialist organisations in the 1880s and then the growth of the new unions of unskilled workers from 1888 (often led by socialists) that the possibility of even mass, class-based action really arose. Again in the US and Britain from the 1940s to the 1960s, emerging victorious from the Second World War and experiencing the longest boom in world history, a period of rising prosperity led to social peace. Japan and Germany experienced similar sorts of political stability during the 1970s and 1980s based on rapid economic growth. During such periods, capitalism seems able to offer real material advance and security for the bulk of its inhabitants. Consequently the political adherence of the mass of workers is to, at best, a reformed version of this system, since it appears that higher living standards, shorter hours and more welfare can all be established without any sort of dramatic struggle. These times therefore foster the development of sets of ideologies which bind the exploited to their exploiters. This was true of Britain during the latter half of the 19th century[3] so much so that in 1889 Engels wrote of the country:

> The most repulsive thing here is the bourgeois 'respectability' which has grown deep into the bones of the workers. The division of society into innumerable strata, each recognised without question, each with its own pride but also its inborn respect for its 'betters' and 'superiors', is so old and firmly established that the bourgeois still find it fairly easy to get their bait accepted.[4]

A few years earlier he had written in similar vein:

> You ask me what the English workers think about colonial policy. Well, exactly the same as they think about politics in general: the same as the bourgeois think. There is no workers' party here, you see, there are only Conservatives and Liberal-Radicals, and the workers gaily share the feast of England's monopoly of the world market and the colonies.[5]

Yet by the end of the 1880s the working class had erupted into the mass strikes around new unions of the unskilled. Relationships which seemed fixed, hierarchical and conservative were suddenly transformed as the old ideas clashed with the new ones developing from struggle. Out of these strikes developed a new working class party, the Labour Party, and further social upheaval and crisis continued until put into temporary abeyance by the First World War.

Typically, the long periods of calm, social peace and low class struggle have tended to end like this, with massive explosions of discontent, as the system begins to break down. When capitalism cannot deliver as much, or not in the way that it had done previously, the old ideas also begin to crumble. Then, often quite suddenly, the old order begins to look shaky and tenuous. Those who believed that the system would continue expanding for ever now search desperately for explanations. The class divisions which had appeared to recede are once more to the fore. The future is approached with uncertainty and fear. So, just as today it is the 'commonsense' of society that revolution will never happen, at other points in history the commonsense has been to see them as inevitable.

The 1920s and 1930s internationally were marked by crises, revolutions, slump and the rise of fascism. Far from revolution seeming a distant possibility, it had actually succeeded in Russia and exploded in countries as far apart as China and Germany. In the years immediately after the First World War there were revolutionary upheavals in Finland, Germany, Italy and Hungary. Revolution was only finally defeated in Germany by the advent of Hitler in 1933. Throughout the 1930s revolution or at least violent upheaval seemed a strong likelihood in many of the major capitalist powers, especially in France and Spain. In the late 1960s and early 1970s, the rise in political and industrial struggle pushed countries such as the US, France, Italy and Britain into turmoil, so much so that revolution seemed at least on the agenda in these countries.

Today it is common even on the left to see revolution as belonging to the past, not a possibility for the future. Yet even in the lifetimes of most people active in politics today, social change has been far from smooth, gradual or piecemeal. Societies and groups within them which seemed unchanging and stable have been replaced and toppled; in many instances it was at least potentially possible for events to have gone further. The 1990s looks likely to raise the spectre of revolution in many parts of the world, as the ruling classes grapple with but fail to solve their problems. The key for socialists therefore is to try to understand the process of revolution; the contradictions in society from which the need and the impetus for revolution arises and the importance of the various subjective factors of class consciousness and organisation which can enhance or hinder the revolutionary mood. We also need to appreciate what makes the long periods of calm come to an end. Why does the system break down at certain times and—perhaps even more importantly—what puts it back together again? The theory of revolution developed by Marx and Engels remains essential to understanding these questions.

The Marxist theory of revolution

Marx and Engels were both touched directly by revolution: their active involvement in the German revolution of 1848 led to their life long political exile in England and confirmed their view that history was shaped by class struggle. As Lenin wrote of them:

> the period of their participation in the mass revolutionary struggle of 1848-1849 stands out as the central point. This was their point of departure when determining the future pattern of the workers' movement and democracy in different countries. It was to this point that they always returned in order to determine the essential nature of the different classes and their tendencies in the most striking and purest form. It was from the standpoint of the revolutionary period of that time that they always judged the later, lesser, political formations and organisations, political aims and political conflicts.[6]

Their theory is usually regarded by both favourable and hostile commentators as about workers' revolution; in reality it is about the whole process of revolution and incorporates the condensed experience of 1848 in attempting to understand how revolutions happen, how they affect all classes and what are the limitations and possibilities of the struggles and activity of each class. In Marx and Engels' view revolution is seen as much more than an immediate overthrow of existing social relations. Rather it is a process which can and often does stretch over years rather than weeks or months, a prolonged period of crisis where no fundamental questions are resolved and where society therefore erupts quite suddenly. Struggles move backwards and forwards, confidence ebbs and flows, and sometimes the social crisis seems hidden for long periods of time before it once again moves into the open, a movement which is marked by explosions which allow a qualitative move forward.

This was true of the great bourgeois revolutions in 17th century England, 18th century France and of the American revolution which began in 1776. In the turmoil brought about by the revolutionary process, the whole of society is thrown into crisis: so the crop failures and famines of the mid-1840s and the economic slump of 1847 which heralded the 1848 revolutions were felt most bitterly by the very poorest but affected all classes, driving some to starvation and others to financial ruin. Such events allowed revolutionary ideas to take hold.

The revolutions which swept Europe in 1848 involved workers and poor peasants, but they were primarily bourgeois, not workers' revolutions—attempts by the emerging capitalist class to overthrow the old order. The bourgeoisie was a revolutionary class in its struggle for power, but the more the working class emerged as an independent social force in countries such as France (which had already overthrown absolutism half a century earlier) and Germany the more the bourgeoisie feared any upheaval which might threaten its property, and so the more cowardly and timid it became.[7]

At first the 1848 revolutions produced unity across the classes—a feature of most revolutions before and since. When Marx describes the composition of the Provisional Government established after the February 1848 revolution in France as 'a compromise between the various classes who together overthrew the July monarchy' or when he describes the poet Lamartine as representing the revolution itself 'with its illusions, its poetry, its imaginary content and its phrases'[8] he could have been describing Vaclav Havel's role in the Czech revolution of 1989, or Portugal's 'revolution of the flowers' which overthrew the dictatorship in 1974. Rapidly, however, the class divisions become more apparent, a point that Engels highlighted:

> But it is the fate of all revolutions that this union of different classes, which in some degree is always the necessary condition of any revolution, can not subsist long. No sooner is the victory gained against the common enemy, than the victors become divided among themselves into different camps and turn their weapons against each other. It is this rapid and passionate development of class antagonism which, in old and complicated social organisms, makes a revolution such a powerful agent of social and political progress; it is this incessantly quick upshooting of new parties succeeding each other in power which, during these violent commotions, makes a nation pass in five years over more ground than it would have done in a century under ordinary circumstances.[9]

But neither Marx nor Engels regarded the class divisions and antagonisms which emerged as necessarily disadvantageous to workers; rather they saw that capitalist class interests would clearly emerge in contradiction to those of workers, and that the mass of the classes in between would be pulled in one direction or another. Although many of these classes might initially and instinctively be conservative rather than revolutionary the pressure of events could effect a massive change in their consciousness, leading them towards radical or socialist ideas and forcing them into alliance with workers. Marx made this point time and again in *The Class Struggles in France*, written after 1848, when he described how sections of the French peasantry moved towards socialism, echoing Engels' point about the speed with which ideas changed:

> *The peasant's claim to property is the talisman with which capital has hith-erto held him under its spell, the pretext on which it set him against the in-dustrial proletariat. Only the fall of capital can raise the peasant, only an anti-capitalist, proletarian government can break his economic poverty and social degradation...This is the way the socialists spoke in pamphlets, al-manacs, calendars and leaflets of all kinds. This language became more comprehensible to the peasant as a result of the counter-publications of the party of Order, which also addressed him and, striking the true peasant tone with their crude exaggeration and brutal interpretation and represen-tation of the intentions and ideas of the socialists, over-stimulated his lust for forbidden fruit. But most comprehensible of all was the language of the actual experience which the peasant had gained from the use of the fran-chise and the disappointments which had overwhelmed him, blow upon blow, with revolutionary speed.* **Revolutions are the locomotives of history**.[10]

Revolution involved all the oppressed and exploited classes rising up and joining together to fight their oppressor. But in every case the working class had to take the leading role in this alliance if it was to be successful in overthrowing society. Why was this? Even before the 1848 revolutions, Marx and Engels had set out their theory in *The Communist Manifesto*, where they argued that the development of modern industry and the market destroyed old forms of society and cre-ated the modern urban working class, turning peasants, artisans and sections of the middle classes into wage labourers. The class which is the source of wealth for the capitalist, the working class, also possesses the power to collectively overthrow this exploitative system and create the basis for socialism. Capitalist development proletarianises ever larger sections of the population, worsening their conditions of work, since the use of machinery leads to speed up, increased productivity, shift work and the like, while wages remain static or decrease relative to the total wealth of society. Such conditions lead workers towards or-ganising themselves as a class, the 'movement of the immense major-ity' which has to overthrow capitalist society if its interests as a class are to triumph.[11] The working class is the only class which can success-fully carry through the revolution, precisely because it is the only one with the cohesion and organisation to do so. Initially, of course, the working class is atomised and overcomes this atomisation only through the course of struggle when it comes together collectively to achieve even the most basic aims; it is thus a collective and a *potentially* revo-lutionary class.

For the working class to liberate itself, rather than force partial changes in the system, it has ultimately to pose its interests *separately* from other classes. Revolution to be successful therefore has to be working class revolution. But it also has to draw in all the other oppressed groups in society. These groups, who by no means see their aim as collective struggle, can be forced by the level of crisis to look to workers and to socialist ideas for relief. Lenin developed Marx and Engels' ideas when he spelled out conditions for revolution in 1920:

> *For a revolution to take place it is not enough for the exploited and oppressed masses to realise the impossibility of living in the old way, and demand changes; for a revolution to take place it is essential that the exploiters should not be able to live and rule in the old way. It is only when the **'lower classes' do not want** to live in the old way and the 'upper classes' **cannot carry on in the old way** that the revolution can triumph. This truth can be expressed in other words: revolution is impossible without a nationwide crisis (affecting both the exploited and the exploiters). It follows that, for a revolution to take place, it is essential, first, that a majority of the workers (or at least a majority of the class-conscious, thinking, and politically active workers) should fully realise that revolution is necessary, and that they should be prepared to die for it; second, that the ruling classes should be going through a governmental crisis, which draws even the most backward masses into politics (symptomatic of any genuine revolution is a rapid, tenfold and even hundredfold increase in the size of the working and oppressed masses—hitherto apathetic—who are capable of waging the political struggle), weakens the government, and makes it possible for the revolutionaries to rapidly overthrow it.*[12]

Here Lenin brings into the picture the whole of society, not just the key protagonists of the two major contending classes; the aim is human emancipation, but with the working class playing a leading role in the process. The potential for social crisis which Lenin points to exists long before the working class arrives centre stage. When society begins to break down, we see the previously passive or apathetic mass of workers and oppressed move into activity on the one hand; on the other, the crisis spreads through the intermediate classes who most of the time play a central role as the ideological glue of the whole system. This was perhaps most clearly true of the impact of the 1930s slump on the middle classes in countries like the US and Germany, where groups like farmers and shop keepers were driven to economic ruin.[13] But there is, of course, no single trigger for such a crisis: it can come from government crises, failed imperialist ventures, wars, slumps, plus the impact of struggle from below.[14]

The extent to which such crises change the ideas of these groupings is important in understanding the nature of bourgeois hegemony as a period moves from relative social calm to upheaval. It is true that such hegemony is strengthened by the allegiance of the various intermediate groups in society, but once their allegiance disappears, such hegemony looks decidedly shaky and is not the stable, seemingly permanent feature that it once appeared.

There is no automatic relationship between economic and ideological crisis and a high level of class struggle, in fact there are many instances where the working class remains quiescent. But when crises arise then even a fairly low level of working class struggle can suddenly transform the situation: 'the whole of society quivers when the working class stirs; when a substantial sector of it undertakes a large scale battle, the authorities react as to civil war'. [15]

Events in the earlier part of this century have tended to vindicate this theory: the collapse of the old European empires after 1918, given impetus by the Russian revolution a year earlier, led to revolutions throughout Europe which demonstrated the need for working class leadership, the possibility of winning the peasantry and other classes to such a strategy and the disastrous consequences of failure to put the working class at the centre of any revolutionary change.[16] We are entering today into a crisis which in many ways mirrors that of the interwar years: intractable economic crisis—perhaps even more intractable than the 1930s—and political and ideological turmoil. How then does Marx's theory of revolution measure up today?

The disappearing working class?

The power and revolutionary potential of the working class, at the centre of the above analysis, is today regarded as a thing of the past. It is widely accepted that the working class is smaller or less powerful than in Marx's time, although this is untrue: in 1848 the working class existed only in Britain, Belgium, parts of France and in the north eastern states of the US. By far the biggest class in Europe was the peasantry, and this remained the case in most countries well into the 20th century. The working class today is, by any definition, much larger and with a greater social weight than its 19th century counterpart.

The current argument all too often takes the form that, regardless of the size of the working class, most workers in the advanced capitalist countries are too prosperous to aspire to revolution; it has become common to view British society as being two-thirds prosperous/one-third under privileged. Peter Jenkins, supporter of the now defunct Social Democratic Party, explained the underpinning of Margaret

Thatcher's electoral success in precisely these terms.[17] He argued that key sections of workers identified with the middle classes through income levels and through ideological conservatism; those less fortunate formed a sort of underclass. So the working class was split down the middle, separated into an increasingly better off white collar and skilled manual section, which has material and political interests akin to the middle classes, and an underclass which is poor, deprived and unable to help itself.

There are material reasons why this theory has become popular with a whole range of sociologists, politicians and commentators: throughout the 1980s the situation of the poorest deteriorated in Britain,[18] with much more obvious levels of homelessness and begging. In Britain in 1989 over 400,000 people were officially classified as homeless, another 120,000 were living in temporary bed and breakfast accommodation and another 180,000 were estimated in 1986 to be the 'hidden' young single homeless. Many thousands more lived in substandard or overcrowded accommodation.[19] The grim reality illustrated by these figures helped to fuel the popular assumption of an underclass cut off from the bulk of the working class. The theory of the underclass is now so widespread that all rioters, those begging or sleeping rough, immigrant workers and all those living on benefits are included in this category by government ministers, the media and many experts. John Kenneth Galbraith talks in a recent book about the gulf between the 'contented majority' and the underclass.[20]

How do these arguments correspond with reality? Firstly, there is no massive army of the unemployed which is permanently unemployable, parasitic on society, living off benefits and so on—although this is a central notion of the underclass theorists. Particular estates or districts are heavy unemployment blackspots and recent rises in unemployment, lack of proper training for school leavers and the growth of rioting have all fuelled the notion of a growing discontented pool of unemployed, including many young people who have never worked and have no job prospects. But the picture is much more complicated than that, as the employment figures for 1990 show. By far the largest numbers of young men claiming benefit had been unemployed for a year or less. So of 16-19 year olds, 48.3 percent had been out of work up to 13 weeks, with another 42.7 percent between 13 weeks and a year. The number of young long-term claimants slumped dramatically after that, with 7.3 percent unemployed between one and two years, and 1.1 percent between two and three years. For 20-24 year olds, the figures rose to 13.9 percent between one and two years, and nearly 10 percent longer than that.

The real bulk of long-term unemployed was among older men, where 22.1 percent of 35-49 year old claimants and 38.2 percent of those between 50 and 59 years old had been unemployed for over three years.[21] The possibilities of these men gaining any sort of reasonable employment are extremely limited. But they are very often former trade unionists with many years' experience of work and they cannot be considered as outside the working class but as a section of it which is surplus to the requirements of the capitalist class. They are part, too, of a general trend towards an increase in the workforce between the ages of 35 and 59 and of a decrease in the age groups before and after these years.

Put simply, workers are entering work later (through higher education, staying longer at school, entering full time work after childbirth and childcare) and are leaving it earlier (through early retirement and voluntary redundancy).[22] This in turn has led to a greater proliferation of part time, temporary and flexible jobs, which do not in themselves represent the growth of an underclass, but of an increasing definition of occupation by age. As Harry Braverman wrote nearly 20 years ago, the long term tendency in capitalist society towards every individual being defined in terms of the market throws more people, not fewer, onto the labour market—including the pensioners and students we see working in Tesco.[23] In the 1980s there was a proliferation of such jobs but it is a mistake to see them as divorced from the main workforce or as in some way peripheral. Many part time workers have the same sort of stability of employment as full time workers; they are often less flexible and more stable than many groups of full time workers.[24] And even the large supermarkets which employ so many supposedly peripheral workers are increasingly keen on a level of skills, corporate identity and long term commitment to the firm.[25]

The common view of the underclass as parasitic—living off benefits and therefore off the taxes of the 'two-thirds'—is completely untrue: large sections of the 'underclass' are workers by any definition. Galbraith makes the point when he argues that today US capitalism simply would not work without a massive 'underclass'.[26] As he points out, the 'underclass' is not a disparate group of people living on benefits but an essential group of workers within the capitalist economy:

> the underclass is integrally a part of a larger economic process and more importantly...it serves the living standard and the comfort of the more favoured community. Economic progress would be far more uncertain and certainly far less rapid without it. The economically fortunate....are heavily dependent on its presence.[27]

A similar point was made by Marx when he talked about the gangs of labourers who hung around in port cities looking for work in the 19th century; they were casual workers, with uncertain incomes who often lived in great poverty, but they were an essential part of the working class.[28]

Even those not working at any particular time are mainly workers who for a specific and often short term reason are outside the labour market. Single mothers on benefits are usually workers who cannot enter the labour market because of the lack of childcare, and the vast majority will return to paid employment when their children are older. Pensioners are permanently surplus to the capitalists' labour requirements, hence the very low level of pensions and the unemployed are those who are either temporarily or permanently surplus to the labour requirements of the capitalist class. Immigrant workers suffer poor conditions and lack of union organisation because of their position but even the least organised and sometimes illegal immigrants can see themselves as part of a working class which has to fight collectively.[29]

The working class is not homogeneous. There are divisions within it. Income and lifestyle differences can be quite substantial but while it is true that those workers on higher wages will be earning something around four times that paid to those who exist on benefits (although it should be remembered that a large majority of workers are below the 'average' wage),[30] compared with a recent survey of executives' pay which showed that the average *perks* of executives in British companies (bonuses, company cars and pensions) added up to over £22,000 a year —far more than the average industrial wage—this differential pales into insignificance. The gap between workers and executives is actually much greater (in the same survey executives' basic average pay was £57,359 a year) than the differentials which exist within the working class. Even the lowest paid managers in this survey earned £27,578 basic, £36,409 with perks.[31] And a recent *Labour Research* survey found 462 executives who earned at least £250,000 a year.[32] A recent Low Pay Unit analysis of government employment statistics shows that nearly 10 million employees, or two-fifths of the adult workforce, earn 'less than the Council of Europe's "decency threshold" of £207.13 per week or £5.52 per hour. The threshold is 68 percent of full time average earnings'.[33] These figures hardly demonstrate a two-thirds/one-third society, but rather one where one-third are prosperous, two-thirds poor.[34]

There are also major differences between the classes when we look at the rise of earnings in the 1980s. Of the lowest decile (which contains a considerable number of workers), the percentage rise after housing costs were taken into account between 1981 and 1987 was only 2.3 percent. For the top decile (which will contain no workers), the rise was

13 percent.[35] Although real wages rose in the 1980s, they did not do so anyhere near as fast as management salaries.[36]

The bulk of the wealth produced stays with those already best off. Of a Gross National Product in Britain in 1988 of $12,810 per head, the lowest 40 percent of households—including a large section of the working class—had only $4,820, an income share of only 17.3 percent. The richest fifth was 6.8 percent richer than the poorest fifth.[37] In addition, levels of poverty have risen quite considerably:

> *The extent of poverty declined during the 1960s and the early 1970s but it started to rise again during the late 1970s and far more sharply during the early 1980s so that by 1987 it was higher than it was at the beginning of the 1970s. In brief, any progress made in the 1960s has all but been wiped out during the 1980s. Thus despite the rise in economic affluence in the country, the portion of the population in the most stringent poverty as well in other degrees of severe poverty has fluctuated but it has not declined. In fact it has risen sharply during the 1980s.[38]*

While divisions and sectionalism exist inside the working class there is no basic separation between workers in work and those out of work, or those with homes or without them; indeed, the impact of government policies has been to dramatically increase homelessness and unemployment among the 'respectable' working class. There can be few workers in Britain in 1992 who feel that their job is safe in the long term, or who do not have a housing problem (mortgage debt, overcrowding, inadequate council accommodation or homelessness) among their immediate family. It is therefore quite wrong to see 'affluent workers' and the 'underclass' as two separate groups, as Leadbeter does, living 'in two different worlds. The more entrenched the affluent working class becomes in its world the less recognisable become the disenfranchised as members of the same community'.[39] Many of the workers most associated in recent decades with relative prosperity have seen their wages and conditions under direct attack: print workers, dockers, building workers and others who seemed to be doing well out of the mid-1980s boom have seen the levels of wages in their industries fall, often quite dramatically. This has been coupled with a massive reduction in the numbers employed in their industries. 'Affluent' workers are wracked with insecurity; for many of them, the huge increase in personal debt during the 1980s was the main reason for increased living standards—the 'debt hangover' caused by high mortgage and other credit repayments has led to, at least, the perception of worsening living standards. The newly redundant BAe, Ford or IBM workers in the south of

England will have been especially hard hit already by high debt repayments. Many will now be plunged into real poverty.

Working class divisions are in any case not enough to prevent common struggle, as we can see historically. In the late 19th century in the Trafalgar Square riot of 1887 the unemployed of London who rebelled were not hermetically sealed from the wave of industrial unrest and unionisation which began in London a year later.[40] The riots of unemployed workers in Liverpool and elsewhere in the early 1930s similarly paved the way for the industrial struggles in the new industries later in that decade.[41] The poll tax riot of 1990 was not separate from the working class, but part of it—and remarkably well received by those workers who did not participate in it.

But, it will be argued, there have been such huge changes in the working class that even if there is no underclass there are still far fewer manual workers, far less manufacturing workers, less militant workers such as dockers or miners. Doesn't this destroy the traditional base for socialism and working class organisation? The problem here is that any analysis of class has to take into account the continual changes within capitalism and so the constant recomposition of the working class. It is impossible to define the working class statically, on the basis of how it exists at a single moment of time. On any such model a contemporary working class which departs from the picture of the working class as it was, for example in the 1930s, must show a decline. But in reality we can only regard the working class as declining if we take an extremely narrow (and male dominated) view of the working class which has been out of date now for nearly half a century, by excluding white collar workers from any definition of the working class, or consigning them to such a privileged position within it that they cannot be won to a collective fight. This is what Eric Hobsbawm's 1978 essay *The Forward March of Labour Halted?* did when it explicitly tied the decline of the labour movement to the decline of the manual working class during this century, and argued that white collar workers are a new form of 'aristocracy of labour' which identifies with the middle class.[42]

The decline of manual workers and the growth of white collar workers has been one of the main features of the labour force since the interwar years. It is not a specific feature of Thatcherism, post-Fordism or any of the other theories which supposedly herald the end of the working class, but is a trend which has continued over decades through periods of high class struggle as well as years of low struggle. Recent figures number manual workers at 10.7 million and non-manual at 14.4 million.[43] This is still a very high number of manual workers in absolute terms, even if we were to disregard white collar workers. But it would be quite wrong to do so, for alongside the growth of non-manual workers has developed a *proletarianisation* of white collar work, as it has changed from a minority occupation mainly of the middle classes at the beginning of the 20th century to being subject to productivity increases, the massive introduction of machinery, the imposition of strict time controls, including the time clock, and even the introduction of uniforms (in areas such as banking and finance). The bulk of low grade white collar workers work in similar sorts of jobs and conditions as manual workers traditionally have done. So the clerical worker who operates a sophisticated photocopier in a big office is classified as white collar, but there is very little difference between this job and sorts of simple printing which are designated manual. The shift in advanced capitalist economies from blue collar to white collar and from manufacturing to services has not been a shift which has resulted in a shrinkage of the working class but in its expansion—crucially through pulling millions of women into the paid workforce. White collar workers are typically the daughters, wives and mothers of manual workers.[44]

Of course, not all white collar workers can be defined as working class. Some—bosses of big companies and the like—comprise part of the ruling class, essentially controlling capital, even if not always directly owning it. A much bigger section of society comprises what can be termed the 'new middle class': middle managers, professionals in areas such as advertising and the media, higher lecturers and school heads, council or health service administrators. They are divorced by salary and lifestyle from most white collar and manual workers; they have a high degree of autonomy over their work; they tend not to be exploited but receive salaries high enough to suggest that they live off the surplus value created by others; and they are crucial to ruling class control and dissemination of ideas throughout society.[45]

These people comprise a relatively privileged minority, unlike the bulk of the labour force in this country, which cannot be described as middle class by any definition. Of a workforce of around 26 million in 1991, around six million were in managerial, administrative and professional occupations.[46] This probably overestimates the non-working class, since it will include 'supervisors' of four or five people in an office who do essentially the same work, classroom teachers and others who are part of the working class. Other estimates place the new middle class as slightly larger, but at no more than 25 to 30 percent of the workforce. There are at the same time huge numbers of workers: 4 million clerical and secretarial workers, 2 million sales staff, 2.5 million plant and machine operatives and nearly 4 million craft and related workers. And while capitalist society may be able to deliver real benefits for the middle classes who have seen their living standards rise in Britain in recent years,[47] the majority of both manual and white collar workers find their lives dominated by exploitation. They have no control over their work, which is nearly always boring and repetitious, and which they are forced to perform if they want to achieve a living standard above abject poverty.

Indeed the wages of supposedly privileged female white collar workers are on average lower than that of their male manual counterparts.[48] In every other respect there is no fundamental material difference in the living standards or lifestyles of the different groups of workers. And these living standards are themselves nowhere near the levels which so many commentators fondly believe are near universal. Wages are low: average gross weekly earnings of male manual workers in 1989 were £217.8; of female manual workers £134.9, and of female white collar workers £195.[49] The hours worked to gain this sort of sum were the highest in the European Community for men: an average of 43.9 hours a week.[50] And Britain has a very high economic activity rate —over three quarters of all men and over half of all women.[51] So more people work in Britain than in many other countries and for some of the longest hours. Yet their rewards are far from sufficient to finance a comfortable lifestyle. In 1991, even some of the highest paid manual workers received extremely low wages. So miners earned (gross) £261 for 44 hours; metal workers £279 for 41.6 hours.[52] These low wages are reflected in the possession or otherwise of consumer durables. A full 35 percent of households had no access to a car, and the average car is 5-6 years old. Among C2s (skilled manual workers and self employed, foremen etc) 40 percent have no holiday a year, and only 6 percent have a dishwasher, compared with 59 percent of ABs (broadly speaking professional and managerial groups). Only 18 percent of households have home computers.[53]

These figures make nonsense of the idea that most workers are bought off, or that they have any sort of material stake in the system— far from workers really benefiting from the boom in British capitalism in the mid to late-1980s, they saw their rate of exploitation increase with big increases in the productivity of labour, which at least in part account for increases in living standards. And just as Marx remarked that the wages of cotton workers in Lancashire in his day were high only because all members of the family worked, as opposed to previously just the man, so today living standards are only higher in real terms over previous generations because of the 9 million women workers whose wages contribute to higher family living standards.

The picture of a privileged and contented working class does not match reality, with British workers expected to work harder than most of their European counterparts[54] to maintain even a reasonable standard of living. They have found the years of recession hard: lower earnings because of less overtime, high unemployment and insecurity, an increased share of wages going to taxation, higher prices from the privatised monopolies, even if these are not necessarily reflected in lower absolute wage levels. The fact that some have fallen through the welfare net and find themselves jobless or homeless does not necessarily cut them off from better off workers, but on the contrary can create the general feeling that all their living standards are in decline.

In addition, the impact of the world crisis and the particular weakness of British capitalism is likely to exacerbate this trend. The pressure on the capitalists to raise the level of exploitation to compete with, in particular, Japan and Germany, will lead to further worsening of working class wages and conditions, and towards higher levels of absolute immiseration of workers in Britain. When real wages in the US are falling in real terms at over one percent *a year*[55] then the pressure is on British capitalists to attack their own workers in order to maintain competitiveness.

The recent discontent over attacks on living standards through the poll tax and cuts in public spending show anger over relative declines in living standards. Yet it is always assumed that workers only look to revolution when their levels of poverty and misery are so low that they see absolutely no alternative. Since many, though far from all, workers today have cars, foreign holidays and mortgages, it is automatically, although wrongly, assumed that they are incapable of revolutionary action. Yet the history of working class organisation shows differently. The Labour Party itself was not built by the poorest workers but by some of the better paid and organised. Eric Hobsbawm describes how, 'The very people who were the backbone of trade unionism, perhaps with the exception of the miners, were, and were seen as, a labour aristocracy which looked down on the mass of those whom it regarded as unskilled, "mere labourers".'[56]

Relative skills, high wages and status were not a barrier to class consciousness or activity but often were symptomatic of it. During periods of high levels of class struggle narrow working class organisation can be superceded. This was true in 1888 and 1889 with the growth of the new unionism—organisation of women, Irish immigrants and the unskilled—which despite its lack of permanent success laid the basis for later mass general unionism.[57] And the skilled engineering workers in Britain and throughout Europe who led the class struggle against the First World War did so from a position of strength and were able to involve and influence the rest of the working class.[58] The differences between skilled and unskilled, although substantial, did not constitute an unbridgeable gulf between the different sets of workers; in addition, the confidence that higher wages and skills gave to these workers allowed them to feel in a stronger position to challenge the employers.

To solve the problems of British capitalism there have been—and will continue to be—attacks on the wages, conditions and welfare of

British workers. The benefits of relative prosperity will come under
attack, provoking outrage because such living standards have become
accepted. Marx made the point that expectations between different
countries and groups of workers vary, but that once standards are accepted, it is much harder to get workers to take less. 'The value of
labour is in every country determined by a *traditional standard of life*.
It is not mere physical life, but it is the satisfaction of certain wants
springing from the social conditions in which people are placed and
reared up.'[59] Once the 'traditional standard of life' comes under attack
then class consciousness and action can rise quite quickly; then too the
traditional social structures which workers look to and accept come
under pressure. Workers rapidly come to accept higher living standards
and are reluctant to take less; witness the defence of the NHS in
Britain, which has been in existence only 50 years but support for
which is deeply embedded in the consciousness of most workers; or the
assumption that televisions or foreign travel are necessities rather than
luxuries, even though most workers have had access to them for perhaps 30 years. Changes in the availability of these 'accepted standards'
can be key to motivating workers to fight.

The ties that bind

Are British workers much too conservative to change their attitudes in
favour of revolution, and are the ideological structures that bind them
to the system so powerful that it is hard to imagine them being overcome? And surely the complexity of society presents a formidable barrier to change; there are so many different social strata and intermediate
classes that it seems simplistic to look at society in terms of two major
contending classes. The attitudes of the mass of people seem so formed
by tradition, by accepted custom and practice, that even when workers
break out of the straitjacket of exploitation through, for example, striking, they will still accept many of the old ideas. Here a whole plethora
of institutions—the police, the trade union leaders, the media, the
monarchy, the family—can have an influence which precludes revolutionary change. Thus develop a whole range of theories which see revolutionary change as either outdated (not taking into account the huge
changes which have taken place in workers' lives this century) or at
best hopelessly inadequate, because things are too complex. The practical conclusions are either to abandon any idea of revolution and settle
only for piecemeal reform as all that will be acceptable to the majority
of people, or that one simple push at the structures of capitalist state
power in Britain will be unsuccessful because all that it will reveal is a

whole range of the defence structures of civil society which prevent its violent overthrow.

There is, of course, some truth in these arguments. Anyone who believes that a ruling class as old and as sophisticated as the British, with its structure of special schools, elite universities, gentlemen's clubs, secret services, judges and civil servants, various networks throughout the media, finance and industry, will be a rapid pushover, is being extremely naive. A society with such a long established working class also contains many institutions and ideologies which bind those workers to the existing system. The advanced capitalist countries have resources of economic wealth and power and a degree of ideological legitimacy which are often lacking in many more undeveloped countries. Trotsky recognised the difficulties facing revolutionaries in the advanced capitalist countries shortly after the Russian Revolution when he talked about the differences between Russia and the West:

> *The easier it was for the Russian proletariat to seize power, the greater are the obstacles encountered by it in the path of its socialist construction.*
>
> *Our old ruling classes were economically and politically insignificant. We had practically no parliamentary or democratic traditions. This made it easier for us to free the masses from the influence of the bourgeoisie and to overthrow the latter's rule. But for the very reason that our bourgeoisie had come into the field late and had accomplished little, our inheritance was a poor one...the more wealthy and civilised a country is, the older its parliamentary-democratic traditions, the more difficult will it be for the Communist Party to seize power; but also, **the more swift and successful will be the progress of the work of socialist construction after the seizure of power.**[60]*

The weakness of Russian civil society, its autocratic state structure and its dearth of mediating structures all made the initial push easier than in more developed Western democracies. However this backwardness also made it harder to build socialism after the revolution, because there was a much lower level of economic and social development on which to build.

The Italian socialist Antonio Gramsci, whose theories became popular in the 1970s among many who wanted to reject outright revolution, argued that ruling class power in the West rests not on overt repression through the state apparatus, but mainly takes the form of ideological domination exercised through a network of institutions which permeate everyday life—what Gramsci called 'civil society'. These networks include the church, the media, trade unions, cultural associations and political parties. The state machine here becomes not the key defence of capitalist society, but one repressive arm alongside many ideological factors.

Revolutionary strategy has to be based on the fight for ideological dominance or 'hegemony', which can only be won through a long drawn out struggle demanding a high level of patience from the working class. Indeed, the working class can only become 'counter-hegemonic' by winning over sections of other classes, especially sections of intellectuals, because of their key role in running the apparatus of ideological domination. This means the working class compromising over its own interests at least in the short term until it has become the 'hegemonic class'. Various passages in Gramsci's *Prison Notebooks* make clear distinctions between revolution in Russia and in the West, and tries to map out a strategy for revolution in the West.

> *In the East the state was everything, civil society was primordial and gelatinous; in the West, there was a proper relation between state and civil society, and when the state trembled a sturdy structure of civil society was at once revealed. The state was only an outer ditch, behind which there stood a powerful system of fortresses and earthworks.*[61]

According to Gramsci, we can understand the structures of society and how to overcome their resistance through the military analogy of the differences between the two types of war—the war of position and the war of manoeuvre. The war of position is a long drawn out strategy which sees two armies locked in battle, unable to really move forward on either side; the war of manoeuvre involves rapid movement by both armies to try to outflank the other. The last successful example of the war of manoeuvre was the October 1917 revolution. But future revolutionary strategy had to be based on a war of position in 'the most advanced states, where "civil society" has become a very complex structure and one which is resistant to the catastrophic "incursions" of the immediate economic element'.[62] While for Gramsci this concept of hegemony does not obviate the need for struggle, for most of those who claim to be his followers it clearly does. As one writer on the subject has put it:

> *whereas Gramsci sought to integrate the 'war of manoeuvre' with the 'war of position', Eurocommunist theoreticians tend to treat them as **separate** strategic options; while Gramsci attempted to unite hegemony with force, in Eurocommunism a mechanically 'hypostasized' consent serves as the identifying attribute of a separate road to socialism.*[63]

The analysis put forward by Gramsci was not an attempt to move *away* from revolution but to try to come to terms with the differences and difficulties faced by those wanting revolution in the advanced capitalist countries. The Dutch socialist Anton Pannekoek made similar distinctions when he wrote in the period just after the First World War:

> Bourgeois culture exists in the proletariat primarily as a traditional cast of thought. The masses caught up in it think in ideological instead of real terms: bourgeois thought has always been ideological. But this ideology and tradition are not integrated; the mental reflexes left over from the innumerable class struggles of former centuries have survived as political and religious systems of thought which separate the old bourgeois world, and hence the proletarians born of it, into groups, churches, sects, parties, divided according to their ideological perspectives. The bourgeois past thus also survives in the proletariat as an organisational tradition that stands in the way of the class unity necessary for the creation of the new world...The intelligentsia—priests, teachers, literati, journalists, artists, politicians— form a numerous class, the function of which is to foster, develop and propagate bourgeois culture; it passes this on to the masses, and acts as mediator between the hegemony of capital and the interests of the masses.[64]

There are two major problems with the analysis put forward by Gramsci and Pannekoek, however. Firstly, they do not really explain why workers accept certain ideas and how they then break from such ideas. Here it is not simply enough to talk about the mediating structures existing in the same way in which they did 60 or 70 years ago. The world about which Gramsci and Pannekoek wrote had a very different pattern of working class life from the one we know now. Proletarianisation even in the advanced industrial countries was much less developed than it is now. Vast sections of the population still worked on the land and even when they went to the cities they retained many of the old peasant ideas for at least a generation. Women were much more tied to the family and their traditional role than they are now, with their work before the First World War centred around domestic chores in their own homes or 'domestic service' outside. Today there has been a breakdown of the old family structures, of agricultural life, the church and many of the ideological structures which accompanied them.

The priests, lawyers and doctors who feature as key purveyors of bourgeois hegemony in Gramsci's theory play a much less central role today. Even the participatory organisations of the cities and towns— union meetings, cultural organisations and political parties—have suffered a decline in every major industrial country in the past half century. They have been replaced instead by the ideological dominance of television and other mass media, and the various components of the leisure industry—institutions which both increase atomisation but which also centralise and generalise the possibility of struggling against them. This is because the development of capitalism leads to the centralisation of ideological power and to the atomisation of the mass of people. Agricultural life is replaced by urbanisation, old stable societies which existed for generations are uprooted and changed. There is a decline of the old hegemonic institutions. Changes in the labour process, the greater mobility of society and the encroachment of the mass media add to the decline. As this happens, there is a weakening of the mediating influences between ordinary workers and the state.

The old institutions were in any case highly characteristic of Gramsci's own Italian society, and rather less so of, say, Britain or Germany. And Italy, despite its small areas of advanced industry, had at the time he wrote a number of features in common with 'backward' Russia, and therefore could support ideological structures such as the church, the Mafia and the local lawyers which were essentially products of such economic backwardness. Gramsci's characterisation of Western civil society was by no means typical of advanced capitalism even in the 1920s and 1930s, let alone now.

What are the equivalent of these structures today? Far fewer workers find their ideas influenced by key individuals who transmit ruling ideas throughout society. There are still some, although they are more likely to be teachers or community workers than lawyers or priests. The organic links between workers and their political representatives, on the other hand, are probably weaker now in Britain than throughout most of this century. The dominant characteristic of workers' consciousness today is what has often been described as 'apathy' based on atomisation; but whereas in the 1950s this apathy was based on a positive feeling that individual workers could solve their problems by personal effort, today it is based much more on despair.

What replaces the old mediating figures are two main features of modern capitalism—the mass media as a direct line of communication to individual, atomised workers on the one hand and the growing importance of workplace based organisation as the only major form of collective organisation on the other. As the old defensive networks weaken, they are replaced by the ruling class dependent even more on the trade union bureaucracy and the big reformist workers' organisations to prevent revolutionary upsurge.[65]

The truth which Gramsci's theories embody is this: it is impossible to regard revolution as one big push which sweeps capitalism from the board and establishes workers' rule. Instead workers have to win the battle of ideas as well as that for state power, and they have to do so at as many levels of society as they can. They have to recognise that this is no easy task especially in the most developed, rooted and apparently stable societies. All too often Gramsci's view is used to reinforce pessimism: it will always be impossible, the argument goes, to win this battle of ideas totally, and so revolution is doomed to failure. But the experience of recent mass movements shows that the battle for ideas can be won: the Anti Nazi League and Rock against Racism in the late 1970s were mass movements which had a huge ideological impact in defeating the rise of the far right, and are one of the main reasons for its failure to re-emerge in Britain today, despite its strength in Germany and France. The anti poll tax movement of 1989-1990 was a mass popular movement which challenged the legitimacy of government and legislation, brought down a supposedly invincible prime minister and led the Tory government to retreat. In both cases these movements, led by socialists and campaigners, against the opposition of the official Labour Party and unions were able to develop alternatives to the received ideas; but in both cases the key was not just the ideological challenge—important though that was—but its link to activity and struggle capable of defeating the threat.

Gramsci's insights can be very useful, but they are not unique to Gramsci. Lenin's pamphlet *Left Wing Communism an Infantile Disorder*, written in 1920, was designed to polemicise against those who believed that revolution could happen in a short space of time and without recourse to patient work in the unions, parliament and the other institutions of bourgeois society. Revolution will involve not only long term work, but a recognition that:

> *Capitalism would not be capitalism if the proletariat **pur sang** were not surrounded by a large number of exceedingly motley types intermediate between the proletarian and the semi-proletarian (who earns his livelihood in part by the sale of his labour power), between the semi-proletarian and the small peasant (and petty artisan, handicraft worker, and small master in general), between the small peasant and the middle peasant, and so on, and if the proletariat itself were not divided...according to territorial origin, trade, sometimes according to religion, and so on.*[66]

In order to win such diverse groups it is necessary to constantly put forward demands, to implement tactics and to raise slogans which can lead them towards supporting the working class rather than away from it. Lenin points out that this involved all sorts of situations both before and after the October revolution where the Bolsheviks worked alongside the Mensheviks in order to win wider layers of people to their politics. This involved clear, principled politics which took into account the differences inside advanced capitalist society, but which never compromised working class politics to other class interests. Trotsky proposed exactly these sorts of tactic when he stressed the centrality of the united front against fascism during the 1930s. The formation of blocs with

sections of the intelligentsia or the petty bourgeoisie who exercised
hegemony over groups of workers can lead to forms of deference, of
the subordination of workers to other classes, which can make it much
harder for workers to give a lead in changing society, and certainly
much harder for them to hang on more permanently to gains they have
made. Again, these were the sorts of alliances made under Stalin's direction through the Popular Fronts in Spain, France and elswhere
during the 1930s, with dire consequences for the working class
movement.

In any revolutionary situation the working class has to try to give a
lead to all sorts of other groups in society whose ideas and assumptions
are in a state of flux by putting forward demands which can persuade
the best sections of those people to come over to revolution. But
attempts at compromising working class interests in the name of cross-
class alliances in such situations have always ended in defeat for workers. Only by the working class leading other groups of the oppressed
can it move towards successful revolution. Here the key lies in collective struggle which can begin to challenge ruling class ideas and the
relative isolation of individual workers. In the process large numbers of
workers can and do break from the old ideas since mass struggles lead
them to new alternatives.

The second problem with Gramsci and Pannekoek's analysis is that
it is a mistake is to see the backward East and advanced West as two
hermetically sealed sorts of society which need two completely separate strategies for revolution. Some of the best work of both Trotsky
and Rosa Luxemburg makes the point that despite very different economic and social development this is not necessarily so, and the more
that capitalism advances, the less it becomes so. Trotsky's theory of
permanent revolution developed the idea that the combined and uneven
development of capitalism meant that even in backward or undeveloped countries the methods of working class struggle still had to apply
if revolution were to be successful.[67] Rosa Luxemburg's pamphlet *The
Mass Strike* attempted to show that the mass strikes which took place in
Russia in 1905 were increasingly central components of workers' revolution, since they involved challenging not merely state political power,
but the economic power of the employers as well. She argued that the
new and relatively small Russian working class, which lacked the
stable unions and political parties already familiar in countries such as
Germany, nonetheless had a great deal to teach workers in more advanced countries on this point.[68] To both of them particular national circumstances were clearly very important but did not override common
international goals or more fundamental questions of strategy and
tactics.

In addition, the different development of Western and Eastern societies has not, as a matter of fact, led to insurrectionary revolution in the East and peaceful parliamentary evolution in the West. It is true that for long periods in some Western countries the class struggle takes the form of a long, slow war of attrition. Neither side has the confidence to break through and outright class war is often replaced with odd outbreaks of skirmish. However this is also a feature of many of the more backward countries (for example Russia itself before 1905). And political development in the West has always been more than just the slow war of attrition. At various times the class struggle has 'hotted up' to produce much more intense and decisive battles which can either take the working class forward materially and ideologically, or can push it backwards and so increase the confidence of the ruling class.

This sort of battle took place in many of the more developed capitalisms in the years immediately preceding the First World War. The end of that war saw them reborn on a much greater scale and the mid-1930s were times of massive struggles in France and Spain and lesser ones in the US. More recently, such struggles were a feature in much of Western capitalism from 1968 through to the mid or late 1970s. In each case the balance of class forces was disturbed by a transformation of working class activity, which in turn produced the possibility of radical restructuring of working class consciousness. The old ideas which workers held no longer corresponded to reality and therefore many workers became open to new ideas. Their ideas did not *automatically* change—that often depended on the degree to which groups of socialists were organised to help combat the old ideas with argument as well. But the possibility of large scale ideological change was present as a result of the social upheavals which took place. This shows the importance of a revolutionary party in such upheavals, capable of linking the ideological struggle with the concrete fight against capitalism.

If the most important mediating structures in capitalist society take the form of the media, and of workplace organisation, then it is possible to begin to see ways to break down workers' allegiance to the existing system. The media is generally regarded as incredibly powerful, having a decisive influence over the mass of workers. In particular, the view of many left intellectuals of the mass of the working class as unthinking *Sun* readers seems to preclude them being won towards struggle. So Labour's failure to win the election in Britain and the continued existence of racism and sexism are put down to the pernicious influence of the tabloid press. But even when there is no struggle many people who read such newspapers do not believe what is in them. A study during the Gulf War in 1991 showed that less than a third of *Sun* readers believed it told the truth.[69] After the 1992 election, the *New Statesman* reported that the swing to Labour in the constituencies with the ten highest *Sun* readerships was higher than the national average, and much higher than comparable constituencies with a high liberal *Guardian* readership.[70] And a recent study of media coverage of the election makes some important points: that the *Sun* called for an SNP vote in Scotland, yet this was the only region where there was a swing to the Tories. Many of its front pages during the election were on non-party issues and its support for the Tories was less than enthusiastic.[71]

The influence of the mass media is great, but it is often a fairly negative influence in the sense that it takes workers' minds off major political issues rather than campaigning hard for a particular line. As the author of a recent study says:

> research with **Sun** readers shows that news and politics are not what they buy the paper for. The **Sun**'s entertainment value is its main attraction... These elements are delivered in a format which is linguistically brief and undemanding, allowing the paper to be frequented at various points in the day, and thus the paper accommodates itself effectively to the working routines of many people.[72]

The means of undermining the ideological views of the *Sun* lie partly in a different sort of socialist paper which can challenge the dominant views of society. Given, however, the monopoly of control of the mass media by a handful of millionaires, such alternatives cannot seriously challenge the distribution and mass penetration of the tabloids in anything but a revolutionary period. In practice workers and other groups in struggle have often mounted a challenge to the media which can begin to alter the balance of class forces. The workplace can become a centre of political ideas and activity, a means of counter struggle against the dominant ideology. And the struggle can begin to present alternative ideas to those propagated by the media. Workers' struggles—however small—for control over the work process can lead to an understanding of the need to control other aspects of their lives, to begin to achieve a sense of direction and purpose to their lives.

There are a number of examples—during the miners' strike in Britain in 1984-85 and during the early 1970s when printworkers raised questions of editorial control and bias and sometimes struck to prevent a particularly reactionary or one sided view being put. In Portugal the overthrow of fascist dictatorship in 1974 ushered in a period of *saneamento*—the 'cleansing' of secret police, collaborators and so on. Various organs of the mass media came under forms of workers' control, such as the newspaper *Republica* and the radio station *Radio Renasenca*; even the media still controlled by the old bosses gave space to left wing views and those supportive of the revolution. None of these and the many other examples of such direct action played by the rules of bourgeois democracy. Had they done so, they would have been much less effective in their task, since rules of ownership and laws established within capitalist society would have been used to justify the actions of a tiny and unelected group of employers. Actions which move towards greater control of the media immediately begin to raise questions which previously workers had thought did not concern them. They can develop a dawning realisation that such control brings workers into conflict with those who own and control society at present. These actions also raise much more fundamental questions such as the role of parliament; who runs the capitalist state; can it be taken over and used by workers; is there any alternative to parliamentary democracy?

A parliament of the people?

When working people in Britain look for change, their central focus is usually parliament: the election of Labour MPs and, hopefully, a Labour government or lobbies of parliament over specific issues and the backing of certain laws which will benefit workers. They are encouraged in these attitudes by the vast majority of institutions in Britain which stress the importance of constitutional change, of proceeding through the 'proper channels' and of putting one's faith in benign MPs or governments. Nowhere are these ideas more deeply rooted than among the Labour and trade union leaders, who see parliament as the main instrument of social change. How does the experience measure up to reality?

Every Labour government in Britain has ended with disillusion among large sections of workers; even the most successful one, from 1945-51, found itself incapable of carrying through many of its policies and effectively ran out of steam by 1948, so alienating many of its most enthusiastic supporters.[73] The fundamental reason for its failures—and those of its numerous counterparts in other parts of the world—lay not in the characteristics of its ministers but in the nature of the institution it was trying to use to implement change. Parliaments have very little power over the executive, still less over big business, finance, the judiciary and all the other key institutions of capitalist society. There is therefore a gap between popular notions of what parliament can achieve and its actual record of delivery. Moreover, faced with any major economic or social crisis, sustained reform is paralysed by class interests, so parliament is unable to carry through some of the most basic reforms, therefore if the struggle is to advance it must go beyond the existing bourgeois democratic institutions. This was the situation in Russia between February and October 1917. It was a pattern which developed in Germany between the end of the First World War and

Hitler's coming to power in 1933. There the mass working class party, the SPD, was able to do the work of the German ruling class in stabilising a revolutionary situation after the war. It was not however able to cope with the chronic social and economic crisis of slump and mass unemployment which made the Weimar Republic—a 'model' bourgeois democracy—one of the most unstable societies ever. During the 1920s millions of German workers and sections of the middle classes looked beyond any form of parliamentary democracy: some to alternative forms of workers' power, others to the 'strong' right wing dictatorship which eventually triumphed. Society became so divided, struggle so intense that the parliamentary institutions became irrelevant—precisely because they could have little or no influence on German capitalism.

Similar forces were at work in Spain and to a lesser extent France in the mid-1930s. In both cases the scale of the crisis and the inadequacy of the bourgeois democratic institutions led to a polarisation between right and left wnen many on both sides looked beyond parliamentary democracy.

At such points in history the arguments about what form workers' democratic institutions shoul... take becomes highly relevant. It is relatively easy when the level of struggle is low for socialists to agree to differ over whether parliament can bring socialism, whether—as many of the Labour left argue—parliamentary and extra parliamentary activity should be combined or whether a complete alternative to parliament in the form of workers' councils have to be built. When strikes, demonstrations and factory occupations become the order of the day, then what previously appeared as essentially theoretical differences over a far off final goal take on a much sharper form. But, in fact, the question of who controls society arises long before any actual conquest of state power—do workers have the right to occupy private property to provide work or housing? Can laws be broken? Is it right that a mass media controlled by a handful of millionaires should be able to operate freely when it is attacking workers' freedom to organise? Every movement for revolution has to confront these questions. When it does so, it finds that the real power in society lies outside parliament. The press barons, the factory owners and the big landowners will do everything in their power to prevent genuine democracy weakening their control; central to this will be the use of the police, the judiciary and the army. This point was made very strongly by Lenin in 1917, in justifying workers' power rather than parliamentary rule as the only force which could confront ruling class power.[74] We have seen his argument borne out by such events as the coup against a democratically elected government in Chile in 1973, when tens of thousands were killed or exiled, or on a much smaller scale in this country, when the forces of the state were used to attack the miners' strike of 1984-85.[75] In such circumstances the role of the capitalist state, and the inadequacy of parliament in confronting it, becomes more apparent, and parliamentary structures can become an obstacle to revolution, not a step towards it.

Most analyses of the progressive role of parliament tend to omit any understanding of its role in *restabilising* the situation after a revolutionary upsurge, and the class basis of its rule. So it is now commonplace on the left to argue that the dissolution of the Constituent Assembly in Russia after the revolution in favour of the workers' councils was a fundamental mistake on the part of the Bolsheviks.[76] But one reason why so many workers and peasants adhered to the soviets and *opposed* the Constituent Assembly was, as Lenin pointed out at the time, not through devotion to the Bolsheviks but because they identified the Assembly with the White armies, the landowners and counter-revolution.[77]

During the German Revolution of 1918-19 the Constituent Assembly was *counterposed* to workers' and soldiers' councils. It was used by the SPD, acting for German capitalism, to restore 'order'. It has been used in crisis ridden countries from Germany in the 1920s to Portugal in the 1970s to *stifle* democracy, not enhance it.

One of the paradoxes about socialist theory today is that lack of revolution is explained in terms of workers' strong commitment to parliamentary democracy, rather than to the failure of the parliamentary left to map a successful course to revolution. So the belief in parliamentary democracy has been used to explain the defeat of the movements following the upsurge of 1968. It has also been used to argue against any attempt to achieve workers' power—a higher and more participatory form of democracy—in opposition to bourgeois parliamentary democracy. The collapse of Stalinist rule in Eastern Europe has only reinforced the view that parliamentary democracy is the highest form of democratic involvement.

The theory is not new. Karl Kautsky couched many of his arguments for gradualism and reform in terms of Western workers' deep and long-standing commitment to parliamentary democracy. As he put it in *Terrorism and Communism* written in 1919, Western 'democracy did not emerge yesterday, as in Russia. It has been won through a series of revolutions and centuries-long struggles; it has become the very flesh and blood of the masses.' He added that 'here it is quite impossible for entire classes, among them the largest, to be deprived of political rights'.[78]

He argued against workers' councils, and in favour of universal suffrage and forms of parliament rather than the young soviets which existed in Russia at the time, and which German revolutionaries had tried to establish in his own country only that year. Others have stressed the deep rooted nature of bourgeois democracy within the working class in the advanced countries.[79] Perry Anderson in fact places commitment to parliamentary democracy as much higher in workers' consciousness than even the significant material reforms which have been won in the past half century: 'The ideology of bourgeois democracy is far more potent than that of any welfare reformism, and forms the permanent syntax of the consensus instilled by the capitalist state.'[80] And Fernando Claudin talks about the '*cultural* universe in which the Western proletariat is immersed...[its] deep attachment to national and democratic values'.[81]

Parliamentary structures and institutions have deep roots in some advanced capitalist countries, but we should not exaggerate how deep these roots are. The idea that most democracies stretch back hundreds of years in their present form is erroneous. Even Britain, with its long established bourgeois institutions, was characterised until well into the 19th century by lack of any trade union rights and repressive criminalisation of those who opposed its rulers. Universal suffrage was not achieved until 1928 and property based voting was not entirely abolished in Britain until after the Second World War (and even then not in Northern Ireland). Germany, Italy and Spain have all had long periods of dictatorship this century. And the US has a 'democratic' structure which results in a very high level of repression against its black and other minorities and a lack of involvement in democratic process which effectively disenfranchises large sections of its working class.[82]

Although it is commonplace to view the postwar settlement as being a division of the world into a 'democratic' West and 'dictatorial' East, the US government was instrumental in ensuring electoral systems rigged in favour of the European ruling classes and against the indigenous working class parties after 1945 in Germany and Italy, it collaborated with dictatorship in Spain, Greece and Portugal until the 1970s, it fostered dictatorship in its own 'backyard' of Latin America and denied the vote to large sections of its black population until the 1960s. As Galbraith says about the US today:

> *Prior to the great revolt of 1989-90 in Eastern Europe, dissatisfaction and alienation were under the broad gloss of socialism; if the people had socialism, they could not be unhappy. The case is now similar in language in the United States: this is the democratic system; systemically it is above error. The fact that a full half of the population does not participate in presidential elections...does not impair the assumption that democracy is controlling and benign.[83]*

Also characteristic of the advanced capitalist democracies is the growth of unaccountable bureaucracy, both of the state and within the big private monopolies.

But it is true that, however weak and imperfect such democracy, it holds two important attractions for most workers. Firstly, it is often perceived as having been won against the vested interests of those who run society. Secondly, it is quite rightly seen as superior to what exists in countries where universal suffrage, trade union rights and basic civil liberties are denied. So any attempts to encroach upon areas of democratic rights in the advanced capitalist countries are usually opposed by large sections of workers.

However this is not and cannot be the end of the story, because although workers act to defend such rights it is also clear that these fall far short of granting anything approaching real freedom. Workers will only be committed to such institutions in certain circumstances. At times this commitment breaks down. We see this even in periods of relative social peace, when large numbers of people may dispute the legitimacy of various laws. A significant minority of workers will argue that Tory employment laws are not legitimate, since they are class based attempts to tie the unions hands. A larger group of workers were in favour of defiance of the poll tax, despite the fact that it was legally passed through parliament.

It is true that most workers in Britain will not want to accept *less* than the existing parliamentary democracy but surely it is conceivable that in many circumstances they can begin to want much more. When their demands begin to challenge the class and property basis of British society, it is unfortunately all too easy to predict on which side the British parliament will fall. And even if it were to back workers in such a struggle, it would be quickly swept aside by those who really are in control.[84]

Revolution has not failed in the West because workers have a higher and deeper commitment to bourgeois democracy than elsewhere, or because they find revolution and direct workers' power an alien concept. The experience of revolution from Germany in 1918-19 to Spain in 1936 to Portugal in 1974-75 is of objective conditions for revolution, but a failure by the leaders of the workers' movement to match up to the opportunities. The breaking down of old values, ideas and certainties did not translate into the overthrow of the old order and its replacement with workers' control because when it came to bringing about change, too many people, especially those influential in the workers' movement, were not prepared to challenge the power of the employers and their state, and so backed off from the necessary confrontation.

Government and ruling class crises lead to a degree of paralysis among the leaders of the working class. The reformist leaders accept the existing framework of society: a stable capitalism, the existence of national divisions, the possibility of gradual reform. The period of economic crisis ushered in by the end of the long boom in the early 1970s led to a major and persistent ideological crisis on the part of these leaders, just as war and revolution led to ideological paralysis among their forebears at the beginning of the century. The fear of economic collapse and of the ending of the established structures led them to make compromises with their respective ruling classes in the mid-1970s[85] and increasingly to take a share in the running of the system in order to solve the crisis. So Socialist governments ruled in Spain, France, Italy and Greece through much of the 1980s. Their role was both to hold back workers' demands and aspirations while at the same time greatly alienating large groups of workers from socialist rule. In Britain, Labour control of local government (now greatly emasculated) performed the same role.

Britain: a model of gradualism?

There are few countries in the world which seem so untouched by revolutionary change as Britain. Even the bourgeois revolution took place in a time so distant that it is all but ignored by today's rulers, while a number of left wing historians regard it not as a fully fledged revolution but a falling out among the ruling classes: 'no social group was evicted or displaced by the revolution; rather one section of a class fought another and by its victory converted the whole class to a new type of production.'[86] This is exactly the view which our rulers want us to have, since it reinforces the supposed impossibility of revolutionary change, as Trotsky noted when he wrote that 'the English bourgeoisie has erased even the memory of the revolution of the 17th century, and recasts its entire past in the form of "gradual changes".'[87] This view of British 'gradualism' is unfortunately not just the property of the bourgeoisie. The existence of 'the mother of parliaments,' the trappings of the House of Lords and the importance of the monarchy all underline the traditional nature of a society which appears very slow to change, and which has fortuitously escaped the upheavals which have affected continental Europe. As Perry Anderson has put it:

> *Occupation, civil war and revolution were the continuous experience of continental Europe for the next three decades* [from 1914 onwards]. *Hammered down from without or blown from within, not a single major social and political structure survived intact...England, meanwhile, suffered neither invasion nor revolution. No basic institutional change supervened from the turn of the century to the era of the Cold War. Through all the tur-*

moil in Europe, the stability and security of British society were never seriously ruffled.[88]

Such a view is reinforced by the often extremely conservative nature of even the working class structures in British society. Whereas in much of Europe political (often Marxist) socialist parties were established between the 1860s and the 1880s, Britain's peculiar contribution —and then only at the turn of the century—was the Labour Party, created to represent the emerging trade union bureaucracy in parliament, and expressly non-ideological (in other words empiricist and pragmatic). Its mass politics were based purely on electoralism and it eschewed any form of Marxism. Fabianism and similar types of reform socialism have dominated it ideologically. There has never been a mass Marxist organisation in Britain; the Communist Party never became anything approaching a mass party, although its influence on working class militants was greater than its numbers. So the picture of Britain has long been one of a complex civil society, strongly resistant to any sudden or violent change, where riots, barricades and the other popular images of revolution are seen as 'outside the British tradition'.

This picture is highly convenient for those who want to stress continuity and stability but is gravely distorted. The English Revolution involved after all civil war and major social convulsions. The Chartist movement of the first half of the 19th century created a mass movement which challenged the whole basis of the state. The peaceful reforms supposedly handed down to us by our rulers over the generations are in fact the product of campaigns, struggle and organisation, whether over trade union rights, votes for women or the health service. Even the Labour Party, whose leaders have always rejected struggle as a means of achieving their demands, was formed and built its base as a result of both the radicalisation of workers through struggle but also out of the failure of these struggles to succeed in meeting the aspirations of workers. So the defeat in the 1890s of the Manningham strike in Bradford, or of the new unions in London's East End, or the outcome of the waves of strikes which shook the South Wales coalfield from the 1910s through to the lockout of 1926, all helped to build Labour support.[89]

The reason for the continued stability of the British ruling class lay in a number of factors: its 19th century pre-eminence as a world imperial power, the ideological dominance of ideas of empire, its longevity and sophistication as a ruling class. The very lengthy and protracted development of British capitalism also led to a labour movement based much less on generalised class politics than on narrow craft defensiveness. In particular the development of British heavy industry in the second half of the 19th century meant the consolidation of capitalist wealth and social stability in great contrast to that of the first half of the century, with its widespread social and political unrest.[90] Engels wrote:

> The class struggles here in England...were more turbulent during the period of development of large-scale industry and died down just in the period of England's undisputed domination of the world. It is the revolutionising of all traditional relations by industry *as it develops* that also revolutionises people's minds.[91]

The corollary of Engels statement is that as large scale industry passes its initial stages of development and 'settles down' so too does the working class created by it, until a new phase of capitalist development galvanises it into action. Writing in the 1880s he describes how Germany's historic backwardness industrially is now being transformed and so helping the growth of a large socialist movement, whereas in England and France this stage has long been passed:

> The political or directly socialistic movements that arose during the period of industrial revolution—immature as they were—have collapsed and left behind discouragement rather than encouragement: bourgeois capitalist development has shown itself stronger than the revolutionary counter-pressure. For a new revolt against capitalist production a new and more powerful impulse is required, say, the dethronement of England from its present dominance in the world market, or a particularly revolutionary situation in France.[92]

The pattern of working class development in Britain was therefore quite different from much later developing capitalisms such as Russia or Italy, where a very new working class was organised directly into very large factories, leading rapidly to a volatile class struggle. The sheer length of gestation of the British working class movement led to a much higher level of working class sectionalism, bolstered during the second half of the 19th century. From the 1850s to the 1880s, the British ruling class enjoyed world pre-eminence based on its domestic industry and its overseas empire; it was able therefore to ensure a level of social stability and peace which left its mark on the workers' movement. However the stability did not last: Britain's decline as a world economic power—which can be dated from the 1880s and which became increasingly obvious from the beginning of the 20th century—led to unrest, colonial revolt, high unemployment and war. From the late 1880s to 1914 there were outbursts of workers' struggle punctuated by employers' offensives, state repression and, ultimately, bitter defeat.

After the First World War, the crisis affecting British society was acute: during the 1920s there was colonial war in Ireland, a general strike, financial crisis, riots, slump. 'In the past, the British bourgeoisie, oppressing the toilers and plundering the colonies, led the nation along the road of material growth and thereby ensured its own supremacy', wrote Trotsky, adding, 'today, the bourgeois regime is not only incapable of leading the British nation forward, but cannot maintain for itself the level already attained.'[93] Nonetheless, Britain was less badly affected by the 1930s depression than some of her main rivals such as the US and Germany. Although unemployment was high, it was not nearly as severe as in these countries, and the middle classes, far from facing financial ruin, saw their living standards rise, as did most workers in employment.[94] This helped to cushion the ruling class politically and led to less upheaval than in many countries of continental Europe. However it is important to distinguish between the inter-war years and the long period of stability of the 19th century—the latter was based on the strength of being the major world power (in much the way that US stability was in the decades after the Second World War). By the inter-war years, Britain's stability was both relative—greater than the other major capitalist powers but still extremely tenuous—and fragile. High unemployment and economic crisis remained throughout the two decades and led to a degree of social polarisation and unrest. There is also a difference between a long period of stability based on very little struggle and one based on struggle which is defeated. So the victory of the ruling class in the 1926 General Strike ushered in ten years of attacks on workers' wages, conditions, jobs and union organisation, but also bitter opposition from a minority and renewed class struggle and union organisation by the mid-1930s from a new generation of workers. The supposed stability of British society over decades can only be sustained by conflating the very different periods of the 1850s-1880s and the 1920s-1930s together on the one hand and by ignoring the explosions which ended the long period of calm in the late 1880s, plus the constant eruptions of class struggle afterwards: in 1910-1914 when the Great Unrest led to a huge militant strike wave; in 1919 when Britain was touched by the revolutionary wave sweeping Europe and when even the police went on strike; in 1926 when despite the timidity of the trade union leaders millions came out on strike; and in the mid 1930s when militancy was reborn.

A new era emerged in the aftermath of the Second World War which finally established US economic domination and ideological hegemony over Western Europe and much of the rest of the world. British long term decline had been under way since the late 19th century. In the 1870s its share of world output of manufactured goods was 32 percent, by the 1880s it had been overtaken by the US as the biggest producer, but still produced 27 percent, by the outbreak of the First World War this figure was down to 14 percent and by 1938 it stood at only 9 percent of world manufactured goods.[95] The division of the world into spheres of influence for the two superpowers after the Second World War marked further decline for the British ruling class. Britain was well on its way to becoming a medium sized European power rather than a mighty empire, and although Britain ended the war as the second industrial power after the US, there was now both domestically and internationally a steep and sure decline. The 1945 Labour government was rapidly faced with economic crisis symptomatic of its relative industrial weakness and its dependence on the US. In the 1950s, the international boom led to real growth in the British economy, but its rate of growth was very quickly overtaken by all its major rivals. So in the years 1951-73, its annual growth rate of GDP was 2.8 percent, around half that of France, Germany and Italy, less than a third that of Japan, and lower than the US. Productivity growth from 1950 to 1976 was again half or less that of its major rivals, with the exception of the US. Investment in the same period was low.[96] Share of world output of manufactured goods fell to 4 percent by the 1960s.[97] Alongside this economic decline went the collapse of the empire, as Britain disentangled itself from direct rule in most of its former colonies.

The general prosperity which underpinned the long boom enabled the ruling class to establish a relatively long period of calm. But by the early 1960s that was already under pressure, and for the first time in 13 years, there was the return of a Labour government in 1964. The tensions created came to a head internationally in 1968. The events of that year were not in themselves revolutions. But they represented the shattering of what Chris Harman has called 'the calm beyond belief'[98] that overcame Western capitalism during the long boom. It had been widely thought that all the contradictions of the system were being ironed out, that growth would continue on its upward curve and that the ills of the 1930s—unemployment, disease and poverty—had become things of the past. That all changed with 1968. Then the richest country in the world, the US, was plunged into crisis, with divisions over the Vietnam War and mass discontent in the black ghettos. The events of May in France started with mass student unrest and spread to the whole of the working class movement.

Those events are portrayed today as the actions of middle class students, but 1968 also saw a mass workers' movement in France generating the biggest general strike in European history. As importantly, the impact of that year was to be felt in the ensuing decade, not just in the radicalisation of young people, but in struggles which involved workers in challenging some of the fundamental priorities of capitalism for the first time in a generation.[99]

The events had varying impacts on the different countries, but throughout Western capitalism large minorities became completely disaffected with the system in the years following 1968. In a number of countries, the ruling classes feared for future stability and believed that revolution was imminent: this was true in France in 1968, in Britain and Italy as a result of the industrial struggles of the early 1970s, in Spain, Portugal and Greece by the mid-1970s. And in nearly every country it took the best part of a decade to defeat those movements and reimpose 'order'. Indeed, the triumph of capitalism and the free market ideologies of Thatcherism and Reaganism which were propagated so confidently in the 1980s can be seen as the consolidation of a ruling class victory which, even a few years before, was by no means certain.

The great upsurge of the late 1960s was contained but in a number of the Western capitalisms working class discontent did not go away and went on to express itself through strike action. In Italy, 'strikes multiplied fourfold between 1968 and 1969'.[100] The 'hot autumn' of 1969 involved workers often from the south, without trade union or militant traditions, organised in factory committees (CUBs). Mass meetings, 'chessboard' strikes where different sections of the factory struck at different times, and other new forms of struggle involved large numbers of workers and led to mass radicalisation.[101] In Britain, there was an equally spectacular rise in the level of strike days. 'The number of strike days rose from less than five million in 1968 to 13.5 million in 1971 and 23.9 million in 1972. After a fall to seven million in 1973, this rose again to 14.75 million in 1974.'[102] The weakness of British capitalism vis-a-vis its competitors forced first the Labour government in 1969 and then Edward Heath's Tory government from 1970 to attempt to introduce legislation to curtail industrial action and rank and file organisation at work. Industrial protest forced Labour's Barbara Castle to back down with her bill, 'In Place of Strife.' So when Heath introduced swingeing attacks on the unions with a centralised Industrial Relations Court aimed at weakening them, there was already opposition in the form of the Communist Party led Liaison Committee for the Defence of Trade Unions. Demonstrations attracted very large numbers, and when five dockers were jailed under the Industrial Relations Act in 1972, the response of massive strike action led to their speedy release. The Act was effectively dead. The miners struck twice under the Heath government, the second time forcing him to call a three day week and a general election in early 1974. His government was replaced by a Labour government in February that year.

In addition, the effect of the Vietnam war on the US ruling class was both to greatly weaken its authority and destabilise its economy. The oil price shock and the ensuing recession of 1973-74 left many of those who believed in peaceful reform and gradual change completely bewildered. Even the ruling classes felt that the years of the mid-1970s were the prelude to complete social collapse. Typical of their response was that of a British industrialist recorded by Tony Benn in his diaries: 'Had lunch with Roy Wright, the Deputy Chairman of Rio Tinto Zinc, who was very gloomy. He said, "Of course, we are heading for a major slump. We shall have to have direction of labour and wartime rationing".'[103] Everywhere the ruling classes feared that the return of severe slump would bring massive political discontent and social unrest. The old postwar consensus established on the basis of boom would break down, to be replaced with, at least, unknown and dangerous instability and, at most, with revolution itself. Already southern Europe looked shaky as Greece, Spain and Portugal emerged from dictatorship. How long, it was felt by many on both left and right, before revolution spread elsewhere?

Major ideological and political crises among the ruling class in Britain continued through the 1970s. Yet the fears of revolution internationally turned out to be unfounded—the overwhelming reason being that the various capitalist powers restabilised with the essential help of the leaderships of the official workers' movements, who feared economic collapse more than anything else. In country after country, their calls for restraint and austerity, often from a position of government, were essential in winning workers away from action. In Portugal and Spain the newly reformed Socialist Parties were a key factor in ensuring ruling class transition from dictatorship to bourgeois democracy. In Britain, the policies of the Wilson-Callaghan governments and of the union leaders in supporting the Social Contract and officially sanctioning scabbing were central to the restabilisation of British capital, helping to pave the way for Thatcherism and the attacks on workers which marked the 1980s. They managed to replace the old postwar consensus of full employment, mixed economy and welfare spending by a new consensus of high unemployment, privatisation and cuts in welfare. All the components of 'Thatcherism' were already initiated by the previous Callaghan government.

The Thatcher years have been hailed as a watershed in British working class history. Eric Hobsbawm's claim in 1987 was that 'the Thatcher regime now has five more years to complete its reshaping of Britain and make itself irreversible, and there is nothing in Britain to stop it'.[104] In 1987 the ruling classes largely agreed that during the Lawson 'economic miracle' Britain was overtaking the rest of Europe and that the mass of workers accepted Thatcherite values. Today such ideas appear ridiculous in the light of intractable economic crisis, defeat of the poll tax and continued resilience of the working class.[105] This is partly a result of the tenuous nature of the boom of the 1980s, based as it was on massive expansion of credit, debt and property speculation and where the much vaunted gains in labour productivity were mainly as a result of plant closures rather than investment or increased efficiency. But it is also partly a tribute to the level of resistance from working people which Thatcher and her cohorts faced throughout her rule. The hard fought struggles from the steel strike through the miners' to the print workers' strike at Wapping, though defeated, nevertheless meant that the ruling class was not able to get its way as quickly and as painlessly as it wished. Thatcher's whole second term agenda was thrown off balance by the cost of having to fight the miners for a year —much longer than had been estimated. The 1980s were punctuated by public sector strikes, protests and riots over the effects of Tory policy. At the end of all this, union density and organisation still remained much higher than in most comparable countries,[106] and real wages continued to rise. At the same time, the level of dissatisfaction grew.

The move towards the market in economics and increasing 'self-reliance' in terms of welfare has only increased the social problems. The Thatcher experiment was essentially a failure in decisively shifting attitudes. At the same time, attempts to push the burden of taxation much more heavily onto the working class failed abysmally and led to Thatcher's own demise.[107] Although Britain did move from slump to boom by the mid-1980s, it is clear that its manufacturing industry in at least some sections is very weak indeed, and lags well behind its competitors.[108] An indication is its level of profits in the 1980s where 'manufacturing was hit by a real profit fall of 38 percent in the 1980-81 recession, which was only just offset during the subsequent recovery, with another fall beginning in 1989; there was no net increase in real profits between 1979 and 1989.'[109]

More fundamentally, the new period of postwar crisis entered into in 1974 and still not at an end has only exacerbated the problems of the British ruling class. Attempts to place the burden of these problems on workers has had only limited success: Heath's attacks on workers' wages and union organisation led to his electoral defeat, the IMF cuts and austerity introduced by the Callaghan government in 1976 and the continued attack on wages led to the Winter of Discontent and Labour's electoral defeat in 1979, Thatcher went too far with her imposition of the poll tax and therefore precipitated her own demise in 1990. Working class opposition managed to break three governments, which is one reason why even today after years of workers' partial defeats or, at best, stalemate Britain's rulers still fear, and attempt to avoid, direct confrontation.

Prospects for revolution in Britain

The period that opened with the East European revolutions in 1989 marks a qualitative change from that which has existed since 1945. Previous economic crises, in the mid-1970s and the early 1980s, caused major shocks to the system by challenging the assumption that capitalism was an ever expanding system free from the contradictions of its earlier years. But it did not automatically challenge workers' illusions in reformism or in the state capitalist regimes in the East. Economic stagnation during the 1970s led to political crises which were particularly profound in a number of countries: in Poland, the mass workers' movement Solidarity exploded on the scene, in Nicaragua and Iran there were revolutions against the old dictatorships. But essentially the political and ideological structure internationally remained. Economic crisis shook it but did not overturn it.

The year 1989 marks a watershed because the economic crisis continues, exacerbated by the final demise of equilibrium based on high levels of the superpowers' arms spending, but is now accompanied by a global political and ideological crisis as well. This is nowhere more true than in the realms of economic theory, where Keynesianism died around 1975, followed to its grave by Thatcherism at the end of the 1980s. Today no alternative commands respect and the strategies of the ruling classes around the world reflect this ideological impasse. But in all areas the ideological change and confusion has been immense, leading to a widespread questioning of ideas unseen since the 1930s. Political instability worldwide has heightened this ideological confusion.

Prospects are grim internationally: the world has now suffered approaching two decades of moving backwards and forwards from fairly shallow booms to longer recessions. As the major Western economies come out of each recession, more and more casualties are left on the battlefield. So large numbers of countries—much of Africa and Latin America and Poland—have never really recovered from the recession of the 1980s. The consequences of whole economies based on drug dealing, the spread of famine and disease in Africa and the writing off of huge sections of capital are all too apparent today. The situation of the advanced capitalist economies too is becoming much more precarious. Until now the sort of catastrophic collapse which took place in the 1930s has not been repeated, but its avoidance has been because each capitalist state has been unwilling to see huge chunks of its industry go to the wall, for both economic and political reasons. So far this has helped prevent the crisis being of the same magnitude. But this creates new problems for the capitalists which they have tried unsuccessfully to resolve. And they are by no means certain of avoiding a major collapse or collapses which can pull whole economies down.[110]

The 1980s boom has turned out to be an economic disaster. The levels of borrowing and debt which now hamper both the huge merged companies and the increasingly crisis ridden banks are making recovery harder in countries like Britain, fuelling fears of a repeat of a 1930s style slump or depression. But, unlike in the 1930s, the option of autarchic national recovery or big injections of state spending to fuel recovery are much less viable. One effect of the crisis is to make it impossible for ruling classes to spend their way out of their political problems. So far the ruling classes have been successful in avoiding or holding down mass struggle, while at the same time trying to squeeze workers further. But they are fearful of moving too quickly and so provoking a fightback which—because of the nature and scale of their attacks—could generalise very quickly across the working class.

Britain is the weak link of the major Western capitalisms: it has suffered both severe long term economic decline and now faces a very deep particular crisis. British workers demonstrate very high levels of alienation from the traditional institutions of British society since many of the old ways of life have been destroyed without replacing them with anything which appears any better. Within the space of a generation Britain has gone from being a country with relatively high living standards, a standard of welfare which was the envy of many other groups of workers and a widespread belief in 'British' superiority, to a country where poverty is at one of the highest levels in the EC, where the welfare state is crumbling and where the sense of national esteem is probably one of the lowest in Western Europe. At the heart of this long term crisis is Britain's long term decline as an economic power, which weakens its ability to overcome the contradictions it faces.

The weakness of British capitalism has been reflected by the prolonged severity of the recession which began in 1990 and which at the time of writing shows no sign of ending. The attacks of Thatcherism have both served to worsen many aspects of life for workers, who tend to work longer hours, receive fewer benefits if out of work, receive worse health treatment if sick, send their children to crumbling understaffed schools and suffer worse housing, while at the same time expectations have remained relatively high. As a result Britain today is a society marked not by contentment and stability but by exactly the opposite. There is a sense of alienation from society which expresses itself in a number of ways. Take many of the most 'stable' and enduring structures: there has not been a time, certainly in this century, when the standing of the police, the judiciary and even the royal family has been so low. Successive scandals, miscarriages of justice, royal divorces and the like have led to massive cynicism and distrust. But at the root of the disaffection lies the economic crisis and its consequences. The decline in respect for these symbols of state authority has been matched by an erosion of the mediating structures of society. The weakening of political parties, social organisation, religious or other structures leads to much greater atomisation, so when people want to express their discontent, this takes the form much less of orderly protests than of spontaneous outbursts, 'apathy' followed by struggle, forms of struggle such as riots which are becoming more and more frequent.

Within British society there are large groups who are systematically discriminated against: most notably the sizeable number of blacks usually located in the inner cities, who suffer worse housing, job opportunities and education than white workers, as well as often high levels of racism. It was not surprising that the riots of 1981 exploded in inner city areas with large black populations, a reflection of the disaffection felt by the majority of blacks (and by a sizeable number of whites who joined them).[111] Those riots symbolised hatred of Thatcher's attacks which marked so much of the 1980s. But such is the discontent today that the riots of the 1990s have tended to be not in the inner city areas (although levels of alienation from society remain as high as ever in these areas). Instead they have spread to the largely white estates in suburbia, once the 'model' estates of the 1950s and 1960s, now bywords for high levels of deprivation, poverty and just sheer boredom. Unlike the older working class areas of Scotland, the north east or Liverpool, these once prosperous estates and towns are now experiencing mass unemployment often for the first generation, and their younger inhabitants are reacting unpredictably and often violently at the prospect.

The old mediating structures were reliable in providing a stable means of transmitting ruling class ideas but they no longer have the same influence that they once did. For many months or even years, the decline of these structures can have no obvious effect within society; bitterness and resentment can accrue among individual workers, but finds no outlet. The ruling class, the government and its state meanwhile relies more and more on inertia, lack of serious political, let alone collective, opposition to its policies and an increase in powers to the police and other institutions of authority. So the once stable consensus built around the welfare state is replaced by a much more authoritarian ruling class presiding over a less contented mass. This is a potentially explosive combination, as Chris Harman wrote about France in 1968:

> *France is usually thought of as an advanced Western capitalist society. Yet under de Gaulle it had adopted some of the authoritarian features more*

usually associated with the less developed capitalisms of Mediterranean Europe.[112]

The breakdown of that postwar consensus of full employment, the mixed economy and the welfare state means that Britain has become a bitterly divided society since the mid-1970s when the new consensus of privatisation, high unemployment and welfare cuts began to emerge.[113] Now the government neither knows what workers are thinking nor really understands what to do about their problems. One of the reasons for their paralysis is the fear, since the poll tax riots, of what any seemingly minor policy change will provoke. It is a problem for the left that the weakening of mediating structures has made it much more difficult to foretell or predict what the outcome of particular attacks on workers will be; there is not a stable workers' party or trade union movement with links in the locality which can act as a barometer. Nevertheless the problem for the government is greater which is why, even with such a low level of working class struggle as there was in 1992, the government is nervous about which direction it should take. Symptomatic of this was a newspaper report in the summer of 1992 which stated: 'Despite official denials, Touche Ross, the leading City accountancy firm, is understood to have been asked by Whitehall to carry out a secret study into the consequences of a property crash, and whether it could precipitate a slump leading, in the worst case, to economic and social disorder.'[114] It shows how detached the government is from the people it is supposed to represent when it has to ask a firm of accountants to judge the level of social unrest its policies will cause.

Many of the *negative* features which mark the beginning of a path towards revolution—disaffection from government and the ruling class, disillusion with most of the alternatives on offer from society, a deep economic and social crisis—are in place. But how do socialists turn that to their advantage, directing the apathy towards struggle and so towards changing ideas, and how do they prevent it from going in the direction either of despondency and introspection, or towards the scapegoating of some groups of workers for the crisis? The task seems immense. The legacy of defeats over the past decade affect workers' ideas and, to an even greater extent, the ideas of the leadership of the working class. The dominant right wing ideas among the Labour leadership were reinforced by its electoral defeat in April 1992, in turn reinforcing the impression that Labour's old working class base is in terminal decline. Many draw the conclusion that Labour cannot win on its own, that it must enter an alliance with the Liberals in order to make any gains. The trade union leaders have also tended to concede defeat before they even engage in a fight, so making the job of working class militants more difficult. They have stressed conciliation rather than confrontation at every stage, regarding the fall in union membership as a foregone conclusion. And have used trade union ballots as a means of weakening and demoralising a fight rather than building it.

The incorporation of many of the reformist leaders and the organisational decline of the reformist parties, coupled with the collapse of Stalinism, has created a vacuum on the left which has two consequences: it means there are no indicators to show what workers are thinking and so outbreaks of struggle are much more unpredictable, but it also creates more opportunities for revolutionary socialists who have often found themselves marginalised in the past. That does not mean reformism is dying—it will remain as long as capitalism itself survives, that is until sufficient numbers of workers see the need to create a totally new society. Despite the unpopularity or weakness of many reformist parties, they can grow very rapidly when workers begin to look for change. Even those reformists who appear weak, discredited and ideologically confused can gain new leases of life in these circumstances.[115] And tiny reformist organisations can grow to meet such a need.[116] So the vacuum on the left is the product of a specific set of circumstances, not something that will last indefinitely, which is why revolutionary socialists urgently need to engage in a battle of ideas.

The weakening of the working class movement and demoralisation of the left is only half the story. At the same time, workers' organisation remains extremely resilient, with around 250,000 shop stewards and with the growth of union organisation in areas such as banking and local government. Since the demise of Thatcher in November 1990, the government has been loathe to take on particular national unions and attempt to defeat them, as was the pattern under the 'Ridley Plan' throughout the 1980s, which specifically drew up plans to take on one group after another, isolating each one in turn. Then, in the early 1980s, the plan was accompanied by rising real wages for the employed; today there are no such obvious compensations. The most recent stage of the British recession—the forced exit from the ERM—will compel the British government, whatever its preferences, to take a hard line with spending and wages in the public sector. It will be backed by the bulk of the British ruling class. Despite the low levels of strike figures in recent years, we should not assume that workers will acquiesce to a more generalised offensive.

We should not regard the labour and trade union movement as in terminal decline, as so many of its leaders do. After years of crisis, cutbacks, and ideological attacks workers usually feel on the defensive. Their traditional organisations do not maintain their slow but steady growth as they do in periods of boom; instead they often contract in numbers and weaken ideologically, as have both the Labour Party and the TUC over the past decade. The growth of workers' confidence and organisation is much more likely to develop in such times through sudden explosions and outbursts of anger and organisation which are totally unexpected. The lessons of the 1930s demonstrate that sudden isolated struggles can push the movement forward and establish the basis for much stronger working class organisation. So it was when the French working class movement mobilised against the fascist threat in 1934, and turned the tide not simply against the right but decisively in the favour of the working class—resulting in the factory occupations two years later. So too in the US, years of employers' offensive, slump and unemployment were turned round by three key strikes in 1934, all led by socialists and all leading to a rebuilding of confidence among workers. These took place in the face of attacks on workers and completely supine, elitist attitudes among the trade union leaders. Indeed the Teamsters' strike in Minneapolis in 1934—now remembered as one of the greatest pages in US working class history—was nearly called off even by some Trotskyists because they thought it impossible to win, just weeks before the employers finally caved in![117]

When both sides in the war of attrition are weak, the outcome of any battle is by no means a foregone conclusion. But once workers score a decisive victory, then that can lead to further struggles. So the Teamsters' victory led to unionisation drives throughout Minneapolis and to a national union movement of the unskilled and unorganised within two years. While it is important not to underestimate the power of the ruling class, it is equally important—especially after years of defeat and attrition—not to overestimate its strength.

In any great social crisis there are advances and retreats in the class struggle; revolution is not simply one great push, where the revolutionary aims are suddenly accomplished; nor is it a steady transition from the mass of workers holding right wing ideas, then moving to social democratic ideas, and finally seeing the light of revolutionary socialist ideas. It is about a polarisation of society often over a period of years which moves backwards and forwards from left to right time and again. Engels wrote sceptically of the notion of instant revolution, deriding the idea of 'all the official parties united in one lump *here*, just like all the Socialists in one column *there*—great decisive battle; victory all along the line at one blow'. As he says, in reality:

> *the revolution begins the other way round, by the great majority of the people and also of the official parties rallying **against** the government, which is thereby isolated, and overthrowing it; and it is only after those of the official parties whose existence is still possible have mutually, jointly, and successively accomplished one another's destruction that* [the] *great division takes place, bringing with it the last chance of our rule.*[118]

That is why the revolutionary process is an era, not just an event. This is inevitable in most situations, both because the revolutionary crisis may have varying depths for the ruling class and because the working class movement usually lacks confidence, experience and sometimes even any sort of revolutionary party. So the revolutionary crisis in Spain in the 1930s lasted the best part of a decade, from the establishment of a republic in 1931 until Franco finally achieved victory in the civil war in 1939. Trotsky compared this situation with Russia, which had its revolutionary 'dress rehearsal' in 1905, and which gained its revolutionary impetus in 1917 from the hatred of imperialist war, the dealing with which could not be postponed:

> The present generation of Spaniards has known no revolution, has gone through no 'dress rehearsal' in the past. The Communist Party went into the events in an extremely weak condition. Spain is not carrying on any foreign war; the Spanish peasants are not concentrated by the millions in the barracks and trenches, and are not in immediate danger of extermination. All these circumstances compel us to expect a slower development of events.[119]

Given the lack of revolutionary tradition in Britain, the small size of revolutionary organisation and the still immense ideological and economic reserves of the British ruling class we can talk about a revolutionary situation lasting many years rather than months. The key here is not whether such a crisis can develop, but whether there are sufficient numbers of workers who begin to see the need to create a complete alternative to the capitalist system. This in turn requires the minority of workers who understand the need to challenge bourgeois society to organise themselves into a party committed to fighting against the old ideas and so winning large numbers of workers whose ideas are changing. The experience from the founding of the Communist International after the First World War to the struggles of the 1960s and 1970s has been the same: when ideas change on a large scale the role of organised revolutionaries is absolutely central. The combination of organisation —having even a handful of individuals in every major town and workplace—and ideological clarity is key in winning a strategy of revolution rather than acceptance of the old leaders and the old ideas. While it is absolutely true that workers' consciousness under capitalism is contradictory, and that it often lags behind events, it is also true that the contradictions in the material world are much more fundamental than those in people's heads. In periods of great social turmoil revolutionary organisations can grow from tiny groups on the margins of the workers' movement to parties with real influence. For over 60 years now the influence of Stalinism among those who wanted to fight the system was massive. It led to a derailing of many of the movements which could have begun a revolutionary breakthrough. Even in the 1960s and 1970s many of the left groups which had broken organisationally with Stalinism still retained elements of its politics. Recent events in Eastern Europe and the USSR have sounded the death knell of those politics as a major ideological and organisational block to real revolutionary politics. That has led to much confusion on the left, but it has also cleared the ground for new organisations to be built, and for a genuine revolutionary politics based on democratic workers' control and socialism from below.

The irrational and catastrophic aspects of capitalism which have become so sickeningly commonplace in large parts of the world have now arrived bang in the middle of Europe. Economic crisis has brought nationalism, war and instability, at the same time that most of the major capitalist powers find it harder and harder to deliver the most basic reforms and most commonly accepted standards of living. In Britain the capitalist class cannot deliver working class housing to the standards of 40 years ago, it cannot build a new tube line to match those built a hundred years ago, it cannot eradicate poverty although this has been the aim of governments since the beginning of the century.

As the scenario unfolds, the question is surely not *if* but *when* will the present Western rulers be challenged? Even more importantly, will the outcome be further barbarism, or can it be the start of a move towards a new form of socialist society? The answer depends on the conscious activity of socialists now, who operate in the day to day struggles of workers around a host of issues, while at the same time trying to answer the major ideological questions which confront us all. Unless those who want socialism stop despairing at what they think is a fixed working class consciousness, and look instead to linking the economic grievances of workers to an ideological assault against the system, the left can fail the next major test as well as the last. We have to ensure that does not happen. As Trotsky put it:

> The question is not one of fixing the 'day' of the revolution—we are still a long way from that—but of clearly understanding that all the objective conditions are bringing this 'day' nearer, are bringing it within the range of the proletarian party's educational and preparatory politics, and creating at the same time the conditions for the rapid revolutionary development of the party.[120]

Notes

1 *Independent*, 7 July 1992.
2 See C Leadbeter, *New Statesman*, 21 August 1987.
3 For a very interesting discussion of how this happened see J Foster, *Class Struggle and the Industrial Revolution* (London, 1974), ch 7, pp203-250.

4   Engels' letter to Sorge in 1889 in Marx and Engels, *Selected Correspondence* (Moscow, 1975), p386.

5   Engels' letter to Kautsky in 1882, ibid, pp330-1.

6   Lenin, *Collected Works,* vol 13, (Moscow, 1977), p37.

7   K Marx and F Engels, 'Address of the Central Committee to the Communist League', in *The Revolutions of 1848,* ed D Fernbach (London, 1973), pp320-321.

8   K Marx, 'The Class Struggles in France', in *Surveys from Exile,* ed D Fernbach, (London, 1973), pp41-42.

9   Engels quoted in H Draper, *Karl Marx's Theory of Revolution,* vol II (London, 1978), p258.

10 *Surveys from Exile,* op cit, p117.

11 K Marx, *The Communist Manifesto* (Tirana, 1981) p40.

12 V I Lenin, 'Left Wing Communism—An Infantile Disorder' in *Selected Works* (London and Moscow, 1969) p566.

13 See H James, *The German Slump* (Oxford, 1986) ch 7 and 8.

14 And the very economic development of society leads to an intensification of the contradictions which give rise to revolution, as Marx pointed out: 'At a certain stage in their development the material productive forces of society come into conflict with the existing relations of production, or the property relations within which they have been at work hitherto. From forms of development of the productive forces, these relations turn into fetters. Then begins an epoch of social revolution.' K Marx, *Preface to Contribution to the Critique of Political Economy* (Peking, 1976), p3.

15 H Draper, op cit, p47.

16 See *The Communist International in Lenin's Time Proceedings of the 2nd Congress,* vol I and II (London, 1991).

17 P Jenkins, *Mrs Thatcher's Revolution* (London, 1989) p379.

18 See *Social Trends 21,* 1991, p95.

19 *Human Development Report* (Oxford, 1991), p31.

20 J K Galbraith, *The Culture of Contentment* (London, 1992).

21 *Social Trends 21,* 1991, p77.

22 Ibid, p67.

23 For an analysis of the pressure on every member of society to make themselves available on the labour market see the chapter on 'The universal market' in H Braverman, *Labor and Monopoly Capital* (London, 1974) especially pp271-276.

24 L German, 'The Last Days of Thatcher', in *International Socialism* 48 Autumn 1990 and A Rogers, 'Is There a New Underclass', in *International Socialism* 40, Autumn 1988.

25 I am grateful to Kevin Dougan for this point.

26 J K Galbraith, op cit, p31.

27 Ibid, p31.

28 K Marx, *The Grundrisse* (London, 1973) pp272-3.

29 See for example the strike in Southern California of Mexican construction workers, many of them deemed 'illegal', all non-union, reported in the US *Socialist Worker* (Chicago, July 1992) p15. See also M Davis, 'The Rebellion that rocked a Superpower' in *Socialist Review* (London, June 1992), for the wide working class support and participation in the LA riots.

30 See *Households below average income 1979-1989* (Department of Social Security, London).

31 Nobel Lowndes quarterly survey on executive pay in *Financial Times,* 29 September 1992.

32 '"Bosses" pay: no sign of recession' *Labour Research* (London, August 1992).

33 Reported in *Financial Times,* 29 September 1992.

34 And the gap between bosses and employed workers has widened. Galbraith makes the startling point that 'in 1980, the chief executive officers of the three hundred largest American companies had incomes 29 times that of the average manufacturing worker. Ten years later the incomes of the top executives were 93 times greater'. Galbraith, op cit, p55.

35 V George and I Howards, *Poverty amidst Affluence* (Aldershot, 1991), p54.

36 See S Ash, 'War of attrition', *Socialist Review* July/August 1992, p9.

37 *Human Development Report* (Oxford, 1991) fig 38, p186.

38 George and Howards, op cit, p27.

39 C Leadbeter, op cit.

40 See Y Kapp, *Eleanor Marx, vol II* (New York, 1976) for details of the riots and the upsurge of new unionism.

41 See R Croucher, *Engineers at War* (London, 1982) ch. 1.

42 E Hobsbawm et al, *The Forward March of Labour Halted* (London, 1981) p6.

43 *Employment Gazette* (Department of Employment, London, March 1992).

44 For a more detailed explanation of what has happened to the working class since the Second World War, see H Braverman, *Labor and Monopoly Capital,* op cit, and C Harman and A Callinicos, *The Changing Working Class* (London, 1987).

45 See C Harman and A Callinicos, ibid.

46 See *Labour Force Survey* in *Employment Gazette* (March, 1992). See also A Callinicos, 'The New Middle Class and Socialist Politics', in *The Changing Working Class,* ibid, for a much fuller discussion of various definitions of the middle class.

47 See *Social Trends* 22 1992, p101.

48 See *Social Trends* 21, 1991, p86, which also shows that male non-manual workers earn much more than male manual, but these are usually professional or supervisory grades.

49 Ibid 1991, p86.

50 Ibid, fig 4.18, p73.

51 Ibid, fig 4.8, p69.

52 *Labour Force Survey,* op cit.

53 *Social Trends* 21, 1991, op cit, pp101, 152, 171, 180.

54 Reported in *Independent,* 23 September 1992.

55 See L Thurow, *Head to Head* (New York, 1992), p53.

56 E Hobsbawm et al, op cit, p6.

57 See Kapp, ibid, pp318-363.

58 J Hinton, *The First Shop Stewards Movement* (London, 1973), especially ch 12 p298-329. Also for a European view of this phenomenon see D Gluckstein, *The Western Soviets* (London, 1985).

59 'Wages, Price and Profit' in *Marx and Engels Selected Works* (London and Moscow, 1980) p222.

60 *Leon Trotsky on Britain* (New York, 1973) pp47-48.

61 A Gramsci, *Selections from Prison Notebooks* (London, 1971) p238.

62 Ibid, p235

63 J Hoffman, *The Gramscian Challenge* (Oxford, 1984) p150.

64 A Pannekoek, 'World Revolution and Communist Tactics', reprinted in D A Smart (ed) *Pannekoek and Gorter's Marxism* (London, 1978) p105.

65 I am grateful to Chris Harman for his unpublished analysis of these questions on which I have drawn heavily.

66 V I Lenin, 'Left Wing Communism an Infantile Disorder' in *Selected Works* (London, 1969) p558.

67 L Trotsky, *Results and Prospects* and *Permanent Revolution* (London, 1982).

68 R Luxemburg, *The Mass Strike* (London).

69 *Socialist Worker,* 23 February 1991.

70 *New Statesman*, 17 April 1992.
71 'The Sun wot done it?' by M Daly in *Tribune*, 31 July 1992.
72 Ibid, pp6-7.
73 K O Morgan, *The People's Peace* (London, 1992) ch.3 pp71-111.
74 V I Lenin, 'The State and Revolution' in *Selected Works*, op cit, p264.
75 See, on Chile C Barker (ed) *Revolutionary Rehearsals*, on the miners' strike A Callinicos and M Simons, *The Great Strike* (London, 1985)
76 For a full critique of this argument see J Rees, 'In Defence of October', in *International Socialism* 52 (London, Autumn 1991).
77 Lenin, *Collected Works*, vol 32 (Moscow, 1977) p486.
78 K Kautsky, quoted in M Salvadori, *Karl Kautsky and the Socialist Revolution* (London, 1979) p278.
79 See R Miliband, *Divided Societies* (Oxford, 1989) pp75-76.
80 P Anderson, 'The Antinomies of Antonio Gramsci', in *New Left Revew* 100, p9.
81 F Claudin, *The Communist Movement* (Harmondsworth, 1975) p60.
82 A recent newspaper report stated that an estimated 90 million Americans (40 percent of the electorate) failed to register to vote in the 1992 presidential election. Turnout was predicted to be only about half (in 1988 it was 50.1 percent). The top 33 percent of Americans by wealth cast 44 percent of the votes. A recent attempt to make voter registration automatic when one applied for a driving licence or welfare failed to get through the Senate after being vetoed by Bush. See *Independent*, 1 October 1992.
83 J K Galbraith, op cit, p151.
84 For a chilling fictional account of the experiences of a left Labour government, which I fear would be only too accurate see C Mullin, *A Very British Coup* (London, 1982).
85 The Social Contract between government and TUC in Britain; the Pact of Moncloa between government and unions in Spain; the Historic Compromise between the Communists and Christian Democrats in Italy.
86 P Anderson, 'Origins of the Present Crisis', in *English Questions* (London, 1992) p19.
87 *Leon Trotsky on Britain*, (New York, 1973) p111.
88 P Anderson, 'Components of the National Culture' in *English Questions*, op cit, p61.
89 For more on the origins of Labour see D Howell, *British Workers and the Independent Labour Party* (Manchester, 1984), and T Cliff and D Gluckstein, *The Labour Party* (London, 1988) pp5-53.
90 See J Foster, *Class Struggle and the Industrial Revolution*, op cit, on the changes in the working class of Oldham in this period.
91 Engels' letter to Sorge, *Selected Correspondence*, op cit, p427.
92 Engels letter to Kautsky quoted in Draper, op cit, p272.
93 *Leon Trotsky on Britain*, op cit, p182.
94 See J Stevenson and C Cook, *The Slump* (London, 1979) pp16-18.
95 A Glyn and B Sutcliffe, *British Capitalism and the Profits Squeeze* (Harmondsworth, 1972) p17.
96 See D Coates, *The Context of British Politics* (London, 1984) pp47-49.
97 A Glyn and B Sutcliffe, op cit, p17.
98 C Harman, *The Fire Last Time* (London, 1988) p1.
99 For a detailed analysis of 1968 and what it led to see ibid.
100 Ibid, p194.
101 See P Ginsborg, *A History of Contemporary Italy* (London, 1990) pp309-322.
102 Harman, op cit, p226.
103 T Benn, *Against the Tide: Diaries 1973-76* (London, 1990) p75.
104 E Hobsbawm, 'Out of the Wilderness', *Marxism Today*, October 1987.

105 See L German 'The Last Days of Thatcher', op cit, for a more detailed analysis of the problems confronting the British ruling class.
106 See 'Sleeping Giants' by H Croft and G Jenkins, *Socialist Review* no 156 September 1992.
107 See L German, op cit.
108 Figures given by S Brittan in *Financial Times*, 19 September 1991, put manufacturing output per worker in the UK at 100 compared with 149 in Italy, 159 in france, 127 in Germany, 139 in Japan and 204 in the US.
109 C Johnson, *The Economy Under Mrs Thatcher* (London, 1991) p198.
110 For a full exposition of this see C Harman, *Explaining the Crisis* (London, 1984), ch 3, pp75-121.
111 See A Callinicos, 'Race and Class', in *International Socialism* 55, Summer 1992.
112 C Harman, *The Fire Last Time*, op cit, pp90-91.
113 See interview with Tony Cliff in *International Socialism* 55, Summer 1992.
114 'Homes Slump Crisis Worries Tories', *Independent on Sunday*, 2 August 1992.
115 It would, for example, be a mistake to write off, say, the Italian or Spanish former Communist Parties which, despite ideological confusion and political compromise, maintain the allegiance of large sections of workers.
116 The ruling PSOE in Spain had 4,000 members at the time of Franco's death, 2,000 of them in exile. It was consciously rebuilt by European Social Democracy (especially the German SPD) as a bulwark against revolution and to ease a smooth transition from dictatorship to bourgeois monarchy. See D Gilmour, *The Transformation of Spain* (London, 1985) pp102-3, 165-7.
117 F Dobbs, *The Teamster Rebellion* (New York, 1972), pp176-177; for the trade union leaders' attitudes see D Guérin, *One Hundred Years of Labor in the USA* (London, 1979) pp93-101.
118 Engels letter to Bebel 1882 in *Selected Correspondence*, op cit, p333.
119 L Trotsky, *The Spanish Revolution* (New York, 1973) p130.
120 *Leon Trotsky on Britain*, op cit, p183.

Columbus, the Americas and the rise of capitalism

MIKE HAYNES

The 500th anniversary of the 'discovery' of the Americas by Christopher Columbus in 1492 has generated an avalanche of publications. These have been dominated by the debate on Columbus as an individual and his relationship to European imperialism and the vast human and ecological changes that followed 1492. This is quite understandable. The incorporation of the Americas into a European empire in the 16th and 17th centuries laid part of the foundations of modern Latin America. But discussion of this process has traditionally been dominated by a celebration of the mythology of the victors. History has often been no more than a romantic tradition where a glorious past meets a glorious present to lead on to a glorious future. As one poet put it at the 1876 American Centennial, in which Columbus figured prominently (having been adopted as a symbol by those in revolt in the War of Independence):

Come back across the bridge of time
And swear an oath that holds you fast,
To make the future as sublime
As is the memory of the past.[1]

In this 'sublime' history the native peoples and their sufferings at best became a backcloth and at worst were completely invisible. The assertion of the centrality of their experience, therefore, and a related focus on the initial catastrophe created by European disease, European exploitation and European plunder in which, on some estimates, between as much as 10 to 15 percent of humanity may have perished is clearly an important one.[2] But not only does the critical history of 1492 and its consequences establish a proper balance, it also leads to a better detailed historical understanding. This is the significance of cutting down an individual like Columbus to his real size. It is now often argued in Columbus's defence that he was a man of his time. But it is precisely this that the old myths denied. For the myth makers Columbus crystallises the virtues of the great Italian, the great Spaniard, the great American and so on even to the extent of a failed attempt to get him canonised.[3]

Yet, however justified and understandable, this critical focus slights a deeper set of problems either by ignoring them or relegating them to second place. These problems relate to the relationship between European 'discovery' and conquest in the 16th and 17th centuries and the rise of capitalism in Europe and the Atlantic economy.

We can identify four main perspectives that are critical of the establishment accounts of 1492 and its aftermath. The one with the longest pedigree is a nationalistic focus on the impact of an undifferentiated Western imperialism on Latin America. This view tries to encapsulate world history over the past five centuries in terms of a simple conflict between the 'advanced world' and the 'underdeveloped world'. Although frequently seen as a Marxist view and often using Marxist terminology this approach in practice displaces the centrality of class in favour of national units or abstract conflicts between the 'core' and the 'periphery' of a long standing 'world system'.

Such discussions have implicitly tended to define the 'exploited' in the Americas as the descendants of Columbus and those who followed him. Against this a second tradition, submerged over much of the history of the Americas, focuses more on the struggles of the native peoples themselves. The Indian story is one of continuing horror as Ronald Wright has powerfully shown in his *Stolen Continents: the Indian Story*.[4] This book is the most recent of a small but honourable tradition which has tried to give a voice to the other side of the history of the Americas. Inevitably it poses uncomfortable questions for an analysis based around the idea of the national group for it raises the obvious question of how that is defined and who is really the victim and of what system?

To the last question a third environmentalist tradition answers 'modern life'. It is this approach, often attempting to subsume parts of the second, that has been given most attention in the 1992 anniversary. The environmentalist-green account is best exemplified in Kirkpatrick Sale's *The Conquest of Paradise*. Here Sale, a founder of the New

York Green Party, offers a sophisticated defence of the 'good old days before 1492' thesis in which the native populations are celebrated for their harmony with the land. In the 16th century Bartolomé de las Casas—one of the most powerful Spanish chroniclers of the real story of the conquest—reported that he had 'heard divers Spaniards confess' that the native populations had 'nothing else to hinder them from enjoying Heaven, but their ignorance of the true God'.[5] By the same token a modern cynic might well feel after reading this kind of literature that the only failing of the pre-Columbian systems was that their peoples did not have their own copies of the *Gaia Atlas*. Sale and others want not only to marvel at the native past but also see it as a model for the future. 'There is only one way to live in America, and that is as Americans—the original Americans—for that is what the earth demands. We have tried for five centuries to resist this simple truth.'[6]

A fourth critical tradition derives from an attempt to understand the conquest and its impact through the development of Marx's analysis of the rise of capitalism. This is by far the weakest developed and not least because it poses formidable analytical and empirical problems to which answers are only just beginning to be given. Indeed in some cases the questions themselves are only just beginning to be posed. In particular, unlike the other approaches, such an analysis has to try to differentiate history—to understand the particular changing forms of the pre-Columbian societies, the changing forms of the post-Columbian societies and above all the changing nature of their interaction. This differentiation is necessary because the history of class society in general is the history of changing and developing forms. When it comes to the development of capitalism, however, we must go further and recognise that as a mode of production it, above all others, has been characterised by its dynamic of change. In these terms we can identify four specific areas of interest:

i) to what extent were discovery and conquest a product of a prior embryonic development of capitalism in the 15th and 16th centuries?

ii) what was the nature of the native American societies that the Europeans encountered?

iii) what was the nature of the new societies created by conquest as they developed in the Americas and especially central and South America in the 16th and 17th centuries?

iv) what was the impact of the American empires on the subsequent development of European capitalism in the 16th and 17th centuries?

Each of these questions has generated an enormous literature and here we can do no more than try to establish more clearly the economic and social structures and connections which need to be focused on in order to find answers. To do this is important because in the attempt to better understand the significance of 1492 there is a danger of lurching from one myth to another and misunderstanding the whole dynamic of development in both the Americas, Europe and the world at large.

'Discovery', conquest and the question of pre-existing capitalist development in Europe

In 1500 the world already contained a number of relatively advanced centres whether defined in terms of economic development, technology or culture. These are shown on map 1. Of those identified the most important were Ming China, Muslim India, the developing Ottoman and Saffayid Empires in the Middle East and Persia and the monarchies of western Europe.

It was, however, from only one of these—the monarchies of western Europe—that the process of discovery and conquest developed. Here the importance of Columbus was as a beginning. His voyages had already been preceded by a number of significant voyages of exploration but more importantly were to be followed by many more during the 16th century. Yet if we view the world from the perspective of 1500 it would not have been obvious that Europe would be the area of explosive expansion. Most famously Ming China had already anticipated European oceanic exploration nearly a century before with the seven voyages of Zheng He (Cheng Ho). Commanding fleets far more impressive than anything the Europeans would be capable of developing for almost another two centuries, Zheng He explored the Indian Ocean between 1405 and 1433 as can be seen in map 2. But unlike the voyages of Columbus to the west and Vasco da Gama to the east these Chinese explorations were not sustained. Ming China turned in on itself with its ruling groups deliberately choosing to avoid further overseas commitments leaving a vacuum in the Indian ocean and the potential for future European dominance.[7]

Historians who have studied this problem all agree that what distinguished the Europeans from the Chinese at this point was motivation rather than capacity. As three American historians of China put it:

> The contrast between capacity and performance, if looked at by our modern world of trade and overseas expansion, is truly striking... [Chinese leaders] ...refused to join in the great commercial revolution which was beginning to sweep the world.[8]

This contrast in motivation is apparent not only in the fact that the Chinese leadership deliberately turned away from continued explo-

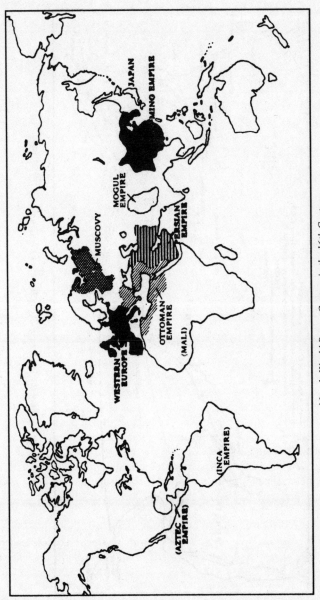

Map 1: World Power Centres in the 16th Century

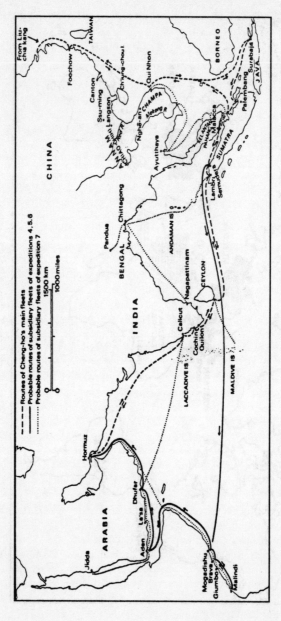

Map 2: The Routes of the Voyages of Zheng He (Cheng Ho) in the early 15th Century

ration but also in the nature of the exploration itself. So far as we know this did not involve plunder, did not involve missionary activity and placed a high premium on scientific knowledge and good relations with natives albeit within a system in which local leaders were expected to show their recognition of the leading role of the Chinese Emperor.

But identifying the differences in motivation is the lesser problem. The difficulty is to explain them. This is further complicated by the fact that the main expansive European powers at the end of the 15th century and during the 16th century were the Portuguese and Spanish monarchies. Yet during the 17th and 18th centuries these societies became relative European backwaters and the momentum of capitalist development shifted from southern to north western Europe. The problem of explaining the dynamic of sustained discovery and conquest has, therefore, also to relate to the precocious but abortive development of these two powers.

A difficulty often arises here because this problem is posed in terms of 'national' and 'state' bound categories: 'why did Spain sponsor Columbus?', 'what happened to the Spanish golden age?' and so on. To us these seem natural ways of asking questions but they presuppose that, as Europe began to emerge from the medieval world, states existed in the way that we think of them today. They did not. European history from the 15th century is a history of continuous and ongoing state making. The modern state had to be created. Once these states have been put in place history is then often rewritten as if they had always existed (think of the books on 'Roman Britain' or 'Anglo-Saxon England'). In this way the development of unified states, with central political authorities, is made to seem natural and inevitable, underpinned by some transcendent national consciousness. More recently still some commentators (who do not share the extremes of such conscious and unconscious nationalist writing) have been attracted to the idea that the modern world is to be defined in terms of the centrality of inter-state rivalry.[9] With this stress few readers of this journal will disagree but these commentators then argue that such a systemic state rivalry is independent of capitalism, pre-dates it and provides an important stimulus to the development of capitalism itself. In this way they believe that they have found a missing ingredient in explanations of the rise of capitalism.

In both instances what happens is that a point of arrival—the world of modern states, national conflicts and state rivalries—is taken as a point of departure, and what should be the end becomes the beginning. The result is both empirically and theoretically debilitating. It is empirically debilitating in that it ignores the protracted process of state formation, forcing history into inappropriate categories. Spain is a notorious example of this. So loose was it as a political entity and so deep was

what has been called its geographical, economic, social and cultural
'cantonalism' that 16th and 17th century contemporaries often referred
to it as 'the Spains' rather than 'Spain'. In the early 17th century
Olivares, a leading politician, advised his monarch that:

> The most important piece of business in your Monarchy is to make yourself
> King of Spain by which I mean that Your Majesty should not be content with
> being King of Portugal, of Aragon, of Valencia, and Count of Barcelona,
> but should secretly work and plan to reduce these kingdoms of which Spain
> is composed to the style and laws of Castile.[10]

In fact such 17th century attempts as were made to achieve this end
in 'Spain' failed. But such arguments are also theoretically debilitating
in the way that they displace attention from the way that the development of capitalism itself sponsored the development of the modern
state. By insisting on the opposite it is necessary either to have the
modern state system born prematurely or to delay the birth of capitalism so that cause and effect can be established.

To avoid these problems, therefore, we must turn first to examine
not some illusory 'Spain' in 1492 but the Mediterranean world of
which the Iberian Peninsula was a part and whose expansive drives lay
behind the initial expansion of Southern Europe both around the coast
of Africa and out to the unknown Americas in the west.

European expansion and the Mediterranean world

In the 16th century some 60 million people lived in the lands bordering
all sides of the Mediterranean (compared to around 100 million in 16th
century Europe). For the majority of this population the Mediterranean
was, as it had been for centuries, 'a world of peasants and landlords, a
world of rigid structures'. The phrase is that of the French historian
Fernand Braudel. If we follow his analysis then the labour of the peasantry in the Mediterranean area produced around three quarters of
output, if measured in money terms. But only a small part of what they
produced actually went to the market to be sold for the money they
needed to pay the taxes and dues to their lords and the monarchies of
the area, or to enable them to buy what they could not produce themselves. The major part of their production was consumed on the land
and in the villages where it was produced. Industry was weakly and un-
evenly developed with craft workers in the towns making up around 5
percent of the population and craft workers in the countryside another 5
percent. A further small proportion of the population was engaged in

the different types of commerce that moved goods around both local and long distance trade routes.[11]

In this general sense the world of the Mediterranean and especially its European side was no different to the world of northern Europe save in one respect—its overall level of development was marginally higher. It is in this slight difference that we find the key component that enabled the Mediterranean to provide the initial base for the more general expansion of Europe. One measure of this difference can be found in the estimate that whereas in northern Europe some 10 percent of the population lived in towns, in the southern European world the figure was perhaps 15 percent.[12] But it was not simply a quantitative gap. In southern Europe too we find a greater sophistication in trade and financial networks by comparison with what yet existed in the north. This is important in trying to understand the rise of capitalism.

Many historians have confused the rise of capitalism with the rise of the market and the money economy. In fact markets and money long pre-date capitalism and they played an important part in articulating the feudal economy of medieval Europe.[13] What characterises capitalism is the increasing generalisation of the market to relations of production and especially the buying and selling of labour and the subordination of this generalised commodity production to the dictates of capital accumulation.

In the Mediterranean world we find elements of this beginning to appear in the medieval period but not yet able to impose their dynamic as the decisive force motivating and controlling production and exchange. 'Capital' at this stage was primarily 'merchant capital' in which merchants sought to expand their wealth through seizing the opportunities presented by trade and finance rather than production. In particular the Italian city states, trading towns like Pisa and Florence and most notably Genoa and Venice, became centres of merchant capitalism whose tentacles stretched out impressively over land and sea and whose innovations in banking, insurance and the first joint stock companies laid part of the institutional basis for a later and wider capitalist development.

Generally in the medieval economy the surplus produced was too limited to allow significant capital accumulation. Production aimed to satisfy the needs of the peasants and craft workers, and the demands of the feudal classes in the countryside and town. To maintain their status, to rule and defend their positions, the aristocracy, monarchy and church and their merchant supporters squeezed a maximum 'profit' from their subjects but none had a real conception of reinvesting what they got on a sustained scale to achieve bigger 'profits' in the future:

*the idea of reinvesting profit for the purpose of increasing production seems
to have been present in few minds if any. In **practice** the minimum rather
than the maximum seems to have been spent on these goods which go towards capital accumulation...*[14]

On the basis of the most sensible conjectures 'capital accumulation'
(the term is a bad one since this was not how it was seen in the feudal
world) certainly took up no more than 5 percent of output and new capital formation only 1 to 2 percent compared to gross accumulation figures of over 10 percent as capitalism matured in its 19th century
industrial form and around 20 percent for many economies today.

As feudalism began to give way more opportunities opened up to increase the surplus exploited from peasants and workers but the attraction of profit through the exploitation of trading opportunities still
outweighed the attraction of profit through the direct organisation of
production itself. It seems that merchant profits were higher on average
and certainly offered the potential of greatest windfall reward.[15]

And in the Mediterranean it was the spice trade that appeared to
offer the greatest potential gains. Spices were central to the European
diet, especially of the rich, because food was so difficult to store and
therefore needed to be spiced with peppers, cinnamon, cloves and the
like to make it edible.[16] Arab traders in the east brought spices from the
Moluccas (part of modern Indonesia), Java, Sri Lanka and India to the
Red Sea and Alexandria where they were transferred to ships financed
and directed by European merchants, especially those from the trading
cities of the Italian peninsula. Spices also came overland from the east
but it was the disruption of this trade that helped to force up prices even
higher at the turn of the 16th century. In return European goods trickled
eastwards—it was a trickle because there was little that the east wanted
from Europe and the balance therefore had to be made up in payments
in silver and gold causing a monetary drain on the European economy.

There was thus a specific incentive to move outwards in search of
alternative routes that might give Europeans direct access to Asia and
the spice trade. There was also a related general incentive to move outwards to try to locate new sources of gold and silver as the prices of
these metals rose because of European shortages. Portugal and Castile
were to be the basis of these moves not simply because of their position
on the geographical periphery of the Mediterranean world but also because of the way that they were developing as socio-economic and cultural crossroads at the turn of the 16th century.[17]

In the 8th century the Iberian peninsula had been integrated into the
Islamic Empire save for small Christian sovereignties in the far north.
From these small enclaves the world of Islamic al-Andalus, which for
five centuries covered most of the peninsula, was gradually pushed

back with an independent Portuguese monarchy emerging in 1139. In the 13th century the monarchies of Castile, Aragon and Navarre emerged in the rest of the country leaving an Islamic kingdom in Granada. This remaining Islamic kingdom was finally to be overcome in January 1492 by the united efforts of Isabella of Castile and Ferdinand of Aragon who had married in 1469. When Isabella became Queen of Castile in 1474 and Ferdinand King of Aragon in 1479 the territories of the two crowns were united in dynastic marriage. The propagandists of Isabella and Ferdinand and generations of later historians saw this process as a centuries long 'reconquest' of Christian Spain from 'the infidels'. It was nothing of the kind. It could not be a 're-conquest' since a unified Christian Spanish state had not previously existed in any meaningful sense. Nor was there anything coherent or sustained in the relations between the different kingdoms of the peninsula for much of the period. Equally the marriage of Isabella and Ferdinand was not intended to create, nor did it create, a unified Spanish state. It was a joining of two monarchs whose lands would retain considerable independence from one another not only while they lived but also under their successors. Nevertheless in the peninsula lands of both the Portuguese Crown and those of Castile and Aragon (there were also lands held by them outside of the peninsula) could be found new pressures and syntheses that help us to understand the expansion that was already under way when Isabella and Ferdinand decided to sponsor Columbus's first voyage in 1492. Castile in particular brought together three elements of immediate importance to Columbus and the wider European conquest of the Americas.

The first was the integration of parts of the Iberian peninsula with the Mediterranean. 'What was distinctive about the Age of Discovery in the 15th and 16th centuries was the combination of Iberian initiative and more general European involvement', writes one recent historian.[18] From the 13th to the 15th centuries it was the Aragonese city of Barcelona that had been 'the greatest city in Spain and one of the leading Mediterranean cities, rivalling Genoa and Florence in the volume of its trade and the power of its combined merchant marine navy'.[19] During the 15th century, however, internal turmoil and stagnation in Aragon saw a shift towards the territories of the Castilian monarchy and especially its Andalusian ports of which Seville was the most outstanding. To Seville came merchants, traders and financiers from the Italian cities and especially Genoa. By the late 15th century the scale of their activities probably put the efforts of the more numerous native merchant capitalists in the shade. There was therefore an element of cosmopolitanism in the first stirrings of capitalism. Columbus himself may have reflected this, for, on the basis of very limited evidence, it is usually conjectured that he was born in Genoa in 1451 and then moved around the Mediterranean to Portugal, gaining experience in Atlantic shipping and then pleading his case for help for a westward voyage before the monarchs of both Portugal and Castile before gaining the support of the latter.[20]

A second element was the dynamism of parts of the economy of Castile itself. As the French Marxist historian Pierre Vilar has put it:

> if Castile came to the fore then, it was because it was, from the 15th century on, a dynamic and creative country with its association of sheep-breeders (the Mesta), its Andalusian and Basque navy, its fairs (eg at Medina).[21]

After the catastrophe of the Black Death in the mid-14th century, the population of Europe recovered. Historians are reluctant to give population figures for the Iberian peninsula but we know that in Aragon the recovery was weak but in Castile it is much more substantial. This was primarily due to an increase in the amount of land cultivated but the additional elements that Vilar identifies were new innovative forces growing in importance in life on the peninsula. Sheep breeding had grown in the 14th century to allow Castile to become the chief area of wool production in Europe. The number of sheep appears to have increased from 1.5 million in 1300 to 2.7 million by 1467. The second component, Andalusian and Basque shipping, reflected the way in which, in the south, Sevillian sailors and ship owners were successful in the Mediterranean and the growing trade on the shores of the Atlantic, while in the north traders and seamen from Burgos and Bilbao played an important role in trade between Bordeaux and England and other parts of northern Europe. Vilar's last component was the great fairs of which that at Medina del Campo was the most important: 'with its world famous fairs [it] was the financial and commercial centre of Castile. It was the city of London of 16th century Spain.'[22]

The third general element that explains the Iberian base of exploration was the way in which the populations of the Iberian peninsula could draw on the interactions of Islamic, Jewish and Christian traditions. The centuries long dominance of Islam on the peninsula was a brilliant period of social and cultural development during which the Islamic parts were far ahead of the rest of Europe and the peninsula, although later generations of historians suppressed or distorted the memory of this. In particular it was thanks to Islamic scholars that much medieval knowledge became more widely available in Europe. It was through the world of al-Andalus that knowledge of ancient Greek culture and of Arab culture and science became available. In Toledo a school of translators was set up by a 13th century Christian king and they translated Greek and Arabic treatises from Arabic into Romance and then into Latin. Included in this were not only the works of philosophers like Aristotle but also the works and scientific conceptions that formed the basis of the idea that the world was round and gave measures, however inaccurate, of its dimensions. (The idea that the world was believed to be flat is a notorious 19th century invention.)[23] The peninsula also had the largest Jewish community in Europe although its exact size is disputed. This community not only carried its own traditions but was an important vehicle for the transmission of others. Jewish translators, for example, played a prominent role in the transmission of knowledge. For centuries these cultures had coexisted especially in al-Andalus but also in the Christian areas where Alfonso X of Castile had called himself the 'king of the three religions' in the 13th century. But from the 14th century Christian intolerance increased and in the Castilian and Aragonese kingdoms pressures developed to squeeze out the non-Christian, though not before the absorption of the knowledge and talents of the other traditions had helped to push this part of Europe further forward.

This Castilian synthesis was partly activated by feudal elements that derived from the old medieval society of southern Europe, of which the 'crusading spirit', which helped to sustain the conquest of the Islamic kingdoms of Spain, is the best example. Some have found in these traditional elements a sufficient explanation for the role of Spain (and Portugal) and therefore argued that overseas expansion was simply a product of European feudalism.[24] But this is a mistake. The synthesis, which was itself an increasingly new force, was also activated by deeper changes which reflected the decay of this old society and the prolonged and halting birth of something new. It is the combination of these new elements with the old and their increasing dominance that enables us to explain not only the origin of European overseas expansion but more importantly its *sustained* character.[25]

For capitalism to develop requires not just markets and trade, it needs the development of productive capital itself. Merchants and towns lived comfortably within the structures of feudal Europe so long as they simply moved goods around. They began to act as a solvent when their power was reinforced by changes in production itself. This process was painfully slow but it lay beneath the broader social conflicts that marked the end of feudalism.[26] In particular it helped to begin to decisively influence the change in political forms that began to push the medieval monarchies towards the modern state.

It was able to do this because of the fragmentation of political authority in medieval Europe. Feudal Europe had seen clashes between lords and monarchs, and monarchs and international Catholicism for authority. There was no single power, no single bureaucracy imposing unified policies. Therefore, when feudalism decayed and new forces arose—the possibility developed of the emergence of embryonic state forms within which divergent policies could develop. Out of this came a broad differentiation between eastern Europe, where the peasantry became less free in the 16th century, and western Europe, where the chains binding lord and peasant were loosened. But out of it also came a differentiation within western Europe and more locally still within the Iberian peninsula where Castile showed more vigour compared to Aragon. Culture too was changing and a distinctive materialism was emerging which reflected and reinforced capitalist development and the dissolution of feudal values. 'Wealth' was being redefined and revalued. Its most characteristic expression was the growing lust for gold and the idea that through its acquisition could come power and advancement. 'Gold is most excellent', wrote Columbus on his final voyage, 'Whoever has it may do what he wishes in the world.' In the journal of Columbus's first voyage Kirkpatrick Sale has counted 130 times when gold is mentioned and the fervour for gold continued to oscillate with a fervour for 'the Lord' in the minds of the conquistadors.[27] 'We came here to serve God and to get rich', Cortés famously said. For Bartolomé de las Casas, the great humanist critic of the conquest of Latin America, the Spanish had an 'unlimited and close fitted avarice'. The rapacity with which this unlimited avarice was to be pursued was not, as some have argued, a reflection of a 'failure of imagination' when confronted with a new and different world, rather it was the most extreme expression of the crystallisation of an emerging new social imagination in Europe.[28]

The scale of Iberian 'discovery' and conquest

The outward thrust of Europe was partly one of 'discovery' as adventurers expanded the area of the world known to Europe. There were some three dozen major voyages in what can be called the heroic phase of exploration from the 1490s to the 1630s when the search for a north west passage was finally abandoned. Thereafter a period of consolidation set in until the second half of the 18th century when Cook was central to exploring the remaining areas of the Pacific unknown to Europeans.

What drove this first period of exploration was the attempt to find a route to Asia. Here the Portuguese were successful in navigating around Africa and establishing a commercial relationship to compete with the old routes of the spice trade. Columbus and the Castilians went west and unexpectedly found the Americas though subsequently Magellen and Elcano were able to establish a non-commercial route to Asia around South America. It was Spanish and Portuguese control of these possibilities that led other adventurers, sponsored by northern

European crowns, to search for a north west passage around north America and a north east passage around Russia. Both proved dead ends but in the process other possibilities were revealed.

But alongside discovery went conquest. Here there was a fundamental difference in the early days between the European impact in west and east. The 'discovery' of the Americas, largely by Spain, was also primarily an act of direct conquest. The French historian Pierre Chaunu has argued that a cyclical pattern developed in the occupation of the Americas and subsequent Spanish-American commerce. The first 25 years of conquest and plunder gave the Spanish crown a territory of some 250,000sq.km. in the form of the early Spanish Main. By the middle of the second decade of the century, however, the outward thrust appeared to have exhausted itself against a disappointing economic background. A second wave of expansion followed in the 1520s and 1530s with the conquest of the Aztec and Inca empires. The Aztec empire is reckoned to have covered some 300,000sq.km. and by 1522 Cortés was in control of two thirds of it doubling the size of the Spanish empire in the Americas to 400,000 to 500,000sq.kms. The drive south into Peru and Chile expanded it even further. By the mid-century some 4 to 5 million sq.km. had been explored by conquistadors and control established over some 1.5 million sq.km. in the form of the two Vice-Royalties centred on modern day Mexico and Peru. Portugal too established its own colonial base on the coasts of Brazil to add to the total size of the European empire in the Americas.[29]

The precise size of the pre-conquest Indian populations is a matter of controversy on which we will comment later. However, it seems that by the end of the first wave of conquest (circa 1515) some 200,000 to 300,000 Indians and some 10,000 colonists were part of the empire. By 1550 this had increased to some 9 to 10 million Indians and some 30,000 to 40,000 colonists. Given that at this point the Spanish Crown was part of a wider dynastic Habsburg Empire in Europe this meant that the Habsburg Emperor and Spanish King Charles V ruled over some 30 millions.[30]

But this second phase of expansion exhausted itself in the 1540s and 1550s. A new third wave developed, based on the more intensive development of the existing American empire and especially Mexico and Peru as a result of the discovery of silver and the mercury amalgam technique which allowed its easier recovery, which dates from 1555-66 in Mexico and 1575-8 in Peru. This was also the period of more intensive development in Brazil with the development of plantations which made it the world's largest sugar producer.

In the east Portuguese expansion was not based primarily on direct conquest and colonisation because the Europeans were not highly enough developed to have a decisive superiority. Instead an attempt was made to control trade and by the mid-century more than 50 forts stretched from Sofala (in modern Mozambique) to Nanking in China. Some of these were precarious toeholds but the most important were Mozambique itself, the island of Ormuz controlling the Persian Gulf, Goa on the west coast of India, Malacca (in modern Malaya) for the spice market, east Mulucca and Macao, first occupied in 1557. Spain too was present in the east and in 1565 established a proper colonial base in the Philippines that it was to hold until the late 19th century.

As a result the first phase of European expansion was dominated by Spain and Portugal. In 1580, as a result of family ties, bribery and threat, the crown of Portugal fell into the lap of Philip II of Spain. The resulting union under the Spanish crown (until 1640) meant that Spain was 'in the impressive position of controlling Europe's every overseas colony and foothold from China to Peru'. 'And were there more lands still to discover they would be there too', wrote Cameons, the great Portuguese literary chronicler of this first phase of European conquest and penetration.[31] In fact this was not to be. By the beginning of the 18th century European possessions covered around 10 percent of the land area of the world and 2 percent of its population—to expand beyond this would require a vigour lacking in the imperial centres of the first wave of European expansion.[32]

The nature of pre-Columbian American societies

When Columbus arrived in the Caribbean he found the islands 'thickly peopled' but the question of how many people there were in the whole of the Americas in the autumn of 1492 has produced one of the most intriguing 'technical' problems in history. Most early commentators, sceptical of the stories of the vastness of the loss of life that followed the arrival of the Europeans, inclined to low figures. More recent writers, taking account of the potential populations that could have been sustained by native agricultural techniques and the rapidity with which newly introduced diseases can kill, have pushed the figures up, in one case to around 100 million which would put the population on a par with that of Europe at the time. Table 1 sets out some of the estimates that have been made with what looks to be a sensible middle figure in the last column though even here the suggested margin for error is plus or minus 25 percent giving a population range of from 43 to 72 million.

TABLE 1: THE RANGE OF ESTIMATES OF THE NATIVE POPULATION
IN THE AMERICAS IN 1492 IN MILLIONS [33]

Region of Americas	Sapper 1924	Koebner 1939	Steward 1949	Rosenblat 1954	Dobyns 1966	Denevan 1976
North	2-3.5	0.9	1.0	1.0	9.8-12.3	4.4
Mexico	12-15	3.2	4.5	4.5	30.0-37.5	21.4
Central	5-6	0.1	0.7	0.8	10.8-13.5	5.7
Caribbean	3-4	0.2	0.2	0.3	0.4-0.6	5.9
Andes	12-15	3.0	6.1	4.7	30.0-37.5	11.5
Lowland South	3-5	1.0	2.9	2.3	9.0-11.3	8.5
Total	37-48.5	8.4	15.5	13.4	90.4-112.6	57.3

Whatever the precise numbers, clearly by 1492 most parts of the Americas had been touched by human settlement and in many parts settlement was very extensive. Overall a wide range of societies existed from primitive hunter-gatherers to the classic civilisations of the Aztecs and the Incas. The question of the nature of these native American societies has provoked widely differing reactions from sensationalist stories of mass blood sacrifice to highly politicised accounts. In the case of the Incas, for example, in 1928 Louis Baudin, a right wing French economist, published his *A Socialist Empire. The Incas of Peru*. Here he attacked Inca society as a form of socialist despotism based on a society with collective property—though he had to admit the influence of the Inca example on later socialists 'was very slight'![34] Ironically it was in the same year that José Carlos Mariátegui (1894-1930), little known in Europe but the greatest Latin American Marxist of the inter-war period, published the first edition of his *Seven Interpretative Essays on Peruvian Reality*.[35] For Mariátegui it was the positive elements of primitive agrarian communism that were outstanding. He believed that elements of these had survived over the centuries in the Indian communities to make a point of contact with modern day socialism.[36] Today, by contrast, the Inca and Aztec societies are presented neither as embryonic Stalinisms nor primitive socialisms but as environmental utopias where productivity was raised at minimum cost to nature.[37]

Such arguments are largely myth making masquerading as history. It is important to begin, therefore, by saying that when we look at the evolution of native society in the Americas we are exploring the evolution of class societies. These existed in some form of development everywhere in 1492 except in a small number of isolated areas and even here the characterisation of such exceptions has been disputed. Equally we must also insist that the fact that these societies were about

to be overtaken by another form of brutal class society should not lead
us to lose perspective on the real contradictions and class antagonisms
that they contained before the arrival of Columbus.

Traditionally it has been argued that the ancestors of the 1492 population entered the Americas across the Bering Strait land bridge some
12,000 years ago and then gradually worked their way southwards, possibly by both land and sea. But this argument is increasingly challenged
by archeological finds that are claimed to go back as far as 40,000 BC
or earlier—though accepting such early dates poses serious problems
in explaining the lack of comparable Siberian sites as well as explaining how early populations could have survived in more hostile climatic
ages. Whatever the solution to this conundrum people did arrive and
social organisation did develop.[38]

The first peoples that Columbus met in the Caribbean were some of
the less developed on the continent. In the Caribbean Columbus found
two groups—the Arawak Indians 'gentle and timid people...without
armaments or laws' as he put it and what were seen as ruthless, canni-
balistic Caribs. In fact there is good reason to think that much of the
terrifying picture painted of the Caribs was invention—a conscious and
unconscious reflection of the way that they proved a greater hindrance
to expansion than the Arawaks.[39] In North America too the native populations were still at relatively low levels though in some regions more
complex societies had developed. Similarly development was patchy in
the lowland areas of south America.[40]

It was in the areas of modern day central America and the Andes
that the greatest development had taken place. In Meso America (north
of Mexico City and south of Nicaragua) Olmec culture had flourished
from 1500-500 BC. This gave way to city states like Teotihuacan in
central Mexico—larger than imperial Rome at its peak with a population of perhaps 200,000. This city was burned and abandoned in the
mid-8th century. In Yucatan, the 4th century AD saw the rise of the society of the classic Maya civilisation which attained impressive levels
until it collapsed around 900 AD. This was a civilisation which was
characterised by its high level of astronomy and its development of a
true hieroglyph based writing system. In South America, in modern
Peru, a similar development of city states had occurred especially with
the Moches in the north and the Nascas in the south. The main period
of growth of the Nascas was from 200 BC to 600 AD and that of the
Moches from the first century AD to the mid-8th century.

Thus the final stages of development in these areas—the rise of the
Aztecs in central America and the Incas in modern day Peru—both occurred against a long background of development and change.
Although Aztec and Inca society developed independently they shared
the fact that they both emerged explosively in the 15th century as

rapidly expanding empires. In central Mexico the Aztecs moved from being one group amongst several to imposing their domination over large areas from the Atlantic to the Pacific. The Incas developed in a similar way from 1438 so that by 1500 the territory covered by the Inca empire was greater than that covered by Ming China or the Ottoman empire in Europe.

Both Aztec and Inca societies depended upon tribute flowing from the periphery to the centre, the countryside to the town, the lower classes to the different components of the ruling class. Although the Americas lacked the wheel and the plough a relatively productive agriculture existed that seemed to have avoided the Malthusian cycle that some historians claim dominated feudal Europe. Agriculture was based on maize in Mexico and the potato and quinoa in the higher regions of Peru and Bolivia. In both instances the diet was supplemented by beans, marrows, tomatoes, chillies etc. The fertility of the soil was increased in both areas by irrigation work and it was these practices that formed the basis of latter day claims that agriculture was better adapted than modern farming.[41] However it must be remembered that the real benefits flowed upwards to the Aztec and Inca ruling class—to aid their wars and maintain their own patterns of consumption as well as to allow their class societies to reproduce in difficult times such as those of famine.

Surplus was transferred upwards in the form of both labour and produce. In the case of the Aztecs, for example, annual tribute to the Emperor Montezuma and his regime flowed from some 370 towns and included over 30,000 tons of foodstuffs—enough to feed nearly 400,000. Although there was no real sense in which an analogy could be drawn between this society and that of the Iberian peninsula it is not surprising that when Cortés first saw the splendour and wealth in which the Aztec rulers and their supporters lived in the capital, Tenochtitlan, (on which parts of modern Mexico city were to be built) it was exactly the class identity he was drawn to, commenting on the houses of 'the nobles of the country' and its 'many wealthy burghers'.[42]

This exploitation depended upon production within village communities. It was from here that the main agricultural surplus was drawn to supply the wants of the aristocratic-bureaucratic class whose power was based on their military, religious and political control.[43] To hold such societies together and allow a surplus to be removed it was necessary to rely on more than force alone. Ideology and religion played a crucial role in legitimating rule and enforcing tribute in terms of not only goods and labour but also the sacrifice of human life. The completeness of this religious submission which, particularly amongst the Aztecs involved large scale sacrifices, is an indication of the tightness of control needed to hold this form of class society together. This was also apparent in the legal systems where the power of the rulers was reflected in the codification of their rights, privileges and morality. In the case of the Inca empire, for example:

> *Inca criminal law has characteristics which reflect much of what was true of the social and political system as a whole: the emphasis on the sacredness of the central government, its symbols, prosperity and officials; the punitive distinction made between criminals on the basis of rank and sex; the reservation of the power to condemn to death; the placing of sexual crimes on a level with offences meriting the death penalty—all these reflected the dominance of government power, the strict social divisions and the puritanical streak in Inca society.*[44]

Many discussions of both Inca and Aztec society present their class systems as being impositions from above on basically egalitarian village communities. This view fits in well with the idealisation of the peasant community in a substantial part of the indigenist movement. However, it is dangerous to underestimate the extent to which internal class differentiation existed within the villages and the links that this had to the wider class systems of these empires.[45]

Internal tensions like these and conflicts with other groups such as merchants combined with strains that were a product of the explosive expansion of these societies and the difficulties of digesting conquered areas to produce a highly volatile mixture on the eve of European conquest. The consequent fragility of control from the centre enables us to understand better why the Aztec and Inca empires disintegrated so quickly in the face of the European challenge. Indeed the probability is that some form of disintegration might well have occurred even if the European conquerors had not arrived when they did. This is so not only in the sense that both the Aztec and Inca empires were politically fragile but also in the wider sense that these societies were in movement socially towards higher forms. The degree to which this is true is disputed, but the Marxist anthropologist Godelier has argued that in broader social terms if they were to advance and not simply collapse inwards two roads were open—towards a form of slave society, or more likely, as he sees it, towards a variant of feudalism.[46]

As it was, when the conquistadors followed Columbus and penetrated inland they were able to rely on three elements which together enabled them to subordinate large parts of the continent. Firstly, they had the element of surprise over both societies because of European technological superiority.[47] Secondly, they were preceded and accompanied by huge epidemics of disease that left those who did not die demoralised and confused. In the Inca empire, for example, smallpox carried off the Emperor Huaya Capat and his designated successor, leaving a succession battle in its wake. Thirdly, and crucially in terms of our preceding discussion, they were able to exploit internal divisions created by the contradictions of the rapid expansion of Aztec and Inca society and turn them to their own advantage. W H Prescott, the great 19th century American historian of the conquest of the Aztecs, concluded that 'the Aztec monarchy fell by the hands of its own subjects' and the conquistador Francisco Pizarro similarly reported of the Inca empire that 'had the land not been divided we would not have been able to enter and win'.

The immediate impact

The immediate impact of the conquest of the Americas is dominated by the demographic catastrophe it created. Depending on the initial population estimate some 75 to 90 percent of the native population died within three to four generations of 1492. This was 'the very greatest demographic carnage in human history'.[48] Its most important cause was disease, what Pierre Chaunu has called 'a fantastic biological war of the worlds' as smallpox, measles, typhus, plague, yellow fever and malaria swept through populations with no experience of them and no resistance.[49] To this was then added the shock of conquest and the subsequent cruelties of colonial rule.

TABLE 2: EXAMPLES OF ESTIMATED DECLINES OF NATIVE
POPULATIONS IN THE AMERICAS[50]

	San Domingo	Central Mexico	Peru
1493-4	4-8,000,000		
1496	2.5-3,000,000		
1500	90-100,000		
1509	60,000		
1512	30,000		
1514	25-30,000		
1518	15,000	25,200,000	9,000,000
1532		16,800,000	
1540	250	—	
1548		6,300,000	
1568		2,650,000	
1570	125		1,000,000
1585		1,900,000	
1595		1,400,000	
1607	0	1,100,000	
1620		700,000	670,000

Table 2 gives some examples of the scale of the human losses and Table 3 the resulting change in the composition of the population of the Americas by the turn of the 19th century.

The scale of this catastrophe was not uniform. On the islands and mainland fringes of the Caribbean the native populations became more or less completely extinct as their more primitive communities were disrupted and overwhelmed. On the mainland the more complex communities showed some demographic resistance, maintaining some community structures and social organisation. Missions which sought to remould local society had a catastrophic effect, so too did slavery. Officially in the lands of the Spanish crown this was banned from 1542 but it persisted in some areas and in Portuguese Brazil, and the deaths in capture, as a result of overwork and indirectly through community disruption, pulled numbers further down. Forced labour also encouraged direct and indirect demographic decline but some recovery was possible as free labour was established in Mexico in the 17th century and Peru in the 18th. This gave the native population more control over their lives and communities but ultimately the freer labour market encouraged mobility and intermarriage and led to an increase in the mestizo (Indian-European) community as can be seen in table 3.[51]

TABLE 3: THE ETHNIC COMPOSITION OF THE POST-1492
POPULATION OF THE AMERICAS IN 000's[52]

	c.1492	c.1650	c.1825
Indian	57,300	10,035	8,334
Mestizos		401	5,130
Whites		849	13,475
Blacks		857	6,433
Mulattos		269	1,121
Total	57,300	12,000	34,500

Even on the most conservative estimates this catstrophe of conquest is so great that the Indian populations have often seemed to be helpless victims in the face of it. All they could do was to retain a degree of dignity. As the widely quoted lines of an Aztec manuscript put it:

Let us die, then,
Let us die, then,
For our gods are already dead.

But it is now recognised that this is misleading. In a pioneering study in the 1950s, J H Rowe bluntly insisted of the Incas that their 'resistance to the Spanish invasion was bitter, obstinate and frequently effective' and this is now recognised to be true much more widely in the

Americas.[53] Indians were both victims and actors struggling to make their own response. This took a number of forms.

One was simply flight ahead of the advancing frontier. The extent of this depended on the nature of the European conquest—it was easier nearer the frontier than in other areas. Flight was also the response of slaves brought to areas like Brazil. In both instances such flight did not necessarily mean a journey into a primitive unknown as apparently vibrant organised communities were maintained in areas outside European control. Such communities though were subject to disruption as in Brazil by brutish raiding parties seeking labour, slaves and anything else they could find. In the long run they were also under pressure as the European frontier advanced further across the surface of the Americas.

A second response was the Indian defence of their own communities within the colonial systems through concessions to preserve the essentials.[54] This could take positive forms involving the incorporation of more advanced elements of European life, including techniques, into the Indian community (eg crops in agriculture, the use of the horse and so on). It could also take the negative form of formal obedience and identification with European culture and religion to avoid more detailed direct European control. Communities could and did negotiate degrees of autonomy for themselves by working within the system and trying to turn it to their advantage including using their rights under the Spanish legal system.[55] But care has to be taken in analysing this. Such a search for a negotiated space could always become too accommodating, leaving little real freedom because too much ground had been given. Secondly, it is also important to avoid idealising such communities since the twin pressures of exactions from the outside and pressures for conformity from within could make them repressive structures for the Indians themselves.

A third type of response was open resistance. In the first place the expansion of the frontier was often resisted and this could last for long periods. Once the frontier had been established there was still the possibility of fighting back. In the case of the Incas, for example, armed resistance lasted until the 1570s. It rose again in the 17th century and there were partial revolts in the 18th century in 1737-1738, 1739, 1762 before 'the greatest of all Inca Rebellions in 1780-1782' with the final revolt as late as 1814-15.[56] Similarly there was a no less important tradition of revolt in central America too.

But behind this newer history of resistance lies a deeper problem —just what kind of system was it that was oppressing and exploiting the Indian populations? What were they fighting back against? To

answer this we have to turn to the long term economic and social structures that were created by conquest.

The economic and social structure of the early colonial Americas

In the first half century or so of European conquest little short of a
'plunder economy' existed in the Americas as native communities were
stripped of things the Europeans valued. By the second half of the 16th
century a more systematic social and economic structure was being created. This involved the transplanting and remodelling of many of the
institutions of the Iberian peninsula to the new conditions of the
Americas. In the 19th century Latin American liberals interpreted this
as the imposition of feudalism and looked forward to encouraging
bourgeois reforms and revolutions which would 'modernise' their societies. In the middle decades of the 20th century this idea solidified on
the left under the influence of Stalinism which could only see national
roads from 'feudalism' to 'capitalism' and then, at some far distant
point, to 'socialism'. Yet the 'classic bourgeois revolution' failed to
materialise in central and south America and the notion that these areas
were developing separately from the overall evolution of world capitalism became increasingly difficult to sustain.

In reaction to this an interpretative revolution developed associated
with the writings of Andre Gunder Frank and, later, Immanuel
Wallerstein.[57] Although their arguments were not identical they had
three great strengths. Firstly, they both insisted that capitalism can only
be understood as a world economy so that the evolution of the parts
cannot be seen in isolation from the development of the whole.
Secondly, they insisted no less that 'underdevelopment' was not a pre-
capitalist state but the distorted form taken by capitalist development
outside the main cores of the system—Latin American social relations,
therefore, were not those of feudalism and even less of some virgin
state untouched by development. Thirdly, they argued that in trying to
understand what had been created it was important to recognise that
various forms of unfree labour were compatible with capitalism so that
it was not sufficient, as many had done, to point to the weakness of the
free labour market to deduce that capitalism was something that had
still to develop. But from these arguments they then jumped to the conclusion that a capitalist world economy was created in the 16th century
and that the Americas after 1492, as part of the periphery of this world
economy, were therefore also capitalist. What defined capitalism was
simply whether or not there was production for the world market. Since
that production existed, the problem was solved.

Against this, critics of their work like Ernesto Laclau and Robert Brenner offered a solution of no less illusory simplicity. For them the key question was not the market but wage labour—the essence of capitalism. Since simple wage labour did not dominate in Latin America at this time then it could not be capitalist. For Laclau, in particular, it was still a feudal society. The subsequent debate has found it hard to transcend these entrenched positions and Frank himself has oscillated between them.[58] Others have argued that they cannot be transcended and have instead gone for an apparent middle position arguing that what existed were 'social formations' which combined different modes of production side by side. Still others have tried to invent new categories such as colonial modes of production or—the final concept of despair —a Latin American mode of production.[59] But these arguments have produced little more than classification schemes.

This will not do either theoretically or empirically. Theoretically what this discussion does is to deal with relatively abstract categories like 'the world market', 'free wage labour' and so on. History then becomes a simple checking of abstract criteria. This is history and theory without the sweat of understanding because it is not informed by a real attempt to grapple with the way in which, as capitalism develops, it historically transforms the concepts that we need to understand it.

Take the issue of 'feudalism'. Frank and Wallerstein are right to suggest that the structures created in the Americas were not simple extensions of medieval Europe. Firstly, what was transplanted was itself a product of societies in which feudalism was decaying and something new emerging. Secondly, the very act of transplantation could accentuate the new elements. The Americas, for example, combined forced labour with elements of free labour that may well have been 'freer' than labour in Europe. Certainly the colonial state was interested in encouraging formal wage labour.[60] Thirdly, the logic of production did indeed derive in part from the demands expressed through the commerce of the Atlantic, the core of the then world market. But just because capitalism was relatively weak everywhere at this stage it follows that we cannot then jump to impose the categories of the modern capitalist world economy on the 16th or 17th centuries as Frank and Wallerstein do.

Rather, what we have to analyse are complex transitional forms which are a product of the uneven development of capitalism. They are not totally subordinate to the dictates of the full cycle of capital reproduction and accumulation precisely because the system is weak and as yet partially formed. To understand them, therefore, we have to dig beneath the form to look at the underlying dynamic of production and reproduction. Agricultural estate work, forced labour in mines, and slave plantation work cannot be declared either capitalist or non-capitalist in the abstract. There is a world of difference between, say, slave labour in the Roman world, slave labour in 16th century Brazil and slave labour in the American South in the 19th century. But at a formal level 'slave labour' appears the same in each case. It is only when we look underneath this to explore the dynamics of these forms that enormous differences emerge and it becomes possible to see how in some instances, as Banaji argues, slave labour can be a part of the capitalist system producing surplus value, while in other cases it is not.

In these terms how did 16th and 17th century Latin America fare once the plunder economy began to be replaced by longer term economic forms? The answer is that the decisive factor has to be the very partial nature of 'capitalism'. Here there was a compulsion to accumulate but there were other forms of motion too including what Banaji calls 'the compulsion to defend and improve social consumption'. The exact balance varied in place and time as we can see if we look at the organisation and dynamic of production in this period.[61]

At the core of the new economy in the Americas was silver production in Mexico and Peru. Between 1560 and 1685 colonial mines produced some 25,000 to 30,000 tons of silver and a further 60,000 tons between 1686 and 1810. In the early part of the period production was dominated by the Potosí silver mountain in Peru—by 1600 some two thirds of silver produced in the Americas was coming from here and one third from Mexico. However, during the 17th century Potosí went into decline and in the last quarter of the 17th century it was overtaken by Mexico as the main producer. Mexican silver production was also spread more evenly around a group of mines than in Peru (where Potosí itself was still producing 40 percent of that region's silver in the 1780s).[62] A second base of integration into the world market developed in Portuguese Brazil where the focus was the sugar estate. The number of sugar estates rose from 60 in 1570 to 346 in 1629 and 528 in 1710. Here, however, we will largely concentrate on silver although the analysis applies as much to sugar.

The silver that was produced was minted into coin and a part of this was then used to pay for imports and government taxes and transfers as well as profits repatriated to Spain. Such silver therefore entered the wider Atlantic economy (and to a lesser extent the Pacific economy). In particular silver paid for the import of consumption goods not available in the Americas and part of the mercury that was needed for the mercury amalgam process to release the silver from the ore. Mercury was imported from Almaden in Spain and Indria (formerly Idrija) in Italy. A second part of the coined silver stayed in the Americas where it was used for taxes, the purchases of goods, payments of wages and loans as well as for further investment.

Around this process of silver production there developed the wider linkages of colonial organisation. Backward linkages fed into the Indian communities in terms of demand for forced and voluntary labour. Some small scale industrial production also existed to supply consumption and production needs. But the main backward linkage was to the hacienda system of agricultural estates supplying foodstuffs. The seizure of large areas of land for estates at one level served to force parts of the Indian population into the labour market, at another level it widened the consumer market. Foodstuffs produced on the haciendas then fed the populations of the mining areas and the colonial urban centres. In assessing the degree of penetration of capitalist relations the extent of the hacienda system is therefore crucial. But it is important not to exaggerate the size of individual haciendas and the overall land they occupied. Forward linkages also developed in the core urban centres concentrating the commercial and administrative centres necessary to support colonial rule and life.[63]

Enormous attention has been devoted to the conditions and nature of Indian labour in these different colonial structures. The condition of labour has been at the centre of debate over the so called 'Black Legend'—the cruelty of colonial exploitation. Apologists for the system have sought to diminish the force of the evidence of contemporary critics and especially the evidence of Bartolomé de las Casas, but his damning commentary has stood up extraordinarily well.[64] No less, apologists have tried to explain the evidence away by arguing that the Spanish crown tried to enforce humane laws but was defeated by the private cruelty of the colonialists. But this will not do because the Crown was quite capable of rigidly enforcing cruel laws of its own and its attempt to control the system amounted to no more than what one contemporary called a proposal 'to commit inequities humanely, and to consummate injustices equitably.' But, of course, the system here was not peculiarly Spanish in origin. Theodore de Bry, a Dutchman who later popularised the evidence of cruelty put together by las Casas, wrote, 'Let us not be so hasty in condemning the Spaniards, but let us rather examine ourselves to see whether we are any better.'[65] With hindsight the answer must be no, for the system that lay behind the cruelty would grow in strength and produce worse barbarisms in the future.

But the nature of the labour process is also central, as we have seen, to the debate on the mode of production question. In both Peru and Mexico forced labour initially played an important role in mining but in Mexico wage labour forms quickly became more important. In Peru, however, continued labour shortages and higher costs meant that it was only possible to maintain production 'on the condition of not paying for the costs of the production and reproduction of labour power.' This meant that the *mit' a*—the forced labour of workers from Indian communities—remained a decisive part of mining until very late on though even in Peru elements of free labour developed albeit in a 'labour market' that was closely conditioned by this central unfree element. African slaves were also to be found in parts of the Spanish Empire though their main contribution at this time was on the sugar plantations of Portuguese Brazil. Because of the collapse of the Indian populations these sugar estates came to depend on slaves from Africa. 'No slaves, no sugar, no Brazil' was the saying. Slavery was not abolished in Brazil until 1888.[66] The slave population increased accordingly from some 13,000 to 15,000 in 1600, to 150,000 in 1680. This growth was based on imports of slaves which averaged 7,000 to 8,000 in the 17th century. The plantations therefore created an enormous slave mortality which reflected the poor conditions and the attendant disease. In the 17th century such conditions also came to characterise the growing sugar plantations of the Caribbean.[67]

But the real issue is less the balance of forced or free labour than what drove the production in which both were engaged. We can see the partial nature of their subordination to the dictates to produce surplus value (rather than just a surplus) in three crucial respects. The first is that the ties to the wider world, though real, were still weak. How much of production was determined by the wider world? Since we have only the haziest idea of the value and volume of trade, we cannot say. Because trade across the Atlantic was expensive it had to involve not only the export of high value silver but also the import of high value goods. Its relative importance may well, therefore, have been more significant than any volume figures suggest. However, even if we allow for multiplier effects we must still recognise the limited role these wider connections played. With fleets sailing at limited, set times and with a six month round trip from Spain to Mexico and an 18 month trip to Peru and back we are inevitably looking at a production process which *in general* had at this stage a significant degree of autonomy. The parts that were closely tied to the wider world were not yet representative of the whole.

Secondly, the degree of integration into the Atlantic economy itself varied over time. In particular, in the 17th century silver production fell off although at different rates and for different lengths of time in different areas. This was a part of the 'depression' of the 17th century in the Americas. Its precise scale is still disputed but we know that it did disrupt the trade networks and forced the Latin American economy to look inward leading to a 'compartmentalisation' of the different colonial regions. This response reflected the partial way in which the logic of capital imposed itself in the sense that were the system fully developed then a retreat to a greater degree of self sufficiency would not have been a real option. The system was not yet restructuring as a fully capitalist system would require it to do. As one historian puts it in a telling phrase about one region, 'for more than a century Peru lacked an engine to drive the economy.'[68]

The third expression of this partial integration occurs at a microlevel and it is to be found in an examination of the way in which individual enterprises and estates functioned at this time. It is here that we can trace in detail the complexity of the degree of subordination to the requirements of the reproduction of capital. It is here that we can see how the enterprises of this time contained other dynamics too. Instead of 'reconstructing them in the image of capital' we can therefore construct them as the complex transitional forms that they were.

But having said this it is important to conclude by stressing that this argument also points to the historical limits of such transitional forms. Because they reflect the weakness of capitalism in its initial stages of development they become increasingly more unusual as capitalism matures. The very development of capitalism means that imperatives of the reproduction of capital become more dominant and these forms are subsumed more directly into the capitalist mode of production. This does not automatically mean that the outer form changes—its shell can continue but the inner content is transformed and it is this that those who see capitalism sponsoring the continued existence (or even the creation) of other modes of production miss. But for capitalism to develop its full power to undermine and transform from within and without, as it would later do in the Americas and other parts of the world, then it had itself to be transformed into a more mature form. This transformation could only come from deeper changes in the core of the system.

The Americas and European capitalism

If we turn from the Americas themselves to the question of the impact of their conquest on Europe we enter a no less intriguing area of debate. A long historical tradition, especially on the left, has seen the development of capitalism in Europe in terms of an expansion in the 16th century but crisis in the 17th century. This crisis was only resolved by underlying economic and social change and, in a number of countries, an assertion of political power or influence by the emerging bourgeoisie.[69] Since we have seen that the development of the Americas also involved expansion in the 16th century to be followed by signs of crisis in the 17th then it is tempting to see a link between the two processes and make the colonial development of the Americas the factor that explains the rhythms of the rise of capitalism in Europe. This argument has taken many forms. In its crudest, nationalist, version Europe is pictured as developing by a simple transfer of wealth and resources to such an extent that the process of internal capital accumulation in Europe is ignored. More sophisticated versions suggest more intricate connections with the exploitation of the Americas creating the primary accumulation of capital which could then set in motion capitalist development in Europe. In the famous thesis of the American historian Earl J Hamilton it was the import of American treasure which led to a price revolution in which profits rose faster than wages, leading to the growth in the power of capital.[70] More recently the various aspects of this tradition have been subsumed in the European side of the writings of the so-called 'world system theorists' who have been inspired by the work of Andre Gunder Frank and Immanuel Wallerstein.

If we are simply interested in quotation mongering it is not difficult to find support for these general positions in the writings of Marx and those in the classical Marxist tradition. Most famously Marx wrote that 'capital comes into the world dripping from head to foot, from every pore, with blood and dirt' and that:

> *the discovery of gold and silver in America, the extirpation, enslavement and entombment in mines of the aboriginal population, the beginning of the conquest and looting of the East Indies, the turning of Africa into a warren for the commercial hunting of black skins, signalled the rosy dawn of capitalist production.*[71]

But neither Marx nor the other classical Marxists attempted a sustained analysis of the relationship of the Americas to the rise of capitalism so that by themselves these quotations mean little. What we need to develop is an empirical understanding of what happened that is consistent with what we know of the longer run dynamics of capitalist expansion. In this respect there ought to be no doubt that capitalist development depended on the creation of a working class and the development of increasing exploitation in Europe. It is this that forms the core of Marx's historical analysis in *Capital* and it is this that has correctly been at the centre of attention in the best accounts of those who have written on the rise of capitalism.

This process was brutal and it was supplemented by brutal processes of primitive accumulation outside of Europe, of which the experience of the Americas formed a important part. This is the point of Marx's comment and our earlier analysis—but it was only supplemented by this. Neither directly nor indirectly were the extra-European processes the decisive ones. Indeed if the question is posed in terms of what is the key—exploitation in the European core or on the periphery of the world economy—then the answer empirically and theoretically always has to be exploitation in the cores.[72] But this is not a helpful way of posing the question of capitalist development because in reality it is not based or 'either/or' processes. The construction of national income accounts which try to measure external trade, capital and labour flows and then set them against 'internal' national flows can do a violence to the reality of capitalism as a functioning whole. Here Wallerstein and Frank are right and it is not a point peculiar to them. Marx recognised it as did John Stuart Mill when he wrote, of a later period, that 'the trade with the West Indies is hardly to be considered an external trade, but more resembles the traffic between town and country.'[73]

The important point is to see that this greater whole and the network of relations within it are based upon a structured inequality. Capitalism as a world economy is an assymetrical system in which there is necessarily unevenness in the level of development and also a resulting unevenness in the value of the flows between the different parts. Moreover, to fully explain how this world economy develops it is also necessary in the advanced world to allow that the world economy has a history and to see its commanding position in modern life developing out of the growth of capitalism. The alternative is simply to see the world economy as a category that can be imposed from the outside. To this extent the same criticism must be made of those in the 'world system' tradition when their ideas are applied to Europe, as we have made clear in the context of the relevance of their ideas to the early history of the Americas after Columbus. We can put some flesh on these terse comments about method by looking more closely at the evidence of change in Europe in the 16th and 17th centuries.

We do not know the precise values or volume of trade between Europe and the Americas but thanks to the work of two French historians, Pierre and Huguette Chaunu, we have fairly precise measures of the Atlantic sailings and gross shipping tonnage from the port of Seville. The importance of this was that until the mid-17th century Seville had a general (though not perfectly complete) monopoly of European trade with the Americas, so the records of the Casa de la Contratación which organised trade give us a good measure of trends and scale.[74] The statistics we now have show that sailings both ways rose from 226 in 1506-10 to a peak of 965 in the years 1606-10 falling to only 366 between 1646 and 1650 as part of the general depression in trade with the Americas. Thereafter the picture becomes confused with trade recovering more in value terms and becoming more diversified and therefore difficult to track in the second half of the 17th century. In the peak individual year of 1608 there were 202 sailings involving a gross tonnage of 54,000 tons. The main imports that this trade brought from the Americas were precious metals. In the 16th century gold and especially silver made up 90 to 95 percent of European imports by value. There was then some diversification, particularly in the trade with Mexico, but precious metals were still dominant—especially if the growing unofficial inflow of silver is taken into account. In the 16th century exports to the Americas were largely agricultural goods but in the next century there was a growing demand for manufactured goods that Spanish industry found it difficult to respond to, so that the trade ramifications of American demand were felt more widely in the European economy.

But how big was the overall impact of the Americas on European development? There is no doubt that Seville and its immediate region benefited enormously and the feedback into parts of the European economy was significant. But it is dangerous to leap from a regional analysis to the emerging capitalist economy of Europe as a whole.

For Adam Smith 'the discovery of the America, and that of a passage to the East Indies by the Cape of Good Hope, are the two greatest and most important events recorded in the history of the world'.[75] From our perspective of a dominant world economy with the United States playing a leading role it is even easier to understand this view. But this is not necessarily how it seemed in the 16th and 17th centuries. After an initial enthusiasm for Columbus's achievement we now know that European activities in the Americas had a limited impact on European consciousness. One reason for this is that Europeans found it difficult to integrate knowledge of the Americas into their mental view of the world.[76] More importantly, contemporaries viewed the east as more important than the west both because there was an immediate threat from the expanding Ottoman empire and because, beyond it, lay what appeared to be the even greater opportunities of Asia.[77] This relative indifference or ignorance of the Americas was reflected in the reputation of Columbus at the time. Although he did not suffer in his old age in the way he himself suggested it is important that when he died in Valladolid the city chronicle did not even record his death. In a very real sense his reputation appears to have risen with the importance of the Americas to world capitalism and was therefore more a product of the 18th century onwards.

In this instance the consciousness of contemporaries matched real economic forces. In particular the impact of trade and silver flows has been much overplayed in many accounts of capitalist development. So far as Spain is concerned the central point is that the wealth that flowed into Spain did not assist the development of capitalism there but helped to freeze its level of development. One of the early commentators on Spain's growing problems, Gonzalez de Cellorigo, recognised this contradiction, that it was the wealth of the Indies that was a part of the undoing of the emergence of Spanish capitalism, though he was not conscious of our modern concepts:

and so the fact that there is neither money, gold nor silver in Spain, is because there is; and the fact that Spain is not rich is because she is; Making two true and contradictory statements about one subject, Spain.[78]

Let us examine why this was so. In the first place a part of the treasure that came to Spain went straight to the Castilian crown to enable it to maintain an imperial role in Europe that would overwise have been far beyond the means of the Habsburg monarchy. In 1516 Charles I became ruler of the crowns of Castile and Aragon and in 1519 he was elected Charles V, Emperor of the wider Habsburg lands in Europe. In this way Castile became the core of a huge dynastic monarchy that included the Low Countries, Burgundy, Austria, Naples and Sicily as well as the lands of the Spanish crown in Africa and the Americas. It is sometimes suggested that Charles V saw himself as the potential monarch of a world empire. This was not so. His empire was always under pressure and he and his followers knew this. But they felt unable to abandon the role of defending what accidents of birth, marriage and death had brought together. This put Charles and his successors in enormously contradictory positions. As Paul Kennedy has expressed it, the Habsburg monarchy provides 'one of the greatest examples of strategical overstretch in history, for the price of possessing so many territories was the existence of numerous foes.' The Habsburg throne was, he argues, like a powerful bear, caught in a pit with dogs snapping at its heels, unable to defeat it but able to wound and wear it down.[79] Some countries in this period were able to engage in what Francis Bacon in England called 'lucrative and restorative warre'. This was not the case for the Habsburg crown—such 'warre' was usually at its expense and it was Castile that paid much of the bill. The flow of treasure from the Americas encouraged the throne and its supporters to sustain this drain. This was partly because some American treasure fed directly into the coffers of the state. However, as many historians have pointed out, the treasure that went to the Crown always supplied a lesser part of its revenue. The Habsburg throne also drew support from taxes in Castile, money from its non-Iberian kingdoms and loans from bankers in southern Germany, the Italian cities and Antwerp. As a measure in 1554 only 11 percent of its income came from treasure and when this rose to a peak in the late 16th century in the reign of Philip II treasure still only supplied around 25 percent of income.[80] The greater contribution was indirect. The existence of American treasure meant that the throne was able to get international credit to fight its wars—treasure was even mortgaged to bankers in advance. Even so the Crown still faced a constant growth in its debt and periodic bankruptcy in the face of war and revolt.

This meant it had to put more pressure on Castile where its powers to raise taxes were the greatest. But overall the point is that American treasure helped it to pursue its ambitions to sustain a leading role in Europe. Indeed it was encouraged to go further. To help overcome financial crises the Spanish Crown was prepared to make all sorts of compromises with the aristocracy so that Spain never felt the modernising pressure of absolutism and remained 'a disarticulated state' until the 18th century. But, as we shall now see, the bourgeoisie also failed to develop a challenge that could push Spanish capitalism forward.

The larger part of the wealth from the Americas flowed into private hands but insofar as it stayed in Spain, and we shall see in a moment that it often did not, it was used in a way that helped to restrict the development of Spanish capitalism. As Vilar puts it, 'the profits were not "invested" in the capitalist sense of the term, and the fortunate emigrants dreamed of buying land, of building "castles" and amassing fortunes.'[81] Land was a key to security and position. The Pizzaro family, for example, was typical in using its plunder to increase its estates.[82] Then there was investment in Spanish government bonds which, because of the financial problems of the Crown, offered not only a good rate of interest but a higher one than was probably to be gained from investment in agriculture and industry.[83] It was also important to use the monetary wealth to buy nobility for with nobility came not only social status but real material advantages in exemptions from important taxes. It was not so much therefore that 'the bourgeoisie betrayed its mission', rather that the structures successful merchants, traders and businessmen found themselves in made it rational for them to relocate their wealth and integrate into aristocratic society as quickly as possible. Instead of revolutionising society they became part of what Vilar calls 'a pyramid of parasitism'.[84]

But the impact of colonial success at this early stage had a wider negative impact too. It helped to create a general climate that militated against more vigorous social change. With empire came an imperial consciousness, 'these Italians, although they are not Indians, have to be treated as such, so that they will understand that we are in charge of them and not they in charge of us', wrote the Spanish Governor of Milan to Philip II in 1570.[85] Consciousness of power and position also encouraged enormous conspicuous consumption not only privately but by the state.[86] Those with ambition now found other avenues to advancement—emigration to the Americas only absorbed a relatively small number, around 0.1 percent of the population a year on average, but perhaps played a greater qualitative role. Then there were soldiering and the bureaucracy as avenues of advancement.

The net result, therefore, was to maintain Spanish power at one level but to make the society incapable of allowing capitalism to emerge in a more rounded fashion. It has recently been argued that the 'decline of Spain' is a myth. For some it could not decline because it never rose.[87] For others its ability to maintain a powerful European position until late on is a sign of some vigour.[88] Both these points have some merit but they do not alter the fact that something was going wrong and the easy acquisition of American treasure was playing its part in making it harder to respond to changed circumstances. There are three manifestations of this that are worthy of particular note.

The first is the disastrous population record of Spain in the 17th century. It was made worse by the expulsion of the Moriscos (Muslims forced to convert to Christianity) and war losses but its underlying cause was disease hitting a people relying on a weak agriculture. Thanks to the *Annales* school in France there has been an enormous stress on the Malthusian crisis mechanism where population grows beyond resources until crisis is precipitated. But this is frequently too neat an explanation. In most European countries populations did experience long run growth through such crises. Spain did not in the 17th century. Its population rose from 7.4 million in 1541 to 8.5 million in 1591-94 but then plague devastated the country in 1596-1602, 1647-52 and 1676-85. Perhaps 1.25 million died and population stagnated at around 7 to 7.5 million.[89] The fundamental reason was not that agriculture was 'naturally weak' but it lacked the benefits of 'improvement' undertaken in countries like England. A second manifestation of this development crisis was de-industrialisation. The record is not so uniformly bad as was once thought but, as Lynch points out, in the three major industries embodying capitalist advance in the 17th century—textiles, metallurgy and shipbuilding—Spain fell back.[90] In particular there is little sign of vigour in the development of rural handicraft industries that played such an important role in the areas of Europe that were to become the bases of successful industrialisation.[91] The third manifestation was that as a result of this weakening and the more general integration of the bourgeoisie into the existing structure there was no real bourgeois political challenge in this century. There was regional revolt and the breakaway of Portugal in the 1640s but these events did not reflect the kind of array of social forces that were apparent in the English Revolution. In these terms there is very good reason to resist the temptation to see them as part of a much wider international revolutionary moment in the history of capitalism.[92]

But what then of the wider impact of the Americas in Europe? As a result of conquest there was a surge in demand for European goods which producers on the Iberian peninsula could not satisfy. This demand, therefore, fed back into the rest of Europe. Although it was

significant for some industries its total value was small in comparison
to the European total. The argument about the role of the Americas has
always depended, therefore, much more on the flow of treasure out of
Spain to help to stimulate the wider European economy. This was the
core of Hamilton's thesis; it was American treasure that pushed forward the development of capitalism through profit inflation. When treasure imports fell in the 17th century growth was accordingly held back.
It remains the case that in this view it was American treasure which
caused rising prices in the 16th century. This still forms the core of the
monetarist view of European price history.

But the arguments against a Hamilton view of this period, whether
cast narrowly in terms of inflation or more widely in terms of the
growth of capitalism, are formidable. The one truth he understood was
that American treasure did not stay in Spain but circulated more widely
across Europe. In 1594, for example, of the 10 million ducats that arrived in Seville 3 million flowed out to pay for the costs and debts of
the Spanish monarchy and another 3 million to pay for the costs and
debts of private individuals.[93] But nothing else fits. We now know that
the early figures produced by Hamilton of a decline in treasure imports
in the 17th century and which appeared to correlate with reduced
upward pressure on prices were wrong. Hamilton failed to take sufficient account of fraud and other factors affecting the recording of treasure imports.[94] At the beginning of the period it was understood that
prices had begun to rise before the import of significant treasure but
proponents of the thesis slighted the significance of this. We now also
know much more about how prices moved when the treasure was flowing in but this has not increased the fit of the thesis. Most importantly
food prices appear to have experienced the greatest increase, which
helps to support the alternative view that it was real pressures of increased demand and population growth that were the motive factor in
price increases. But how much did treasure increase the supply of
money? We do not know precisely, but the evidence of Braudel is that
Europe was not awash with silver at this time.[95] Not the least of the reasons for this is something still too little appreciated in popular accounts
—most of the treasure that flooded into Europe flooded back out to pay
for the balance of trade deficit with the east.'Asia, China and India
were sponges that soaked up the streams of silver flowing through
Europe (and the Philippines) from Spanish America.'[96] To the extent
that American treasure made a contribution therefore it was even more
indirect than Hamilton imagined for it was tied to helping the European
economy continue to import from the east rather than directly revolutionising production within Europe.

But if the conquest of the Americas and the linking to the European
economy are not the lynchpin of capitalist development in the 16th and

17th centuries or the explanation of the switch in the economic centre of gravity away from the world of the Mediterranean to the developing capitalism of north western Europe, what is? The answer has to be found in real changes in the European economy which were largely independent of Europe's relations with the wider world at this time. It was the failure to recognise the central importance of an autonomous European change in the nature of the forces and relations of production that was always the key weakness in the Hamilton type thesis and variations on it. At first sight these theories have a pseudo-radicalism in appearing to concentrate on super-profits gained by exploitation. But the radicalism is more apparent than real for the focus is not on the real exploitative mechanisms of capitalism but more on chance, 'windfall' gains. As Pierre Vilar put it in drawing together the arguments against this type of thesis:

> the historian's business is not only to discover favourable conjunctures, but to explain the appearance of economic 'structures'. The appearance of capitalism required a far more complex mechanism than the simple influence of American bullion on European prices. History does not start with Christopher Columbus.[97]

The importance of this is that these other forces not only paved the way for the next stage in the development of capitalism they also paved the way for a transformation in the nature of the Atlantic trade so that in the 18th century the capitalist world economy could move to a higher level of integration than was possible in the first two centuries of its existence (though a still weaker level than would be achieved in the future). They help to explain the dynamic behind the evolution of the world economy to a position of dominance:

> whereas in the 16th and still partially in the 17th centuries the sudden expansion of commerce and the emergence of a new world market decisively contributed to the downfall of the old mode of production and the rise of capitalist production, this process was, conversely, only carried through on the basis of the capitalist mode of production. **The world market itself forms the basis** for this mode of production. **On the other hand**, the immanent necessity of this mode of production to produce on an ever-expanded scale tends to extend the world market continually, so that it is not commerce in this case which revolutionises industry but industry which constantly revolutionises commerce.[98]

These other forces arose from a deeper and more convincing establishment of capitalism in the Low Countries and England at this time. They were reflected in the way in which industry there became more competitive, especially the textile industry. This was at the core of what is now called the 'proto-industrial' stage of capitalist development —the pre-factory expansion of networks of cottage based domestic industry, tied together in the putting out system.[99]

What lay behind this was lower prices and more innovative techniques both in production and organisation than could be found in the Mediterranean world, although initially the northern producers poached many of their methods and skilled workers from the south at the turn of the 17th century. The result was a northern European industry that began to put Mediterranean producers under pressure most notably in the production of lighter cloths, what were called 'new draperies' using Spanish wools to produce lighter textiles. By the end of the 17th century advances in production and its organisation in the Low Countries and England were giving them a commercial dominance in the Mediterranean world and pushing indigenous producers into a backwater. In the late 17th century, for example, only around 10 percent of English exports went outside of Europe but 48 percent of all exports went to the Mediterranean, including Spain and Portugal, and 53 percent of all manufacturers and 57 percent of woollen cloths.[100]

Once this European dominance had been established it was then possible to shift to wider markets and begin a second process of transformation in the Atlantic trade that not only took control away from Spain and Portugal but also changed the pattern from that of the two centuries after Columbus to shift it much more closely to meet the needs of European producers rather than the merchant and financial networks that absorbed the early gold and silver flows.

The explanation of this northern European success is to be found first in the processes that allowed the growing proletarianisation of labour, changing the relations of production as it occurred. In England, for example, by as early as 1500 some 45 percent of land was enclosed, in the next century a small percentage was added and a further massive 24 percent in the 17th century.[101] Here was a much more decisive process of change, a more crucial process of primitive accumulation not only of capital itself but the conditions of sustained capitalist production. Out of this could emerge both an agrarian capitalism and an industrial one. An independent bourgeoisie could develop, merchant capital could be balanced by industrial capital and then give way to industrial capital and they could both find allies in those of the landed classes that were responding to the new opportunities in a way that could not and did not happen in the Mediterranean and especially Spain. This bourgeoisie could also push the state to develop in a way more favourable to long run capitalist expansion even if it needed a revolution, as it did in England, in the mid-17th century to complete the process.

To argue this is in no way to diminish the scale of the transformation in the Americas after Columbus but it is to put it into perspective.
It is this that should be the real aim of any serious history of capitalism.
It is foolish to think that lessons can be drawn from what happened
centuries ago or simple analogies made. What can be gained is something more valuable, an understanding of the long run dynamics of the
system, what determines its structures and their relative importance and
where its real heart lies. To do this we need not only to cut Columbus
down to size as an individual, we need a true sense of proportion about
the historical development of the system of which he was an early
creature.

Notes

1   Quoted in R W Rydell, *All the World's a Fair* (Chicago, 1984) p9.
2   P Chaunu, *L'Espagne de Charles Quint*, vol 2 (Paris, 1973) p425.
3   Columbus Day on 12 October marking the first landfall became a national holiday in
    both the Americas and Spain (though the record is so vague that landfall could have
    been made on 11 October). The best demolition of Columbus is H Koning's
    Columbus: his Enterprise, (Latin American Research Bureau, 1976, reprinted 1991).
4   R Wright, *Stolen Continents: the Indian Story* (London, 1992).
5   B de Las Casas, *The Tears of the Indians*, 1656 (New York, 1972) p2.
6   K Sale, *The Conquest of Paradise: Christopher Columbus and the Columbian
    Legacy* (London, 1991), p369.
7   See Hok-Lam Chan, 'The Chien-Wen, Yung-Lo, Hung-Hsi, and Hsuan-te Reigns,
    1399-1435', in F W Mote and D Twitchett (eds), *The Cambridge History of China*,
    vol 7, *The Ming Dynasty, 1368-1644*, Part 1, (Cambridge, 1988) pp232-236.
8   J K Fairbank et al, *East Asia: Tradition and Transformation*, (London, 1973) p199.
9   See, for example, the work of T Skocpol, *States and Social Revolutions* (Cambridge,
    1979); T Skocpol (ed), *Bringing the State Back In* (Cambridge, 1985), and M Mann,
    *The Sources of Social Power, vol 1, A History of Power from the beginning to
    AD1760* (Cambridge, 1986).
10 Quoted in J H Elliott, *Spain and its World* (Yale, 1989) pp178-179.
11 F Braudel, *The Mediterranean and the Mediterranean World in the Age of Philip II*,
    vol 1 (London, 1972) part 2 ch 3, passim.
12 D Hay, *Europe in the Fourteenth and Fifteenth Centuries* (London, 1966) p77.
13 The general analysis in this discussion owes a great deal to Jairus Banaji's argu-
    ments in 'Modes of Production in a Materialist Conception of History', *Capital and
    Class*, no 3, 1977, though it does not always agree with everything he writes. He is,
    however, especially good on the role of the money and the market in feudal society.
14 R H Hilton, 'Rent and capital accumulation in feudal society', *Second International
    Conference of Economic History* (Aix en Provence, 1962) vol 2, p67; R Roehl,
    'Patterns and structure of demand 1000-1500', in C Cipolla (ed), *The Fontana
    Economic History of Europe vol.1 The Middle Ages* (London, 1972) pp132-139.
15 For some examples of different profit rates see S Thrupp, 'Mediaeval industry 1000-
    1500', in Cipolla (ed), ibid, p261. Braudel further points out that it was long dis-
    tance trade in luxuries such as pepper that attracted merchants rather than the higher
    volume trade in more basic goods. Speaking of one of the leading 16th century
    Spanish merchants, he notes, 'Simon Ruiz was unwilling to commit himself to
    buying grain, because it was riskier for the merchant. Grain was not like pepper or

cochineal, a "royal merchandise" and a relatively safe risk.' F Braudel, op cit, pp442-443.

16 The 'spice trade' at the time actually referred to more than what we understand by spices. It included foods, drugs, dyes, perfumes, cosmetics and oils. J H Parry refers to a 14th century merchant's handbook listing 288 types of 'spices'. See *The Age of Reconnaissance* (London, 1963) p41.

17 P Vilar, *A History of Gold and Money, 1450-1920* (London, 1984) ch 4-8.

18 D Arnold, *The Age of Discovery 1400-1600* (London, 1983) p40.

19 G Jackson, *The Making of Mediaeval Spain* (London, 1972) p119.

20 R Pike, *Enterprise and Adventure: the Genoese in Seville and the Opening of the New World* (Ithica, 1966) passim; R Pike, *Aristocracy and Traders. Sevillian Society in the Sixteenth Century* (Ithica, 1972) p128.

21 P Vilar, 'Problems in the Development of Capitalism', *Past and Present* no.10, November 1956, p32; P Vilar, *Spain a Brief History* (London, 1967) pp19-22.

22 T Davies, *The Golden Century of Spain, 1501-1621* (Oxford, 1937) p43.

23 The latest onslaught against the flat earth myth by Jeffrey Russell is summarised in 'Inventing the Flat Earth', *History Today*, vol 41, no 8, August 1991.

24 For examples of the feudalism approach see J H Parry op cit. and from the left, Banaji, op cit. Banaji sees Columbus and early discovery as a response to a crisis within feudalism. He also appears to misread Pierre Vilar in mistakenly looking to him for support for this view. In his 1956 essay 'The Age of Don Quixote' (see footnote 80) Vilar does use the phrase 'Spanish imperialism—the highest stage of feudalism' but this does not appear consistent with what he writes.

25 It is important here to distinguish the issue of Columbus from European discovery as a whole. Explaining the origin and drive of Columbus himself is a key part of the Columbus industry but in reality this is a trivial question. Columbus after all may not have been the first European to 'discover' America and he was only part of a general movement and a quixotic part at that with his wild and flawed ideas of the world at that time. The important thing was that he was part of a movement of expansion that had begun before him and continued long after him. In this movement his own role had chance elements, the movement itself did not.

26 See the discussion in C Harman, 'From Feudalism to Capitalism', *International Socialism*, no 45, Winter 1989.

27 K Sale, *Conquest* op cit, p106; Vilar in his *History of Gold...* op cit, p65, counts 65 mentions of gold in Columbus's diary between his first landing in and leaving the Caribbean. However, it should be noted that we only have this diary at second hand —something that creates serious difficulties for the assessment of the real Columbus.

28 B de Las Casas went on to write, 'Now the ultimate end and scope that incited the Spaniards to endeavour the extirpation and desolation of this people was gold only, that thereby growing opulent in a short time they might arrive at once at such degrees and dignities as were in no ways consistent with their persons.' In these last lines we see a typical expression of how the new and more liquid forms of wealth were beginning to confuse social divisions.

29 P Chaunu, op cit, pp397-405, 417.

30 Ibid, p438.

31 W Atkinson, *A History of Spain and Portugal* (Harmondsworth, 1960) p160.

32 These figures are given by R Chandra, *Industrialisation and Development in the Third World* (London, 1992) pp19-20. I have not been able to trace the original source but they seem plausible. Later figures are given in G Clark, *The Balance Sheet of Imperialism* (Columbia, 1936).

33 W Denevan (ed), *The Native Population of the Americas in 1492* (Maddison, 1976) pp3, 291. The figures in the table do not sum precisely due to rounding.

34 L Baudin, *A Socialist Empire. The Incas of Peru* (Princeton, 1961) p220. This first English translation has an introduction by Ludwig von Mises which extends the attack on socialism through the Incas.

35 J C Mariátegui, *Seven Interpretative Essays on Peruvian Reality* (Texas, 1971).

36 There is an interesting but perhaps insufficiently critical appreciation of Mariátegui in the Australian sister journal to *International Socialism*, see T O'Lincoln, 'Mariátegui Peruvian Revolutionary', *Socialist Review* (Melbourne), no 2, Winter 1990, pp102-117.

37 K Sale, op cit, passim.

38 Finds relating to early Americans are regularly reported and debated in the scientific press. See, for example, W Bray, 'Finding the earliest Americans', *Nature*, vol 321, no 6072, 19-25 June 1986; N Guidin, 'Carbon 14 dates point to man in the Americas 32,000 years ago', ibid, vol 321, pp769-771; J Benditt, 'Earliest Americans' *Scientific American*, vol 258 no 6, 1988.

39 There is also a strong argument that the Europeans projected images of their own unconscious desires and fears into their perceptions of these peoples mythologising in particular the existence of cannibalism. K Sale, op cit, pp131-135, provides a useful critique of this. There is good reason to doubt the evidence of extensive cannibalism in human history. I cannot, however, resist drawing the attention of ecologically minded readers to a 1970s school which believed it to be widespread and explained it as a rational ecological response to the severe depletion of animal resources in the Americas before 1492! See M J Harmer, 'The Ecological Basis of Aztec Sacrifice', *American Ethnologist*, vol 4, 1977 and the work of Marvin Harris, for example, *Cannibals and Kings: The Origins of Cultures* (New York, 1978).

40 Recent archeological finds have been used to claim that an advanced civilisation developed on the Amazon at Taperinha as early as 6000 BC. But it is too early to evaluate these claims. See the report in *Independent*, 19 December 1991.

41 The achievements of native techniques in this period cannot be doubted but their limitations from the point of view of humans should also be recognised. In particular it is worth drawing attention to the oppressive impact of their limitations on women. The failure to develop a grinding technology meant that 'if one miller-baker in Rome produced enough bread for some 400 households, in Teotihuacan 400 women, each with her metate, would have risen at first light to begin *the six hour daily grind*', (my emphasis). See A J Bauer, 'Millers and Grinders: Technology and Household Economy in Meso-America', *Agricultural History*, vol 64 no 1, Winter 1990, p3.

42 F Katz, 'The Evolution of Aztec society', *Past and Present*, no 13 April 1958, pp18-19.

43 There is a growing debate about whether Inca and Aztec society should be theorised as variants of the Asiatic Mode of Production, a tributary mode of production or social formations reflecting mixtures of modes of production. This debate can be traced in M Godelier, 'The Concept of Social and Economic Formation: the Inca example' in *Perspectives in Marxist Anthropology*, vol 18, 1977; J Golte, 'The economy of the Inca state and the notion of the Asiatic Mode of Production' in A Bailey and J Llbera (eds), *The Asiatic Mode of Production* (London, 1981). See also the discussion in T Patterson, *The Inca Empire: the Formation and Disintegration of a Pre-Capitalist State* (Leamington, 1991). These discussions of the Inca regime all draw heavily on the pioneering work of John Murra. Murra's own arguments are summarised in J Murra, 'Andean Societies before 1532', in L Bethell (ed), *The Cambridge History of Latin America*, vol 1, 1984, pp59-90. For the Aztecs see also M León-Portilla, 'Mesoamerica before 1519', in the same volume. For the general idea of an Asiatic Mode of Production see M Godelier, 'The concept of the Asiatic Mode of Production', in D Seddon (ed), *Relations of Production*, (London, 1978). For the more general argument about whether there was an Asiatic mode of production or whether it is better to talk of a more general form such as a tributary form see

the introductory and somewhat schematic discussion, in J Russell, *Modes of Production in World History* (London, 1989).

44 G Bankes, *Peru before Pizarro* (Oxford, 1977) pp112-113.

45 J Golte, op cit, especially suggests that the extent of internal village differentiation has been misunderstood.

46 M Godelier, 'The Concept ..', op cit.

47 The superiority was so great that the conquistadors may temporarily have seemed 'godlike' but the idea that the leading conquistadors like Cortés were thought to be specific returning Indian gods seems, like the flat earth, to be an invention. See J H Elliott, 'The Mental World of Hernan Cortés', in his *Spain and its World* (Yale, 1989).

48 S Katz, 'Quantity and interpretation. Issues in the comparative analysis of the holocaust', *Holocaust and Genocide Studies*, vol 4 no 2 (1989) p134. Katz's work (summarised here) is a valuable guide to the accountancy of mass deaths in human history. He argues, however, that the Jewish holocaust in the 20th century was qualitatively unique in being intended, planned and directed to the total extermination of a perceived 'racial' category.

49 P Chaunu, op cit, p398. Of the many accounts of this see W H McNeill, *Plagues and Peoples* (Harmondsworth, 1976), on the general role of disease and more specifically on 1492 see A W Crosby Jnr, *The Columbian Exchange* (Greenwood, 1972).

50 This table reports the standard figures of Woodrow Borah and Sherborne Cook and David Cook (on Peru). For a full bibliography see L A Newson, 'Indian Population Patterns in Colonial Spanish America', *Latin American Research Review*, vol 20 no3 (1985) pp41-74. For a taste of the intricacies of the debate see D Henige, 'On the Contact Population of Hispañola: History as Higher Mathematics', *Hispanic American Historical Review*, vol 58 no 2 (1978), and the subsequent debate in vol 58 no 4 (1978).

51 This paragraph summarises Newson, op cit.

52 Figure for 1492 from table 2, later figures from the calculations of A Rosenblat as quoted in S van Bath, 'The Absence of White Contract Labour in Spanish America During the Colonial Period', in P C Emmer (ed), *Colonialism and Migration: Indentured Labour Before and After Slavery* (Comparative Studies in Overseas History, vol.7, 1986) p19.

53 J H Rowe, 'The Incas under Spanish Colonial Institutions', *Hispanic American Historical Review*, vol xxxvii, no 2, May 1957, p155.

54 For a review of some studies of resistance within the system see B Keen, 'Recent Writing on the Spanish Conquest', *Latin American Research Review*, vol xx, no 2 1985. See also the discussion in R Wright, op cit, pp143-199, which draws heavily on Indian chronicles.

55 We now know a lot about the various cultures and rituals of resistance of the native population. One illustrative ritual, according to an 18th century Spaniard 'a custom so depraved and unreasonable' that some may feel worthy of wider emulation, was an Indian insistence that they be allowed to drink and rest not only after work but before work so that 'when they become intoxicated, they will be stronger and more vigorous for work awaiting them'! Quoted in E M Brumfiel, 'Aztec Religion and Warfare. Past and Present Perspectives', *Latin American Research Perspectives*, vol xxv, no 2, 1990, pp253-254.

56 Rowe, op cit.; Patterson, op cit, ch 5; S J Stern, *Peru's Indian Peoples and the Challenge of Spanish Conquest* (Maddison, 1982); S J Stern, 'The Struggle for Solidarity: Class, Culture, and Community in Highland Indian America', *Radical History Review*, no 27, 1983.

57 Both Frank and Wallerstein have written prolifically but the starting point should be A Gunder Frank, *Capitalism and Underdevelopment in Latin America* (Harmondsworth, 1969); I Wallerstein, *The Modern World System I. Capitalist*

Agriculture and the Origins of the European World Economy in the Sixteenth Century (London, 1974); *The Modern World System II. Mercantilism and the Consolidation of the European World Economy 1600-1750* (London, 1980).

58 E Laclau, 'Feudalism and Capitalism in Latin America', *New Left Review*, no 67, 1971; R Brenner, 'The Origins of Capitalist Development: a Critique of Neo-Smithian Marxism', *New Left Review*, no 104, 1977.

59 These positions are reviewed in a useful debate S J Stern, 'Feudalism, capitalism and the world system in the perspective of Latin America and the Caribbean', *American Historical Review*, vol 93, October 1988, and his subsequent debate with Wallerstein in the same issue.

60 This is emphasised by J H Elliott. See *Spain and its World,* op cit, part 1.

61 J Banaji, op cit, and his important review of Frank, J Banaji, 'Gunder Frank in Retreat?' *Journal of Peasant Studies*, 1980.

62 On trends in silver mining see R L Garner, 'Long-run Silver Mining Trends in Spanish America: a Comparative Analysis of Peru and Mexico', *American Historical Review*, vol 93, 1988, pp898-935. For the more general background see D Brading and H Cross, 'Colonial Silver Mining: Mexico and Peru', *Hispanic American Historical Review*, vol 52, 1972, pp545-579; P J Bakewell, 'Mining in Colonial Spanish America', in L Bethell (ed), *The Cambridge History of Latin America: the Colonial Period*, vol 2, 1984, pp105-151.

63 A good up to date description of the colonial economy is given in J Lynch, *The Hispanic World in Crisis and Change, 1598-1700* (Oxford, 1992) ch 8. However, readers tempted to follow this up should take note about our later comments on the need for perspective on the scale of flows as they apply especially to Lynch, amongst others.

64 The accounts of Las Casas (eg *The Tears of the Indians,* op cit) are independently echoed by Indian accounts. See, for example, Wright, op cit. The mistake that Las Casas made was to attribute all the deaths directly to the horrific violence practised by the conquerors to the exclusion of recognising the additional catastrophe of European disease.

65 B Keen, 'The Black Legend Revisited', *Hispanic American Historical Review*, vol 49, no 4, November 1969; B Keen, 'The White Legend Revisited', *Hispanic American Historical Review*, vol 51, no 3, May 1971; Rowe, op cit.

66 It has not been possible within the space available to take up the key issue of racism and its relation to 1492. Interested readers should consult B Davidson, 'Columbus: the Bones and Blood of Racism', *Race and Class*, vol 33, no 3, 1992 and J H Elliott, *The Old World...* op cit, ch 2.

67 On sugar see S Mintz, *Sweetness and Power. The Place of Sugar in Modern History*, (Harmondsworth, 1985). This too little known work is not only fascinating in itself but is valuable empirically and informed by a full awareness of the debates discussed here; Newson, op cit, contains a useful short summary of forms of labour in the colonial era.

68 Garner, op cit, p935. See also S J Stein and B H Stein, *The Colonial Heritage of Latin America* (New York, 1970) p66. Of course the extent of the crisis varied as Garner's analysis of mining trends shows. See also J TePaske and H S Klein 'The 17th century crisis in New Spain: Myth or Reality' *Past and Present*, no 90, 1981, and subsequent debate in no 97, 1982, pp144-161.

69 T Ashton, *Crisis in Europe 1560-1660*. Essays from *Past and Present* (London, 1965).

70 E J Hamilton, 'American Treasure and the Rise of Capitalism', *Economica*, November, 1929; *American Treasure and the Price Revolution in Spain, 1501-1650* (Cambridge, Mass. 1934).

71 K Marx, *Capital*, vol 1 (Harmondsworth, 1976) p915.

72 For the empirical evidence see P O'Brien, 'European economic development and the
    Contribution of the Periphery', *Economic History Review*, vol xxv, no 1 1982; 'The
    Foundations of European Industrialisation: from the Perspective of the World',
    Journal of Historical Sociology, vol 4, no 3, September 1991. The theoretical reason
    is simply that in Marxist terms in normal circumstances a greater level of surplus
    value must be generated by more advanced technologies than less advanced ones.
73 Quoted in S Mintz, op cit, p42.
74 The Chaunus' work runs to thousands of pages. They summarise their approach in
    'The Atlantic Economy and the World Economy', in P Earle (ed), *Essays in
    European economic History 1500-1800* (Oxford, 1974) pp113-126.
75 Quoted in J H Elliott, *The Old World and the New* (London, 1970) p1.
76 Ibid, ch1-2.
77 See the essays in F Chiappelli ed, *First Images of America* vol 2 (Berkeley, 1976)
    part 1.
78 S J Stein and B H Stein, op cit, p12
79 P Kennedy, *The Rise and Fall of the Great Powers: Economic and Military Conflict
    from 1500 to 2000* (London, 1988) p61.
80 Elliott, *Spain and Its World...* op cit, p23.
81 P Vilar, *Spain a Brief History* (London, 1967) p46.
82 R Varon Gabai and A Pieter Jacobs, 'Peruvian Wealth and Spanish Investments: the
    Pizarro Family during the 16th Century', *Hispanic American Historical Review*, vol
    67, no 4 (1987).
83 J Lynch, op cit, pp186, 200-201. There are many informative histories of Spain by J
    H Elliott and H Kamen and others but this is the clearest.
84 On the general defection of the bourgeoisie see Braudel op cit, vol 2, part 5 section
    2. For the idea of 'the pyramid of parasitism' see P Vilar, 'The Age of Don
    Quixote', in P Earle (ed), *Essays in European Economic History 1500-1800*
    (Oxford, 1974).
85 Quoted in Elliott, *Spain and Its World,* op cit, p9.
86 One example of this is the royal palace of Buen Retiro, built and filled at enormous
    cost in the 1630s. See J H Elliott, ibid, p280.
87 'The fundamental fact is that Spain never developed to begin with' according to C
    Cipolla, *Before the Industrial Revolution European Society and Economy 1000-
    1700* (London, 1976) p233.
88 H Kamen, 'The Decline of Spain: a Historical Myth?', *Past and Present*, no 81
    1978, and subsequent debate in no 91. Kamen has continued this argument in a
    number of later works on Spain in this period. See also R A Stradling, '17th Century
    Spain: Decline or Survival?', *European Studies Review*, vol 9, 1979.
89 J Nadal, *La población Española* Siglos XVI a XX (Barcelona, 1976) p16; Lynch, op
    cit, pp173-179.
90 Ibid, p219.
91 See P Kriedte, *Peasants, Landlords and Merchant Capitalists. Europe and the
    World Economy, 1500-1800* (Leamington, 1980).
92 J H Elliott, 'Revolution and Continuity in Early Modern Europe' reprinted in *Spain
    and its World,* op cit. In Segovia, for example, the population fell from 25,000 to
    8,000 during the 17th century and the number of textile looms from 600 in 1580 to
    159 in 1691. Politically textile manufacturers were pushed aside. In 1648 (when
    England was in revolution) a local law was passed that 'no cloth manufacturer, mer-
    chant or dealer, notary or attorney, or their sons can be town councillors'. Lynch, op
    cit, p212, 191.
93 Elliot, *The Old World* ... op cit, p65.
94 The major critique is by M Morineau, *Incroyables Gazettes et Fabuleux Métaux, Les
    Retours des Trésors Americains d'Apres Les Gazettes Hollandaises* (XVIe -XVIIIe
    siècles), (London, 1985).

95 F Braudel, op cit, pp451-453.
96 C Kindleberger, 'Spenders and Hoarders. The World Distribution of Spanish American Silver, 1550-1750' in his *Historical Economics Art or Science* (Brighton, 1990) p34.
97 P Vilar, 'Problems in the Development of Capitalism', *Past and Present* no 10, November 1956, p31.
98 K Marx, *Capital,* vol 3 as quoted in Banaji, 'Gunder Frank ...' op cit, p510.
99 C Wilson, 'Cloth Production and International Competition in the 17th Century', *Economic History Review,* vol xiii, 1960; D Coleman, 'An Innovation and its Diffusion: the "New Draperies"', *Economic History Review,* vol xxii, 1969.
100 R Rapp, 'The Unmaking of the Mediterranean Trade Hegemony: International Trade Rivalry and the Commercial Revolution', *Journal of Economic History,* vol xxxv, no 3, September 1975.
101 J Wordie, 'The Chronology of English Enclosure 1500-1914', *Economic History Review,* vol xxxvi, no 4, November 1983.

The myths of Columbus: a history

MIKE GONZALEZ

The legend created

First, the fiction. There was once a bright eyed young explorer, obsessed with visions of lands beyond the horizon. Like the wandering scholar he went from monarch to blinkered monarch, hawking his wonderful tales of a world as round as an orange. But no one listened. Until, in Spain, a queen saw the light of genius in his eyes and, persuading her sceptical husband into an investment, pawned her own jewels as a mark of her conviction. Thus Columbus's adventure began.[1]

As the weeks passed out of sight of land, a grumbling, scurvied crew began to lose their faith in the young navigator. Then just as mutiny threatened, the Admiral (as he was named by the idealistic young Queen Isabella) spied land. It was 12 October 1492 and the 'discovery' had begun. In the years that followed, the navigator made four further journeys. In the course of them there was violence and barbarism, a massacre of the innocents which Columbus regretted as much as anyone. But what could he do? Men far from home and the worse for drink are occasionally prone to bad behaviour. Disease was the real killer—the invisible enemy borne by unwitting and unwilling carriers. And the savage innocents died at the merest touch, the simple act of meeting was enough to seal their fate. Christopher Columbus could do little to hold back this inexorable historical necessity. In any event he was driven by another need—a restless urge to explore and discover. Like all great misunderstood men ahead of their time, he was destined to die in poverty and neglect, spurned by his patrons, his grave unmarked.

So much for the novel. Its characters, above all its protagonist, are imaginary; its historical frame is an invention. Even its categories of explanation belong to another world. The expeditions that criss-crossed the oceans of the world in the latter half of the 15th century were commercial expeditions, backed by the venture capital of the day. The captains and admirals of these unknown ocean seas were entrepreneurs engaged in a ruthless competitive race. And the notion of the 'explorer', an enthusiastic amateur absorbed by the customs and lore of the unknown is a fabrication produced by a 19th century world anxious to cover its colonising adventures in anthropological clothing. 'Exploration' was more a secular century's version of the evangelism of earlier times. And like that earlier set of explanations, it served to cloak and justify the brutal and material realities of conquest after the event.

Columbus was neither victim nor hero—he was a creature of his age, his mental universe no different from that of his contemporaries and his motivations given by the atmosphere of his time. Subsequent attempts to make a visionary of him have their explanation in the need to underpin the 'accident' school of history which has Columbus stumbling across America while looking for something else. Its great advantage is to divert attention from the dynamics that drove conquest forward, an economic necessity greater than any incidental motivation of its spokespersons. It is true that there were no *Rough Guides* to an as yet unknown America; it is equally true that many people knew that there was *something* there, and that its resources would probably be as open to exploitation as all the other territories occupied or annexed in the course of the 15th century. Columbus had at his disposal not only the accumulated experience of a generation of sailors and navigators, but also the impressively precise work of map makers like Pierre D'Ailly.[2]

More importantly, the determination to make the journey came not from Columbus's own imaginings but from more material causes. The ocean seas of his days were not placid ponds first cut by the swishing bows of his caravels (though that is so often how the myth makers represent it). The caravel itself was developed by the Portuguese navigators who so successfully negotiated the African coast and the route to India from the 1440s onwards; and the Mediterranean was dominated by the vessels of the north African empires. These seas were trade routes for whose domination a struggle was already under way. By 1470 the Portuguese Crown controlled the Gold Coast of west Africa which was producing 10 percent of all the world's ore[3] and which also gave access to the fields of the Sudan. European silver and gold production was in decline and the search for alternative sources of these and other commodities of international exchange (cinnamon, pepper and cloves stood alongside the precious metals)[4] was becoming increasingly intense. The beneficiaries of earlier trade with China and the East now enjoyed a stock of capital which they put at the disposal of one or another competing team in the race to control new resources.

Columbus was just one schemer among many. All had grand plans. When he went to the Portuguese court he was met with little more than contempt, and he was initially received with some scepticism at the court of Ferdinand and Isabella. What changed their minds? Certainly not the swashbuckling heroics of the rather conventional Columbus. The reasons, again, were more directly material. What Columbus offered the King and Queen of Leon and Castile was the possibility of making up for lost time. They had come late to the scramble for resources; their marriage was a first step to unifying the warring and separate regions of Spain under a single state—and until 1492 the Moors, who had controlled Spain in part or in whole for seven centuries, still remained on Iberian soil. Their last redoubt was Granada. The siege and eventual defeat of the defenders of that city had two effects: it marked the final expulsion of the Moors, but more importantly it established the political domination of the Catholic monarchs. They pressed rapidly forward to consolidate their new found hegemony. They were, however, at a disadvantage; access to the markets and resources of Africa was blocked by the north African empires and their Mediterranean fleets, while the other route to both was controlled by Portugal. Spain needed another point of access to the resources of the southern world. The matter was urgent.

A matter of survival

The urgency came from the rapidly changing reality of an emerging mercantile economy on a global scale, a change which echoed through the consciousness of the period with prophecies of doom and auguries of terrible transformations:

> When you perceive the miserable corruption of the whole of Christendom, of all praiseworthy customs, rules and laws, the wretchedness of all classes, the many pestilences, the changes in the epoch and all the strange happenings, you know the end of the world is near.[5]

The central column of the feudal order, the Catholic church, was unable to respond from its corrupt and rotten redoubts; the imminence of the scientific revolution and the Reformation of Luther confirmed that an ancient world was disintegrating—fearsomely represented in

the paintings of Hieronymus Bosch. Earlier intimations of this disintegration must have reached the Iberian kings too and spurred their determination to repress the changes within the country and actively seek
the means of their own survival from without.

That is why they turned at that point in 1492 to an Genoan weaver
with a plan who had been hanging around the court for over three
years. And that is why they simultaneously turned their fire against a
section of the merchant and financial class of Spain by expelling the
Jews. It was neither vision nor philosophy that motivated them, but the
material demands of a bitter and unforgiving race to survive into the
mercantile age.

It is well known that Columbus was promised extraordinary rewards
as he sailed from the port of Palos with his three small ships. The 10
percent of all that he discovered still left a healthy 90 percent (or there-
abouts) for the Crown. Yet when the true extent of the resources available to Spain through his journeys became clear, the Crown reneged on
its promise and embarked on a 23 year lawsuit against Columbus; it
was still going on when he died, and his sons wrote their histories of
his exploits as contributions to a courtroom dispute—praising and ex-
aggerating his vision, insight and bravery accordingly. But Columbus
died a wealthy and honoured man, not in penury as some suggest. It is
true, however, that he thought he should have been a great deal wealth-
ier. There is no honour among thieves![6]

The dynamics of conquest were those of competition; even if it was
weakly developed when compared with full blown capitalism, it nevertheless laid the basis for that explosive development. And the great financial institutions—the Fuggar and the Welser banks and their
ilk—were present and influential at the very outset.[7] There is no mis-
taking the motives of conquest, the acquisition of the means of exchange; nor the framework of that gathering of resources, competition.

And yet there is a paradox, more apparent than real, to be resolved.
The Spanish state, while participating in the burgeoning world market,
was to all appearances an absolutist state. As the 16th century opened it
was the ideological leader of the counter-thrust to the new religious
ideas challenging the Catholic church. While it was led by economic
necessity towards a new world it declared its purposes to be the ideological and religious defence of the old world. The expulsion of the
Jews was rapidly followed by new persecutions against Islam and the
conversos (Jews who had converted to Christianity), culminating in the
assault in 1519 on the Comuneros. Their demand for freedom of commerce and political autonomy and their protests against royal taxes represented the voice of a rising Spanish merchant class. In repressing
them, the Emperor Charles V, who succeeded Ferdinand, reasserted the
centralised autocratic state in Spain and became the major bulwark

against the Reformation in the years to come. Charles's long wars of occupation in the Low Countries and northern Italy reflected his imperial design and were financed by the gold of the Americas. Spain provided the ideological base for the Counter-Reformation; the Inquisition made its home there and the Jesuits, the Catholic Church Militant, distributed their forces from there.

This, then, is the irony. Success in the competitive race for resources ensured the regeneration of a Spanish absolutist state and brought about the destruction of its own merchant class—though to the benefit of the other merchant and manufacturing classes of Europe who provided Spain with its goods and the finance for its expansions. This was to be paid for with the gold and silver to come. The whole of the 16th century is marked by the tension between the demands of exploitation and accumulation on the one hand, and the essentially medieval justifying ideologies on the other. The Great Debate (of which more below) that arose around the purposes and legalities of conquest, the insistence on the ethical and juridical niceties prior to each act of conquest and destruction, are signs of this contradiction. In 1548 the theologians met to discuss the issue, but were unable to reach a conclusion; in the early 1550s the Crown imposed prohibitions on further conquests until religious precepts were satisfied.

Yet the delicate matters of right and justice were marginal to the *practice* of conquest and colonisation; after all, others in the race for resources were unlikely to wait on the resolution of ethical problems. Nonetheless, a bizarre process occurred as the conquest evolved. Spain closed in upon itself, swathed itself and its colonies in the 'cloak and the sword' beloved of its theatrical heroes, and wrote the history of its own recent exploits in the framework of medieval lore. Thus was written the first book of myths—with its two faces. On the one hand, its utopianism enshrined in texts by Thomas More and others and the many practical and literary essays based upon it; on the other, the aggressive evangelism that rediscovered Aristotle in legitimating conquest. Once Spanish colonisation began 'the mental shutters came down'.[8]

Today the early myths of conquest have been reappropriated by the late 20th century. The realities were rewritten almost as soon as they occurred and so what the 20th century inherits are some rare documents and a body of *explanation and interpretation* masked as history.[9] For us, the task is to match realities against myths, but also to explain and locate the myths themselves. For then, as now, the mythification of those realities served contemporary purposes.

And when he got there...

Columbus's three ships made their first landfall at La Gomera in the Canary Islands; its recent history was a prophecy of what was to come since earlier that same year a Spanish expedition had eliminated the local population. Sailing on, Columbus's ships touched land in the Bahamas on 12 October 1492. A second precedent was established. Columbus claimed the 10,000 *maravedis* bonus for the first sighting of land, despite the fact that the lookout had seen it first! That is more than an idle anecdote; it establishes the motives and priorities of the recently elevated Admiral of the Ocean Seas.[10]

His letters and diaries confirm his concerns. His journals are no longer extant, but they exist as reported by Bartolome de Las Casas and confirmed by Columbus's sons.[11] It is clear from the beginning that while he made note of the *newness* of the world he found, he was desultory about describing it. His interest was not ethnographic. He measured what he saw, assessed—or rather assayed—it for its value; it was not a place but a *resource,* and its people simply a component of that source of wealth. As he wrote later this was an opportunity 'for the turning of so many peoples to our holy faith and afterwards for material benefit'.[12] While his comments on the character of the Tainos and Arawaks he encountered on the Caribbean islands were the germs of an expanding utopian literature (see below), Columbus himself showed little or no interest in them. He accepted the generous hospitality of the local peoples, but he very soon set out to destroy the communities he had found. In the first place, this world was a resource to be exploited and used; the humans in it were not different from the commodities. They were 'goods'. And the organisation of that process required the rapid imposition of a known structure of exploitation. The Old World was brought rapidly to the New, not only in the form of direct violence but also in the transposition of the structures of production, agriculture and social organisation. The introduction of domestic animals and Peninsular crops wrought its own havoc:

> One who watched the Caribbean islands from outer space during the years 1492 to 1550 or so might have surmised that the object of the game going on there was to replace the people with pigs, dogs and cattle. Disease and ruthless exploitation had, for all practical purposes, destroyed the aboriginals of Hispaniola by the 1520s. Their Arawak brothers and sisters in Cuba, Puerto Rico and Jamaica followed them into oblivion shortly after.[13]

Between his first and second voyages, the colonists left under the leadership of his brother Bartolomeo massacred the local population. Columbus returned and wreaked his own vengeance on them. Later he imposed the terrible requirement that every three months the natives produce a hawk's bell filled with gold. It was an impossible demand but it reflected Columbus's obsession with gold.

It was the urgency of his task, the baying of the impatient Spanish monarchs that he could hear at his back, and the powerful thrust that came from the knowledge that he was involved in a race with enormously high stakes, that spurred Columbus. It drove him to acts of absolute and wanton cruelty against the peoples he found in the Caribbean: first the Arawaks or Tainos, whose lifestyle so impressed those who read the scant references to them in Columbus's journals, and later the Caribs, in fact another branch of the Arawak people, whose name in its various transmutations became synonomous with satanism, flesh eating etc. The evolution of the myth of the 'Carib' or 'cannibal' or the Caliban of *The Tempest* has much to do with the contemporary need to legitimise conquest on the one hand and with the justification of slavery on the other. In fact Juan de Castellos saw things differently: 'they were called Caribs not because they would eat human flesh, but because they defended their homes well.'[14]

But the first native peoples the Spaniards met saw no need to defend themselves and welcomed the invaders with an innocent generosity that perplexed but pleased them. Peter Martyr reported Columbus's own words:

> The land among these people is as common as sun or water, and that 'mine and thine' the seeds of all mischief have no place with them. They are content with so little, that in so large a country they have rather superfluity than scarceness; so that they seem to live in a golden world, without toil... They deal truly with one another, without laws, without books and without judges...[15]

And Columbus (Santangel letter) confirms that:

> True it is that after they felt confidence and lost their fear of us, they were so liberal with what they possessed, that it would not be believed by those who had not seen it.[16]

There were probably some 10 million people living throughout the Caribbean; within a generation they were virtually wiped out. Their stable agricultural systems were disrupted then destroyed, their flora and fauna overwhelmed by European imports; the carp and the sparrow, for example, seem to have destroyed their American counterparts. It was the collapse of the structure of their social life that was primarily responsible for the collapse of these communities, enshrined and represented by the diseases that ravaged the native peoples.

These communities provided the model and the image of utopia, of a balanced and propertyless collective governed by moral laws unsullied by interest. The realities have long since faded. They were small agricultural communities with a clear internal hierarchy headed by the chief or *cacique*. It is true that local products provided a balanced diet which allowed the communities to become stable, to leave behind the stage of hunting and gathering. They were primitive agricultural communities and they were destroyed by the primitive accumulation of emerging European capitalism.

Even as Columbus and his heirs were cutting and burning their way through their villages, the yearning for a world that the Tainos came to represent had begun. Peter Martyr presented his idealized vision in 1503, Americo Vespucci shortly thereafter; by 1530 Vasco de Quiroga was trying to reproduce such a community in Janitzio in Mexico, and there were many others. In the process, the fragile world of these small agricultural communities was idealised and rewritten as a moral order of the kind dreamed of by the Renaissance humanists. The paintings of Bosch and the writings of the Spanish followers of Erasmus[17] waged a relentless battle against excess, hypocrisy and an order where interest overwhelmed morality; the critique of the Catholic church began with the assertion that they had corrupted the moral balance of Christian teachings.[18]

The Reformation placed conscious human beings at the heart of philosophy, so that it was men and women who bore the responsibility (and had the capacity) to fulfil the moral law. At the end of the 15th century the struggle to reform the Catholic church, to rid it of corruption and hypocrisy, was still being waged *within* Catholicism. It was, of course, a challenge to the old order, the unquestioned hierarchy whose authority derived from revealed truth. The humanists argued that authority had to be earned[19] though this was not meant to suggest that there was no God given authority and order of rank in society.[20] The turn of the century produced some ruthless satires of venal and wealth laden bishops. But this questioning was interwoven with the challenge to the very basis on which the old order rested. The call for reform could call into question the system itself—and that implication explains why Charles V turned so ruthlessly against the merchant class, whose interest in a new social order found expression in the philosophical critique of the old.

For the humanists, Indian America was an ideal world to be preserved as a perfect moral order; but by the time they wrote about it, it was well on its way to complete obliteration. It was already being elevated into a myth. And the Spain that had produced those scathing satires of the corruption of popes and monarchs was now superseded by a burgeoning empire whose discovery of America guaranteed its survival and served to reaffirm the absolute authority of kings.[21] On that basis the Inquisition moved to Spain and began the counter-thrust to the Reformation; on that basis the wealth of the Americas was sufficient to float the Spanish economy, to enable it to borrow from the bankers of northern Europe and repay with gold and silver beaten out of the Indian miners of America.

The New World was born out of the systematic destruction of a world whose population was decimated in a few decades.[22] That act of subjugation set the frame for the characteristic future relations of capitalism—the ruthless exploitation of the majority and their subordination to the accumulation of profit. The denunciation and exposure of that truth has often been expressed in a yearning for the world that went before; and many of those who have unmasked the current Quincentennial celebrations have manifested the same longing.

The search for Utopia[23]

At the very time when the New World that Columbus found was in the throes of destruction, that world began to be idealised. Peter Martyr's writings of 1503-4 and Vespucci's accounts a few years later were widely read and eagerly acclaimed. Medieval utopias (like the Land of Cockaigne) found both confirmation and addition in the American experience. For what the Indians offered Europe was a reassurance as to the 'naturalness' of the moral order and a material representation of man uncorrupted. Taking his lead from La Boetie's *Contr'un*, the French essayist Montaigne celebrated the quality 'of cannibals':

> *I do not find...that there is anything wild and barbarous in this nation, excepting that everyone gives the denomination barbarism to what is not the custom of his country... There the people are wild, just as we call fruits wild which nature produces of itself...whereas in truth we ought rather to call those wild whose natures we have changed by our artifice and diverted from the common order... We have so surcharged the beauty and richness of (Nature's) works by our own inventions, that we have almost smothered her. Yet wherever she shines in her own pure lustre, she wonderfully disgraces our vain and frivolous attempts.[24]*

Montaigne repeated the common sense among some writing in his time that America gave a glimpse of the 'Golden Age', of the 'happy state of mankind' which Peter Martyr had celebrated. And the yearning for that time of harmony stretches across the 16th century and beyond, from Martyr and More, to Montaigne, to Shakespeare's Gonzalo, dreaming of a commonwealth where:

All things in common nature should produce
Without sweat or endeavour. Treason, felony,
Sword, pike, knife, gun, or need of any engine,
Would I not have; but nature should bring forth
Of it own kind all foison, all abundance,
To feed my innocent people.[25]

In the year of the Quincentennial, the inheritors of that vision also share an environmentalist nostalgia enshrined in the contemporary utopian myths. The cinema has offered a contradictory technological representation of innocence. The scenes of joyous plenty in Roland Joffe's *The Mission*, in the curious blonde satyr emerging from *The Emerald Forest*, in the dilemmas of the *Medicine Man* for whom progress itself carries the germ of destruction.

The New World did call into question concepts that were central to the culture of the medieval world—the idea of property, for example, or of hierarchy itself. It was the absence of these features that so outraged Hobbes later, when he described the life of the American natives as 'solitary, poor, nasty, brutish and short'.[26] The 'counter-utopians' were present at the outset too, as debate raged long and furious between the Spanish utopians and the advocates of conquest for whom the indigenous peoples of the Caribbean were 'barbarians' in untamed and rebellious nature, obstacles to the best of human purposes. In 1511, before it became almost impossible to speak, Father Montesinos spoke from the pulpit against the conquest:

> *By what right and by what justice do you hold the Indians in such cruel and horrible bondage? Aren't they dying, or rather, aren't you killing them, to get gold every day? Aren't you obliged to love them as yourselves?*[27]

After that, though at the edges of the Spanish empire continuous attempts were made to set in train 'the commonwealth of equals', these voices became fewer and more difficult to hear. Among those who read the translated versions of Martyr and Vespucci were some who would become the colonists of the north of America: Verazzano and Cartier in France, Raleigh in England, for example.[28]

So America provided both a source of myths and legends that nourished a critical view of an emerging world of property and exploitation *and* the indispensable material *of* competition whose acquisition merited and justified savage exploitation, slavery and murder—all on a hitherto unprecedented scale. The contradiction was most intractable in Spain, where the survival of a world rooted in the moral universe of medieval humanism was ensured only by the adoption of the most extreme form of exploitation, the formative relation of capitalism. At the level of theory, the enlightened despotism of Charles V was an attempt to maintain both positions at once; the royal decrees protecting the Indians are ample testimony to that.[29] At the level of practice, the insistence of his bankers that there should be rapid returns on their loans ensured that there would be no ambiguity.

In part the debate centred on a different description of the American world. The utopians, then as now, rested their descriptions and their arguments on the communities of the pre-conquest Caribbean. The detractors from the myth of American innocence took their evidence from the very different experience of the Aztec and Inca empires of America.[30] If the ideological legitimators of empire laid tendentious stress on the brutalities of Aztec society, the utopian thinkers then and now have chosen to ignore it. In the current discussions the simple Caribbean communities are allowed to stand for the native civilisations of America. The contradictions of the pre-Columbian empires are ignored.

Aztecs and Incas

Aztecs and Incas had much in common. Both had recently imposed their direct rule upon surrounding peoples and nations, and continued to dominate by despotism and fear. In both cases, expansionism had brought these societies to a point of internal crisis and conflict whose resolution could no longer be postponed.[31] The parallels with Spain are irresistible; the three major empires on either side of the ocean had reached points of crisis in their social development. They had of course advanced in different ways, and it would be foolish to pretend that the pre-Columbian empires had reached the point where capital was pressing at the frontiers of the old order. The dynamic of that process, however, *had* begun in those societies, with the consequent crisis in the structure of social relations. And it was internal tension that produced the fissures and cracks that were the key to the outcome of the encounter between Europe and America.

The clash between the Aztecs and the Spaniards was not a simple slaughter of the innocents as Europe's meeting with the Caribbean peoples had largely been. The Aztecs or Mexica settled in their capital city of Tenochtitlan in the mid-14th century;[32] at the time they were the proteges of one of the warring nations around the Lake of Texcoco on the high plateau of Anahuac, where Mexico City now stands. Within a century the Mexica emerged as dominant among the declining and crisis ridden states of the Central Valley. The great Toltec empire housed at the city of the pyramids—Teotihuacan—was now in decline, though many of its cultural and religious elements were assimilated by the

Aztecs. In the course of their rise to dominance, the Mexica assumed the ideological mantle of expansion and control. Their origins in a clan and kinship system (the *calpulli*) were set aside in favour of a ruthless system of social hierarchies and divisions, legitimated by a religion of war which justified expansion. The deity Huitzlipochtli was a terrible and vengeful god whose functionaries were the societies of warriors who wore the emblem of the Jaguar and the Plumed Serpent. And while the wars of assimilation were initially conducted as ritual—what was called the war of flowers[33]—they became real wars of domination some of whose victims at least were sacrificed to the (literally) blood-thirsty god.[34]

The society contained an alternative cult, derived from the civilisation of Texcoco and mystical in content. Its central figure, the Plumed Serpent Quetzalcoatl, was a historical figure transformed into a god whose second coming would set the world to rights. This mystical and contemplative order undoubtedly had adherents at the highest level of the society, and the Emperor Moctezuma, who met Cortes, was certainly influenced by it.[35] But there can be no doubt that the aggressive expansionism of the Aztecs found its rationality in the cult of a warlike and conquering deity. Once the sacrifices were carried out, the dominated peoples maintained their internal organisation but were subject to increasingly heavy tributes to sustain the Aztec apparatus of war. Not every nation was overwhelmed, however; Tlaxcala and the Tarascans successfully fought off the Aztec invasion for years. Later they would provide the battle hardened troops that helped tip the military balance in the Spaniards' favour.

The Aztec empire has been described as 'a system of conquest without consolidation'.[36] By the early 16th century the failure to consolidate had become a serious problem. Expansion and the growth of religion had spawned an unproductive class of priests, warriors and functionaries and produced consequent shortages in the supply of food and other goods. An emergent merchant class (the *pochteca*) traded to and beyond the frontiers of the empire, and developed an independent cultural and political centre at Tlatelolco that came to represent a threat to Moctezuma's imperial core—he attacked and subdued them much as Charles V broke the Comuneros in Spain.[37] But that was only one symptom of rising internal tensions; further expansion was blocked by the resistance of Tarascos, Tlaxcalans and the Mayas of the south. But internal change met the resistance of Moctezuma himself, who stood at the head of a despotic autocracy.

Sacrifice was undoubtedly practiced, though it was a ritual gesture towards the gods and to strike fear into future enemies rather than evidence of cannibalism. The hypocrisy of a Christian civilisation quite willing to murder and torture thousands and impassively witness the decimation of millions drains all meaning from Christian protests at the practice. But in the encounter between Mexico and Spain, the future of two imperial autocracies was the sole issue.[38] Later, Moctezuma tried to negotiate with Cortes, and the Spaniard employed all the diplomatic 'skills' and astuteness which sworn enemies always use. Eventually, Moctezuma died at the hands of his own people, and the warrior caste led by Cuauhtemoc took on the Spaniards and fought back. They were overcome only after an eight month siege by the Spaniards:

> and the walls were spattered with blood
> and worms slithered through the streets
> and our destiny was a network of holes.[39]

The revenge of Hernan Cortes was to raze the city to the ground and build a Spanish urban complex in its place.

Aztec Mexico was overcome. The myth of a tiny knot of Spaniards routing the ignorant and frightened natives is a convenient formula serving every war of colonial oppression from America to Vietnam. But equally mythical is the other version of the same legend—that the indigenous prophecies spoke incessantly of the second coming of an all powerful deity who would rescue a people in agony. Many societies abound with that particular rumour; our own Western civilisation offers regular trips to the top of one mountain or another for those assuring us that 'the end of the world is nigh'—and Europe itself was rife with those same rumours at the same time that Moctezuma was severely exercised by local portents of doom.[40] What is interesting is how the returnee has grown *whiter* in the various retellings. The Aztec deity Quetzalcoatl has paled visibly through his reincarnations! The truth, of course, is that Moctezuma's hesitations derived from his internal crisis and from the possible assumption that these strangers could serve his purposes.

In Mexico, as in Peru, these internal fissures dissipated resistance and precipitated collapse. They released thousands of other native troops to join the enemy of their Aztec enemy and tip the military balance towards the Spanish invaders; and they made it impossible for the Mexica warriors to use their knowledge of the terrain to their advantage.

The causes of Spanish victory were thus far more complex than any racist myth that shows the natives bowing before their natural superiors would allow. And the linked argument that points to Europe's technical superiority is equally partial. There is no denying the degree of European technological development, nor the dynamics that drove it forward and generated new skills and productive techniques in every arena—from boat building and cartography, to printing, to the early transformation of mechanical means of production. That drive to change was overpowering; but the scale of destruction is testimony to the extent to which the American empires did not merely dissolve in the face of European expansion and how far from 'natural' was the consolidation of European dominion.[41]

In 1532, a smaller body of Spaniards came face to face with the Inca empire.[42] It was in some ways a more dramatic and disruptive encounter. Mexico had already been submitted to Spain and the empire was in place; a colonial ruling class now acted on behalf of a confident and expansionist Spanish state that derived both certainty and material wealth from its conquest of the Aztecs. But it was also a class that had developed independent interests which it was disposed to fight for and to which the Spanish state had to respond constantly.[43] That was to emerge clearly in the course of the conquest of Peru. Pizarro, who led the Peruvian expedition, had been with Cortes and gained property and income. This he invested in an expedition spurred by persistent rumours of even greater wealth to the south. The environment in which he operated was a far more competitive and dangerous one than Cortes's. Other expeditions were circling the northern part of the continental land mass—and no one was there for exploration's sake. In this bitter race for riches there was neither sharing nor compromise; the victor took the spoils—until he fell at the hands of yesterday's colleague.

The history of the Incas was even more extraordinary than that of the Aztecs. Their expansion had required less than a century; the Chimu culture dominated the Andean region until about 1475, at which point the Incas emerged the victors from a series of internecine wars. Their dynamism and the speed of their expansion were remarkable. By the time the most important Inca, Huayna Capac, died in 1525, the Inca empire stretched the 6,000 or so kilometres from the central valley of Chile to present day Ecuador. Unlike the Aztecs, the Incas imposed their culture on subject peoples and assimilated their leaders into the Inca ruling class, taking them to the heart of the empire—the city of Cuzco—and training their children in the centre for the *curacas*, the non-Inca chiefs.[44] The intensely centralised structure was maintained by an extremely efficient communications system, via mountain highways and specialised runners, and a cultural hierarchy which worked without writing through a system of oral history and cultural institutions of considerable power. Despite its short history Inca civilisation recorded its own past to the exclusion of all previous cultures.

The speed of growth and consolidation of the Inca civilisation is explained in part by the dynamics of conquest, in part by the urgent necessity to extend both the physical frontiers and the resources of a system of ancestor worship which treated the ancestors as if they still

lived, and accorded to them both property and a share of the social
stock.[45] The tensions that this produced had already interlaced with the
dynastic war that followed on Huayna Capac's death. He had divided
his empire between his sons Huascar and Atahuallpa, who took up arms
in a struggle for absolute control (it is unlikely that the issue of 'legitimacy' which so absorbed Catholic historians was an issue between
them—it was a war over power). In fact it was also a war between different perspectives on the future; the eventual victor, albeit fleetingly,
was the traditionalist Atahuallpa, who exploited the Spaniards' presence to eliminate his rival before he was himself despatched.[46] The encounter between the Inca and Pizarro was a fascinating clash of values,
but there was something inevitable about Pizarro's murder of the Inca,
once he had persuaded him to provide the ransom in gold that finally
sent Europe into paroxyms of delight and appeared to confirm the
wildest rumours about this golden place.[47]

The internal divisions in the empire gave the Spaniards victory; their
weapons of course did have an effect, as did their considerable experience of colonial warfare. But it is unlikely that they would have survived so easily, or at all, had Atahuallpa not seen in them a potential
weapon in his dynastic struggles. It is true that the Spaniards betrayed
the trust of the meeting at Cajamarca, springing on the Inca and his
troops without warning—but they were few and surprise was an important element in their armoury.

What kind of society was this? To all appearances, it was quite
clearly a highly centralised theocracy, where production was conducted
through communal and kinship organisations (the *ayllus*), but where
one third of all production was taken automatically by the Inca or the
ancestors. Yet it has been strongly maintained over the years that Inca
society was collectivist and communal, a basis for a future socialised
production.[48] For the *indigenistas*, in their defence and advocacy of
Indian civilisation, the *ayllu* represents a primitive communism which
has survived the destruction of the Inca empire and persisted into the
present. Thus Sendero Luminoso, for example, advocate that the structures of communal organisation in the communities of the high Andes
must provide the foundation for the kind of society they are setting out
to create. Yet it is a terrifying communalism they advocate, with a hierarchy of absolute rigidity and a reverence for the conditions of primitive accumulation. The continual emphasis on 'purity' and
'authenticity', however, connects them to the thinking of European
utopianism. A paradox indeed.

The conditions of Inca society reveal a producing class sharing a
portion of their agricultural production, collectively worked and har-
vested, among themselves. What they shared, however, was what remained after the deduction of the portion corresponding to the nobility

and the non-producing class, and a second portion corresponding *both* to the ancestors and to the elderly, unable themselves to work or produce. And there was, as in Aztec Mexico, a class of slaves who were not participants in the collective process. Their *treatment* was not the brutality characteristic of the slave owning plantations of a growing capitalism,[49] and their enslavement did not pass from generation to generation. Most importantly their inferiority was not ascribed to racial characteristics. Yet this was a slave society, in which the freedom of some provided an image of other potential forms of social organisation. But the dynamic force was a state accumulating the labour of those who produced. It directed and co-ordinated production, for example, towards the temples, the ancestors, the provision of stocks to maintain the army and so on, and most importantly to feed the noble class which was growing with the incorporation of the chiefs of captured or subjected peoples.

There are two major debates interwoven here. The first is economic and concerns the mode of production in the two pre-Columbian empires.[50] This argument also serves different purposes—either it is demonstrated that their disappearance occurred as a natural consequence of the development of the productive forces on a world scale, and that they represented a mode of production that could not coexist with the higher level of productive relations in a developing capitalism, or they are offered as societies whose internal organisation was free of the exploitation and inequality of the system that destroyed them.

Neither argument is useful or correct. It is clear that both Inca and Aztec societies were class systems. Both had reached a point where a reorganisation of society and of production was required by that very development.[51] The internal conflicts that exposed that dynamic had produced brutal and repressive responses from both states. But both were recently evolving states and had recently established ruling classes. Their imperatives as a social group required further and more rapid expansion and a deepening exploitation; both societies had witnessed a significant development of the technical means to achieve higher productivity: irrigation, efficient use of land, the growing use of indentured or slave labour.

The transition to the new kind of class society was neither smooth nor instantaneous; these ruling classes had barely had time to consolidate the structures of class rule. Yet the dynamics of their system required that they defend it against enemies within and without. Other forms of production—village, communal, subsistence—continued to exist within their frontiers, but all were by one means or another subordinated to the imperatives of the central power. Those who resisted were treated remorselessly; those who accepted incorporation were guaranteed cultural survival within the Inca order.

But in the end, though the mode of cultural organisation and social relationships may serve as a metaphor for the potential of harmonious human integration, these communal forms of organisation were subject to the dominant imperatives of the Inca state, or were in the process of integration into it. To claim otherwise is to romanticise the Inca state and to integrate it back into a simple version of the 'indigenist' message. Within that society there were exploited and exploiters, chiefs and slaves. They were made one by the conquerors, but the internal differentiation was a reality.

The idealisation of the indigenous past corresponds now, as it has so often in the past, to a 'backward glance'. There is within these nostalgic visions of a harmonious past a powerful component of criticism of the brutalities of the order that emerged out of conquest. Those critiques are wholly justified. But if they lead to a romantic vision of the *past* as the alternative, they deny the very real brutalities of that world and they deny the very possibility of emancipation. Thus, curiously, those who look back, who seek the 'restoration' of past worlds, ultimately assume a wholly mechanical view of human and social development, as if the consequences of development *itself* were misery and exploitation.

We may join the utopians in seeing evidence in the past of the historical origin of inequality, the concept of property, of individuality, of competition; that human beings were once capable of existing in a quite different, egalitarian way, setting production to the resolution of need. There *was* a world before profit, a very different human 'nature'. The liberation of that nature, however, requires a concept of the future, of a new direction available in the world that has emerged from conquest and colonisation.

Pinning the blame

The conquest of Latin America was a devastating act of destruction. At every level it seemed to draw out all that was most base and brutal in human beings. From the outset the Spanish conquerors seemed aware of the judgement that history might make of them. In a sometimes bizarre and sometimes ridiculous ceremony the sweating and anxious new arrivals would insist on planting a cross and a banner on the beach and delivering a long Latin disquisition on the legalities of colonisation to the uncomprehending native peoples (if they were there) or otherwise to the unresponsive dunes. This *Requirement* was a statement of the God given rights of a Spanish state accorded dominion over unknown lands by a co-operative pope.

Before they start the rush for gold, for nuggets possibly as big as eggs, lawyer Fernandez de Enciso reads, complete with periods and commas, the ultimatum that the interpreter translates painfully by fits and starts.

Enciso speaks in the name of King Ferdinand and Queen Juana, his daughter, tamers of barbarous peoples. He makes it known to the Indians that God came to the world...and awarded to the King of Castile all the lands of the Indies and of that Peninsula...

The chiefs reply...that the holy father has indeed been generous with others' property but must have been drunk to dispose of what was not his and that the King of Castile is impertinent to come threatening those he doesn't know.

Then the blood flows.

Subsequently the long speech will be read at dead of night... The natives, asleep, won't hear the words that declare them guilty of the crime committed against them.[52]

And yet they still insisted on reading it out. The ideological legitimacy of the conquest mattered to an absolutist state whose internal cohesion flowed from that justifying religious ideology.

Bartolome de las Casas, the Dominican who later became Bishop of Chiapas in Mexico, sustained for nearly 50 years an angry debate on the justice of the enslavement of the Indians.[53] He was not an advocate of withdrawal from the colony—at least not until the very end of his life. On the contrary, he saw in this new and uncorrupted territory the opportunity to establish the medieval 'city of God', a place of harmony and perfect order. The Indians were to be placed under the sovereignty of a Spanish Crown which enshrined and defended the evangelizing mission to found an authentic Christian community. Las Casas accepted for most of his life the Spanish presence in America, but for him its justification lay in the fulfilment of that utopian promise. The exploitation and abuse of the native peoples by the new colonial landowners—the *encomenderos*—made a mockery of those purposes; the *encomienda* was supposed to be an obligation upon the new colonisers to protect and educate their native charges. Instead it simply became the form of the organisation of Indian slavery.

At first the emperor Charles V maintained a dialogue with Las Casas, for the monk spoke with the voice of medieval universality which Charles was now striving to establish in Europe as well as the transatlantic territories. But the inconclusive debate at Valladolid on the theological legitimacy of evangelism and occupation was both Las Casas' highest achievement (together with the Laws of the Indies of 1542) and the final mark of the failure of his enterprise. After two years of intermittent argument, the learned tribunal retired to consider its verdict; it has not yet returned. A year later (in 1550) the Crown decreed

the suspension of conquest. For a few years exploration did cease, but
then the relentless search for land, labour and precious metals began
again. The explicit and implicit purposes of conquest were irreconcileable. Accumulation and the exploitation of the labour required to
extract resources from the ground were the overwhelmingly dominant
purposes. The ideology of conquest stemmed from a medieval
Christian humanism; its practice was resolutely contemporary. 'The
conquest did not seek land, but men to labour'.[54] Gold drove the conquest forward. This is not to deny, of course, that there were acts of
heroism and adventure in those times; they are not testimony to some
other motivation, but rather evidence of how far the conquering class
would go to steal a march on a rival or seek out a route to some hitherto
unmapped field of gold.

That is the fundamental difference between the two public myths of
the time. The search for Utopia was impelled by a medieval, humanist
universal. The myth of El Dorado, on the other hand, was a thoroughly
and unmistakably early primitive dream of accumulation, a place of in-
finite *quantities* of gold. It was a dream of wealth and property, a race
for the power that it brought; and the extraordinary resilience and reck-
less courage of those who sought it bore witness above all to a new law
of motion—not the spirit of exploration but, ultimately, the driving
force of competition.[55]

The implication of this perspective places all that followed
Columbus's voyages at the door of emergent capitalism itself. The destruction was the method of subordinating the New World to the imperatives of the world market born in the Old; the violence was the
characteristic of the crisis of the old order and the bloody emergence of
new relations of production, and the exploitation on which they rested.
The disease and cultural shock that had such a terrible and dramatic
impact on the inhabitants of America were not *distinct* from that over-
arching encounter but aspects of it; it was not the meeting itself that
produced disaster—as if nothing would ever have happened to disrupt
either world if only they had lived in ignorant autonomy—but the circumstances and conditions of it.

In 1792 the Abbe Raynal announced the award of a prize to the best
account of the conquest of Latin America. The replies bolstered 'the
black legend' of Spanish cruelty, a feature apparently of the benighted
Catholic bloodlust of the Iberian peninsula.[56] But capitalism could not
so easily absolve itself of the savagery which was the feature of every
colonial adventure—in Latin America it was the Spaniards, in Virginia
the English, in Canada the French who wrought havoc among the
native peoples. Spain acted on behalf of a wide range of backers and
patrons and under the aegis of a wider system of finance and trade to
which it was deeply indebted and over which it had no control. Within

a single century of the Columbus voyages, Spain was already an economy in decline.[57]

There is another argument offered by some: that the conquest was motivated and justified by racism, by the compulsion to dominate and control subject peoples. Only this, it is argued, can explain the inhuman treatment of the Indian and black populations and the institution of slavery that tore the latter from their own lands. It is a complex argument but one thoroughly dealt with by Alex Callinicos[58] and Basil Davidson:

> *Was there then no racism before the major onset of the Atlantic slave trade?... There was vast misunderstanding, gross abuse, bewildered superstition. But there was no racism in the instrumentalist sense in which the term is rightly used today.*[59]

There were slaves or bondsmen in pre-Columbian societies; there was fear of the stranger and resistance to the unknown. But 'slavery was not born of racism; rather racism, was the consequence of slavery'.[60] In a world of 'free' labour, the 'natural' hierarchies of society belong to a previously existing and unmoving world; now the existence of unfree labour demands another and different *legal* defence —the theory of scientific racism. It is an extreme expression of the central reality of exploitation in *capitalism*. It was not accidental that Marx described the lot of workers there as 'wage slavery'.

Responsibilities

In the course of 1992 the many approaches to the 500 years of conquest have converged on a very few conclusions. In various guises, commentators have argued that the process was the inevitable result of material progress itself—that the development of the productive forces produces violence and destruction of both the human and the physical environment. The case appears strong; in every direction there is evidence of the wreckage and debris that capitalism's development has left behind—the blackened forests, the once green deserts where millions starve to death before our eyes.[61]

It is a curious conclusion to draw, nonetheless, that mankind would have been better never to have progressed at all. It can only be drawn, of course, by thoroughly rewriting the past. If the primitive communities were in perfect and delicate equilibrium with nature, and labour occupied only a small part of life otherwise spent in gentle social pursuits, then there would be some explanation for the persistence of the myth of the utopias of the ancient world.[62] The truth of *that* life is somewhat different; the communities were small and their possibilities narrow. They lived on the edge of catastrophe, and expressed in a multi-theist religion the spectrum of fearsome forces and powers on which they were dependent. Freedom from that fear is one condition for human emancipation; control over the environment and the capacity to mould it to human purposes is the prerequisite for freedom.

> *Freedom...can only consist in socialised man, the associated producers, rationally regulating their interchange with Nature, bringing it under their common control instead of being ruled by it as the blind forces of Nature; and achieving this with the least expenditure of energy and under conditions most favourable to their human nature. But it nonetheless still remains a realm of necessity. Beyond it begins the development of human energy which is an end in itself, the true realm of freedom which, however, can blossom forth only with this realm of necessity as its basis.*[63]

But this freedom is not the mechanical consequence of the development of the productive forces. 'The transformation of Nature by man cannot be isolated from man's transformation of himself'.[64] The paradox is that material progress creates *both* the conditions for human emancipation *and* the conditions for the enslavement of humanity to alienated labour. As society develops the technical possibility of classless society grows—but so does the depth of the crisis that the oppressed class must overcome before that possibility can be realised. In the past lies the fear and inequality that scarcity produces. It is dangerous in the extreme to idealise that past, to deny the want and terror of subjection to a capricious nature.

It is undeniable that those societies so wantonly destroyed by the conquest contained elements of understanding and community which showed humanity at its most co-operative. The irony is that it was those very qualities which were most threatened by the fragile balance between plenty and catastrophe. We would do better to look to harnessing the enormous material resources that capitalism has liberated for its own purposes to a project for human liberation.

And the conditions of capitalist development have ensured that the framework for that project is a world system. The conquest was a first step in creating it, as George Bush acknowledged in one of his rare coherent expositions of the official response to Columbus. Bush's 'New World Order', announced in the aftermath of the Gulf War, stands exposed as a framework for new violence, greater hunger and need, a light veil over mounting social disintegration. How closely the birth of the New echoes the birth of the Old!

It is no response, however, to ignore that global reality and resurrect the discredited nationalisms of previous decades. There is no denying the contradictory reality of nationalism in the contemporary world. On the one hand, it expresses the rage and resistance of the oppressed; on the other, it holds up a promise of a solution—independent national development—which in the integrated world economy of the late 20th century has been exposed as an illusion; never so clearly as in the context of an international debt crisis whose tentacles reach into the most remote corners of the 'Third World'.[65]

The celebration of Columbus's voyages have never been innocent commemorations of an event in the history of navigation or exploration or philosophy. When the US government announced the formation of a Quincentennial Commission it was assumed that the bulk of its finances would come from private enterprise[66]—after all, it was their birthright that was to be feted. It is a particular irony that the Dominican Republic, claiming to be the site of Columbus's first landfall, spent far more than the government of the United States on a monument; all the more ironic, since the land on which it was built was home to 1,500 or so squatter families who were brutally expelled by police using tear gas.[67] Since then Spain's huge expenditure in Seville in Columbus's name has been accompanied by rising unemployment and economic recession, the latter significantly deepened by the as yet undisclosed outlays by a Spanish government anxious above all to take its place among the inheritors of the post-Columbian world capitalist order.[68] It was somehow sickeningly fitting that a demonstration by a group of native Peruvians should have been broken up Spanish police and many of their number expelled. In 1492 or 1992, it is one thing for a Peruvian or Bolivian Indian to arrive bedecked in native costume playing their *zampoña* pipes to the delight of the metropolitan bourgeoisie; it is quite another when they fight back.

The argument from resistance

Christopher Columbus was present at the birth of the world market; since then his name has been invoked by those who see 1492 as the date of birth of a new, progressive world. New actors appeared then on the stage of history; the thrusting individual, the daring entrepreneur, the priest rushing along behind him to anoint his acts of terror with holy water, the despot ruling in the name of progress. The 60 million or so who died within a few years of his arrival (some 85 percent of the existing population) disappeared from the historical narratives—just as they have been absent from each previous centenary of the voyages. But in 1756 Rousseau noted that the outcome of that development was that 'man is born free but is everywhere in chains';[69] beyond that, Rousseau understood that human emancipation is conditional upon collective organisation. In 1892, a Catholic revival and a burgeoning North American capitalism combined to rediscover the origin of their world. And in 1992, polishing here and there, Columbus re-emerges as the all too human herald of a world order now about to enter its 'higher' phase.

Against that the native American organisations of north and south have combined to launch a campaign to remember 500 years of resistance. That history of struggle and rebellion is a continuous one, yet it still has to be written. It begins in the resolute counter-attacks of the native Americans against their oppressors. Racism has developed a myth of passive Indians, barbarians or innocent victims—but at all events *passive*; they have their equivalents in the poignant disaster victims so often portrayed on front pages across the world. But just as the droughts and floods of the late 20th century are the product of man made crises, so the indigenous peoples who faced the conquest were the objects of a remorseless history.

They did not lie down, however. The fear of the flesh eating cannibals, demonised for five centuries from early accounts to children's books, was the fear of rebellion. For after the destruction of the Tainos, the Caribs fought back. The fearful resonance of the term 'voodoo' reflects the fragile social peace in a Caribbean whose black slave communities maintained their culture, language and religion—the instruments of resistance—and revived them under cover of night. Later, within years of the arrival of the first slaves from Africa, the escaped slaves formed independent communities which held off the invaders by force of arms and linked with the Indian communities which had risen in insurrection from the very beginning of the colony. Usually they were crushed. But sometimes, from the resistance in 1530 led by Manco Inca from the mountain fastness of Macchu Picchu, through the refusal of the Chilean Mapuches to submit to Spain, to the great risings of Tupac Amaru and Tupac Katari in the late 18th century, resistance could claim some success.

The rebellions and insurrections were frequent and determined; between confrontations the determination to resist found many forms— the preservation of a language, the playing of forbidden instruments, the enactment of religious and secular rites. And the history was preserved and passed on in myth and legend and symbol. That history is continuous, and continues now. It does *not* belong to the past and, while some rebellious groups identified their struggle through symbols of the past, they were not attempts to *restore* that past. These were struggles against the conditions of life and labour in the society created out of conquest. The fighters organised around their collective experience as propertyless producers of wealth for distant centres. When the peasants of El Salvador rose periodically against the landowners from the 1880s onwards it was to resist the loss of their food producing land to the cultivation of export crops; when the workers of Cordoba and Tucuman in Argentina struck against their employers and the state and closed the factories in those cities, they were fighting against the same priorities. Through time, and since the pre-Columbian world disappeared, the struggles of the exploited have been directed against capitalism and its representatives.

That is where the continuity of resistance is to be found, in the link between struggles, whose forms and symbols may differ, but which are directed against the same priorities and the same imperatives across the world. A future society in which those differences and that enormous diversity of human experience can flourish can only emerge from a *struggle* that is international in vision and in scale.

> *Stick and stone will rise up for the struggle... Dogs will bite their masters... The usurpers will depart to the limits of the waters... Then there will be no more devourers of men... When greed comes to an end, the face of the world will be set free, its hands will be set free, its feet will be set free.*[70]

Notes

1   This mock version of the Columbus story turns out to be the precise plot of the new film *Christopher Columbus the Discovery!*

2   See K Sale, *The Conquest of Paradise* (London, 1990) p15 footnote. Sale's book has been received with some scepticism because it is written from a committed ecologist position. That said it is still in my view the most thorough and accessible of all the crop of Columbus studies. H Koning's *Columbus His Enterprise* (London, 1991) is aimed at a wider popular audience, and is also very good.

3   See E W Bovill, *The Golden Trade of the Moors* (London, 1958) ch 13.

4   See F Braudel, *The Mediterranean and the Mediterranean World in the Age of Philip II* (London, 1972).

5   Quoted in K Sale, op cit, pp29-30

6   In this respect see H Koning and K Sale, op cit, in particular.

7   On the general influence of European finance see P Vilar, *A History of Gold and Money 1450-1920* (London, 1976). The bankers were particularly influential in the exploration and colonisation of Venezuela, documented in detail in J Hemming's *The Search for El Dorado* (London, 1978).

8   J H Elliott, *The Old World and the New* (London, 1970) ch 1.

9   E Salerno, in *Genesis* (London, 1987), orchestrates these differing views brilliantly and provides the richest history of the period.

10   See C Coloin, *Textos y documentos completos* (Madrid, 1984), ed C Varela, for the most comprehensive compilation. See also C Jane (ed), *Four Voyages of Christopher Columbus* (New York, 1988).

11   See *National Geographic*, November 1975.

12   Quoted in K Sale, op cit, p124.

13   A Crosby, 'The Biological Consequences of 1492', in North American Congress on Latin America (NACLA), *Report on the Americas* XXV/2, September 1991, p9. For a fuller account see Crosby's *The Columbian Exchange* (Westport, Conn. 1971).

14   M Stevenson, 'Columbus and the War on Indigenous Peoples' in *Race and Class* 33/3, January-March 1992, p30.

15   Quoted in W Irving, *The Life and Voyages of Christopher Columbus* (London, 1876) p123.

16   Ibid.

17   J H Huizinga, *The Waning of the Middle Ages* (London, 1924), and G Jackson, *The Making of Medieval Spain* (London, 1972).

18   One of the most revealing critiques is the *Dialogo de Mercurio y Caron* (Barcelona, 1987) by Alfonso de Valdes, in which Caron refuses to ferry various corrupt and overweight church dignitaries across his river Styx. Bosch's paintings remain a powerful assault on contemporary hypocrisy.

19   The brilliant *Letter to a King* by the descendant of Indian nobility Felipe Huaman Pomo de Ayala (London, 1978) is a blistering critique of colonial society and the hypocrisy of its priests and administrators. It was written during the second half of the 16th century, then suppressed until its rediscovery in 1911 in the Royal Library of Copenhagen. Since then the woodcuts that accompany the text have become widely known. Its original Spanish title, *New Morality and Good Government*, says much about its source in medieval humanism and the standpoint from which it was written.

20   Martin Luther was later to codify this thought, 'Anyone who can be proved to be a seditious person is an outlaw before God and the emperor; and whoever is the first to put him to death does right and well.' Quoted in W Brandon, *New Worlds for Old* (Ohio, 1986) p127.

21   This theme of the authority of kings as the source of wisdom and true justice is constant in the prolific Spanish theatre of the age. See the recently revived *Fuenteovejuna* by Lope de Vega.

22   On the general and vexed question of population see S F Cook and W Borah, *Essays in Population History. Mexico and the Caribbean* (Berkeley, 1971).

23   W Brandon's *New Worlds for Old* (Ohio, 1986), an excellent and comprehensive account of this issue is an indispensable source.

24   M Montaigne, *Essays* (trans Peter Coste London, 1811), vol 1, p247.

25   *The Tempest*, act 2, scene 1. In Shakespeare's *Complete Works* (Oxford, 1991) p1176.

26   Quoted in Brandon, op cit, p85.

27   E Galeano, op cit, pp57-58.

28   See Brandon, op cit, particularly ch 6.

29   The most complete source of the documents and debates of the period is still L Hanke's classic *History of Latin American Civilisation* (London, 1969). See too F Jennings, *The Invasion of America, Indians, Colonialism and the Cant of Conquest* (New York, 1976).

30   Like Gomara, for example, and Sepulveda.

31   This is comprehensively argued in G H Conrad and A A Demarest's *Religion and Empire* (Cambridge, 1984).

32   Their legends depict the Aztecs as a wandering tribe who settled where they found an eagle with a serpent in its beak resting on a cactus. The spot, an island in the middle of Lake Texcoco, seemed unpropitious at first, but proved to be an impregnable fortress from which to launch their expansionism.

33   See J Canesco Vincourt, *La guerra florida* (Mexico, 1966).

34   The myth had it that Huitzlipochtili had leapt through a fire to keep the world in being during a contest between the gods. His blood, flowing daily at sunset, had to be replaced with the blood of those captured in battle.

35   See D Viñas, *Mexic y Cortes* (Madrid, 1978), M Collis also wrote a novel called *Cortes and Moctezuma* published some years ago by Faber and Faber, London.

36   Conrad and Demarest, op cit, p53.

37   This is expounded by L Sejourne, *The Daily Life of the Aztecs* (Harmondsworth, 1968).

38   See D Viñas, op cit, and also the classic account of the Conquest of Mexico by W H Prescott.

39   This comes from the version of the last Aztec codices, the *Song of Songs of Tlatelolco* in its version by the contemporary Mexican poet Jose Emilio Pacheco. The original is in M Leon Portilla, *Vision de los vencidos* (Mexico, 1961), translated as *The Broken Spear* (Boston, 1962).

40   Portilla gathers the contemporary Aztec accounts of these portents—which included a sight of the ubiquitous Halley's Comet and the wailing of the children at night.

41   See, on Mexico, C Gibsoni, *Los aztecas bajoel domnio espaniol* (Mexico, 1977), and N Wachtel *Vision of the Vanquished* (1976).

42   J Hemming's *The Conquest of the Incas* (London, 1970) remains the definitive work. Until his work appeared the usual reference work was W H Prescott's 19th century *History of the Conquest of Peru*. Prescott, like most others, relied almost entirely on the writing of the Inca Garcilaso de la Vega whose account of Inca society—the *Royal Commentaries of the Incas* of 1615—was very detailed. Its framework, however, was a curious one, since Garcilaso argued that Inca Peru and Spain should *merge* because they had reached an exactly parallel point in their development by independent roads. See too T Patterson, *The Inca Empire, Formation and Disintegration of a Pre-capitalist State* (Oxford 1991).

43   The colonists had already rebelled against the Spanish state in Mexico, under the leadership of Cortes's brother Martin. If Spain kept control of its empire at a vast distance, it was through the work of a skilled and tentacular bureaucracy and, of course, the army. But in the end it was ideology that cemented the whole edifice together—reinforced by interest. For a more general account see F Kirkpatrick, *The Conquistadors* (1934).

44   On the Incas generally see J Hemming, Garcilaso, Huaman Pomo de Ayala, op cit, and W Van Hagen whose *The Ancient Sun Kingdoms of the Americas* (London, 1979) covers Aztecs, Mayas and Incas.

45   See Conrad and Demarest, op cit.

46   See J Hemming, op cit, but particularly Peter Shaffer's marvellous play about the encounter between Pizarro and Atahuallpa, *The Royal Hunt of the Sun* (London 1964).

47   See V Von Hagen's *The Golden Man* (London,1964) and J Hemming, *The Search for El Dorado*.

48   This idea is argued in a work of crucial significance by the great but still largely unknown Peruvian Marxist Jose Carlos Mariategui in his *Seven Interpretive Essays on the Peruvian Reality* published in 1928. His ideas are claimed today as their own by almost every revolutionary organisation in Peru. In another context, the work of the marvellous Peruvian writer Jose Maria Arguedas addresses the same cultural traditions. He committed suicide in 1968 after publishing a final novel, *El zorro de arriba y el zorro de abajo*, which concluded that white and Indian worlds were irreconcileable.

49   See C L R James, *The Black Jacobins* (London, 1980).

50   See here the writing of L Baudin, *L'Empire Socialiste des Incas*, translated as *Daily Life in Peru under the Last Incas* (1961).

51   This is precisely the argument of the Inca Garcilaso de la Vega, see note 42.

52   See E Galeano, op cit, pp59-60.

53   See B de las Casas *Historia de las Indias* (Mexico, 1965), and L Hanke *Aristotle and the American Indians* (London, 1959).

54   P Chaunu, *Conquête et Exploitation des Anciens Mondes* (Paris, 1969) p135.

55   See J Hemming, *The Search for El Dorado,* op cit. The story of Lope de Aguirre, reproduced with analogous madness by Werner Herzog in his film *Aguirre Wrath of God* may stand as an example.

56   The argument is still regularly rolled out for repetition, as for example in the opening programme of Carlos Fuentes' BBC2 series *The Buried Mirror* reproduced (word for pretentious word) in *The Buried Mirror* (London, 1992). The book never uses one word where 12 will do, and in the end is a barely concealed apology for conquest as an event beyond anyone's control.

57   See S and B Stein, *The Colonial Heritage of Latin America* (Oxford,1970) ch 1.

58   In A Callinicos, 'Race and Class', in *International Socialism* 55, Summer 1992, pp3-40.

59   B Davidson, 'Columbus, the Bones and Blood of Racism', in *Race and Class* 33/3, January-March 1992, p20.

60   E Williams quoted in A Callinicos, op cit, p11.

61   See D Treece, 'Why the Earth Summit Failed', in *International Socialism* 56, Autumn 1992.

62   The argument is most powerfully made by Sale and Crosby. See too the edition of NACLA Report entitled *The Conquest of Nature*, XXV/2, September 1991.

63   Marx, *Capital,* vol III (London, 1972), p820, quoted in A Sanchez Vazquez, *The Philosophy of Praxis* (London, 1972) p335.

64   Ibid.

65   See M Gonzalez, *Nicaragua: What Went Wrong?* (London, 1990).

66   NACLA Report XXV/3, December 1991, pp11-12.

67   See A Reid, 'Waiting for Columbus', *New Yorker*, 24 February 1992, pp57-75.

68   See M Carr, 'Spain, the Day of the Race', in *Race and Class* 33/3, Jan-March 1992, pp89-95.

69   The famous opening sentence of J J Rousseau's *Social Contract*.

70   E Galeano, *Faces and Masks* (London, 1990) pp258-9.

Poetry and revolution

A transcipt of a programme originally broadcast on BBC Radio 3

PAUL FOOT

> *These vs are all the versuses of life*
> *From Leeds v Derby Black*
> *White and (as I've known to my cost) man v wife,*
> *Communist v fascist, Left v right,*
> *class versus class as bitter as before,*
> *the unending violence of US and THEM,*
> *personified in 1984*
> *by Coal Board MacGregor and the NUM.*

Tony Harrison's epic poem 'V' was inspired by the desecration of his father's grave. Its theme is the political and social conflicts of our time. But should poets meddle in politics at all? Most English literature teachers think not. An editor of a recent collection of Shelley's poetry for instance left out two political poems because he insisted, 'a great lyric poet had strayed outside his own proper field'. But not all teachers agree about this. Terry Eagleton, professor of English at Oxford University, points out that many of the great English poets were writing at the time of revolution:

Times of revolution do tend to throw up poets and often very major poets, sometimes in direct response to what is going on politically. At a time of revolution you have the feeling that history is actually in the making; you can see history moving before your eyes. That is different from the sense of simply receiving history as a kind of dead tradition, something inert. If you look at revolutionary poetry, particularly around the French Revolution, let's say Blake, or the early Wordsworth, then often you find those poets are responding quite directly to what is going on. On the other hand, a bit more subtly, a bit more indirectly, revolutions tend to unleash the unconscious. There are all kinds of subliminal built up forces which the act of revolution or the process of overthrowing a state or installing a new government or changing economic arrangements tends to catalyse. Now, what you then get, I think, is a sort of liberation, a kind a flood of those very intangible forces into the whole cultural environment. There's a quickening of energy.

The first example of the 'quickening of energy' in our history is the English Revolution of the 1640s led by Cromwell and the Puritans. Here's Christopher Hill, a leading expert on the 17th century:

The first thing is just to say that there was a revolution in 17th century England. There is a fashion among historians these days to say there was not really a revolution, there wasn't anything wrong with English society. There was just a bit of mistaken government and a bit of court intrigue and then by accident the thing blew up. Now whenever people use that argument to me I refer them to English literature in the period where there is any amount of evidence of the deep social divisions and hostilities. Even though the literature is censored it still comes through. If we take, perhaps best of all, Shakespeare. Shakespeare was not a revolutionary, but he's very good at listening to what people are saying in his society and reproducing them fairly, and also safeguarding himself against being too closely associated with revolutionary sentiments. In, for instance, *Henry VI, Part Two*, where he depicts Jack Cade and his rebels, he makes them say a lot of silly things in order to show that he does not take them seriously, but every now and then they make a perfectly shrewd and sensible comment, and they also do ask for things that people in 16th and 17th century society were asking for. For instance, Jack Cade's supporters say, 'Break open the jails and let out the prisoners!' as they did in 1640 when the English Revolution started. 'Kill all the lawyers!' which is something that a lot of people would liked to have done in the 1640s and 1650s. 'Burn all the records of the realm!'—that's a continuing demand. And various social comment is put in biblical terms as people did in the 17th century. 'Adam was a gardener'—we shall meet that often later. Gardeners occur again in *Richard II*, where they have a long discussion saying that they could run the state a lot better than it was being run under Richard II—not that that would have been very difficult. In *King Lear*, because the king is mad he is able to say all sorts of dangerous things that you could not have said on the stage otherwise, unless you were a fool—fools are licensed to say dangerous things. Remember what King Lear says:

> *Thou rascal beadle, hold they bloody hand!*
> *Why dost thou lash that whore? Strip thy own back;*
> *Thou hotly lusts to use her in that kind*
> *For which thou whip'st her. The usurer hands the cozener.*
> *Through tattered clothes small vices do appear;*
> *Robes and furred gowns hide all.*

So there's a lot of social comment which looks forward to things that were actually going to be said in the 1640s and 1650s. There is plenty of evidence for that. It shows pretty clearly that these things were being said in the 1590s and early 1600s and that Shakespeare and other Elizabethan dramatists heard them and reproduced them in a carefully edited way so as to show that they were not in sympathy with these people—which would mean as much as their skins would be worth.

One of the most enthusiastic supporters of that revolution of the 1640s was John Milton. Milton threw himself heart and soul into propaganda for the Puritans and their generals, Cromwell and Fairfax. Marilyn Butler, professor of English literature at Cambridge University, thinks this revolutionary inspiration is inseparable from Milton's great poetry:

Milton, in the period after the revolution (because in the revolution he was very busy being the Latin secretary, so that he wrote a lot of prose during the revolutionary period itself), produces really great work and you feel that Milton sort of went through fire and he matured in the revolutionary period and then wrote *Paradise Lost, Paradise Regained* and *Samson Agonistes*, his great work, in his bitterness in a way, his post-revolutionary period.

In that post-revolutionary period monarchy was restored and supporters of Cromwell, like Milton, were hunted down. Tom Paulin is reader in poetry at Nottingham University. How significant does he feel the political events of the 1660s were to Milton's *Paradise Lost*?

For me one of the most moving passages in *Paradise Lost* is near the beginning of book seven when Milton stands back and talks about himself. He's blind, he's on the wrong side, the restoration has taken place, he's halfway through his great epic poem. He's been hunted, he's been put in jail, he's been very, very nearly executed. Only the intercession of friends, I think, stopped him from being led to the scaffold with the other surviving regicides. This is the voice of a great classical poet who is looking at his subject, looking at his life, looking at the history he's lived through and reaffirming his commitment to the English Revolution.

> *Half yet remains unsung, but narrower bound*
> *Within the visible Diurnal Sphear;*
> *Standing on Earth, not rapt above the Pole,*
> *More safe I Sing with mortal voice, unchang'd*
> *To hoarse or mute, though fall'n on evil days;*
> *On evil days though fall'n, and evil tongues;*
> *In darkness, and with dangers compast round,*
> *And solitude; yet not alone, while thou*
> *Visitst my slumbers Nightly, or when Morn*
> *Purples the East: still govern thou my Song,*
> *Urania, and fit audience find, though few.*
> *But drive far off the barbarous dissonance*
> *of Bacchus and his revellers, the Race*
> *Of that wilde Rout that tore the Thracian Bard*
> *In Rhodope, where Woods and Rocks had Eares*
> *To rapture, till the savage clamor drownd*
> *Both Harp and Voice; nor could the Muse defend*
> *Her Son. So fail not thou, who thee impores:*
> *For thou art Heav'nlie, shee an empty dream.*

What Milton is saying there is 'preserve me, muse', which he saw as the voice of god, 'preserve me from the barbarous dissonance of Bacchus and his revellers', and what he means there is all these Royalist louts rampaging drunk through London, beating up surviving republicans, persecuting them and at times executing them. This is the voice of deep political commitment.

Christopher Hill says of Milton:

'I sing unchanged', he said in 1667. Now in 1667 nobody had ever heard of Milton as a poet. He published one slim volume 22 years earlier. Nobody really took much notice of him. When he says, 'I sing unchanged', people thought of the Milton they did know—the man who defended the Commonwealth in the face of the whole of Europe and won European fame for it, the man who had attacked Charles I after his death, the man who had proclaimed the right of people to call their kings to account and the man who in 1659, just on the eve of Charles II coming back, had gone on record attacking him personally and monarchy in principle in a pamphlet called *A Ready and Easy Way to Establish a Free Commonwealth*.

The *Private Eye* caricature of a left wing writer, Dave Spart, would conclude from all this that good poets support the revolution and bad poets oppose it. Well, another famous supporter of the English Revolution, John Dryden, also supported the reaction that replaced it. Professor John Lucas of the University of Loughborough takes the opposite line to Dave Spart, at least as far as John Dryden is concerned.

I think he's a better poet when he has gone over to the Restoration to be honest. I think the early poetry, perhaps because it is early poetry, is not very skilled. Indeed it is often extremely clumsy. I also think that he is wearing his heart on his sleeve in a lot of that early stuff, whereas I do think by the time he has settled into the great period, roughly say 1675 on, then the poetry is magnificent. I happen not to share his politics but I wouldn't want to take anything away from the stature of the poetry.

But that doesn't mean that the revolution was irrelevant to Dryden. The revolutionary 'quickening of energies', as Terry Eagleton put it, inspires poets of all political persuasions. Eagleton adds:

I think it would come as a great surprise, wouldn't it, to, say, Milton or Pope or Swift or the whole line of major writers if they were told that literature and politics have nothing to do with each other. I mean they would have found that whole conception unintelligible. We're taking the very recent historical definition which is only a century or so old and then reading it back into these people. The moment of the English romantics is perhaps the last moment when you might say that the imagination is operating as a political force.

And who were these romantics? They made up the long line of famous English poets who wrote in the 1780s and 1790s and the first 20 years of the 19th century. This was the period in which the whole culture of Europe was shaken up by the French Revolution. Almost all these poets at one time or another were revolutionaries but they are known as 'romantics' because their poetry has been filleted—the politics taken out and nature left in. As Marilyn Butler says:

The one really great poet that we have got that is directly a revolutionary poet, that is writing in a revolution and really basically about a revolution is clearly Blake. He is writing in this simple anticipatory way with his *Songs of Innocence* which is immediately pre-revolutionary 1789. Then in a few years between 1790 and 1795 he does the majority of his great output. Those are the direct revolutionary years themselves and he begins with a group of epics which imagine the revolution becoming worldwide—America, Europe and then the 'Song of Loss' which is in fact an epic poem about a revolution coming in Asia and in Africa. So what he has actually done is to imagine the revolution coming worldwide in that little group of Continental epics which he wrote between 1791 and 1793. And then he wrote a small strange group of writings which I think in some ways are his very best. The best of those is the first book of 'Urizen'. This is a book that rewrites Genesis and the beginning of the bible, overturning it, oversetting it. It is because Blake identifies the Christian religion as the religion that is the state ideology, the state church, that he writes this great imaginative, indirect poem in which he himself oversets, topples, ideology by writing his own bible so that in future people are not enslaved to the stony laws of received wisdom.

> *Cold, he wander'd on high, over their cities*
> *In weeping & pain & woe;*
> *And where-ever he wander'd in sorrows*
> *Upon the aged heavens*
> *A cold shadow follow'd behind him*
> *Like a spider's web, moist, cold & dim,*
> *Drawing out from his sorrowing soul,*
> *The dungeon-like heaven dividing,*
> *Where ever the footsteps of Urizen*
> *Walk'd over the cities in sorrow;*
>
> *Till a Web, dark & cold, throughout all*
> *The tormented elements stretch'd*
> *From the sorrows of Urizen's soul;*
> *And the Web of Female in embrio:*
> *None could break the Web, no wings of fire,*
>
> *So twisted the cords & so knotted*
> *The meshes, twisted like to the human brain.*
>
> *And all call'd it The Net of Religion*

William Wordsworth, whose best known poem today is about daffodils, was almost hysterical in his support of the French Revolution. By the time he came to write his greatest poem, 'The

Prelude', the revolutionary ardour was cooling fast. But it is quite
impossible to understand the poem without understanding
Wordsworth's relationship to the revolution:

> And we chanc'd
> One day to meet a hunger-bitten Girl,
> Who crept along, fitting her languid gait
> Unto a Heifer's motion, by a cord
> Tied to her arm, and picking thus from the lane
> Its sustenance, while the girl with her two hands
> Was busy knitting, in a heartless mood
> Of solitude, and at the sight my Friend
> In agitation said, ''Tis against that
> Which we are fighting,' I with him believed
> Devoutly that a spirit was abroad
> Which could not be withstood, that poverty
> At least like this, would in no little time
> Be found no more, that we should see the earth
> Unthwarted in her wish to recompense
> The industrious, and the lowly Child of Toil,
> All institutes for ever blotted out
> That legalised exclusion, empty pomp
> Abolish'd, sensual states and cruel power
> Whether by edict of the one or few,
> And finally, a sum and crown of all,
> Should see the People having a strong hand
> In making their own Laws, whence better days
> To all mankind.

Marilyn Butler argues:

You then have a phase, because after all poets don't have to be pro-
revolutionary, they can be counter-revolutionary poets, and we had a
phase of major poetry which is in a way counter-revolutionary.
Wordsworth's poetry is a thoughtful, remorseful, rather guilty reconsid-
eration of his own childhood and youth. There is an argument that
Wordsworth's backward looking poetry, his attempts to tell his own
life story in 'The Prelude', is really an attempt to explain away his involvement with the French revolution. It is the central episode, and
some of the great odes, certainly 'Resolution and Independence' and
'Intimations in Mortality' again have been seen as remorseful rework-
ing of the past.

Tom Paulin says:

I think one's got to read both versions of the poem. The 1805 version, the early version is radical and republican in its whole address to the subject. In the 1850 version Wordsworth holds more or less to that thread but then he cuts bits or he introduces bits which go against it. There is a sort of counter-revolutionary argument going on with the revolutionary argument in the 1850 version. For example, in the 1850 version he introduces a rather tedious passage in praise of the counter-revolutionary writer Edmund Burke which is not there in the 1805 version. He rewrites his own history and his own autobiography and suggests that he actually admired Burke as a young man, but he didn't. He was anti-Burke and then he switched over. The result is a very, very complex, in many ways very vulnerable work. Actually when the 1850 version of 'The Prelude' was published after Wordsworth's death McCaully thought it was a socialist work. He did not see it as in fact a conservative work, so it's very complicated in its whole tenor.

Two other great so-called romantic poets, Byron and Shelley, stayed loyal all their short lives to the principles of the French Revolution. Byron's early work, perhaps because of his infectious sense of humour, was enormously popular, but his publishers and his adoring public were not so happy with his great epic poem, written near the end of his life, 'Don Juan'. This book is one long mockery of the establishment of the day—the Tory government, the church, the army, the poet laureate and the apostate Wordsworth. 'Wordsworth's last quarto by the way is bigger than any since the birthday of typography.

A drowsy, frowsy poem called 'The Excursion',
written in a manner which is my aversion.

And in the middle of 'Don Juan' Byron suddenly spells out a remedy to all the world's ills:

But never mind;—'God save the king!' and kings!
For if he don't, I doubt if men will longer—
I think I hear a little bird, who sings
The people by and by will be the stronger:
The veriest jade will wince whose harness wrings
So much into the raw as quite to wrong her
Beyond the rules of posting,—and the mob
At last fall sick of imitating Job.

At first it grumbles, then it swears, and then,

Like David, flings smooth pebbles' gainst a giant;
At last it takes to weapons such as men
Snatch when despair makes human hearts less pliant.
Then comes 'the tug of war;'—'t will come again,
I rather doubt; and I would fain say 'fie on 't,'
If I had not perceived that revolution
Alone can save the earth from hell's pollution.

Byron was read by almost everyone, but his friend and admirer Shelley was read by almost no one. During all his 30 years Shelley made only £40 from his published work, and that from a trashy novel that he wrote when he was 16. Marilyn Butler says,

Shelley is the among the most, perhaps he is *the* most, directly political of all the British great poets. Really I think his work from first to last is political so that anything you pick out is a bit arbitrary. He wrote long poems which in their different ways act out revolutions. This is a much misunderstood fact about the romantics. It has been fashionable to say recently that what romantics were really good at was lyric poetry, that is short poetry that is like music. On the whole the reason is that the modern period, being rather apolitical as far as literary criticism is concerned, wants to think that great poetry is also apolitical and so the long poems which act out revolution in the romantic period have simply been written out of the record. But in fact there is a whole sequence of them starting really with Robert Southey, who couldn't make up his mind whether to be on the left or on the right in the first decade after the French Revolution, in fact Southey wrote a series of long poems about colonial revolutions and they are very political. The first of them, 'Fallimar the Destroyer', is the most political of the lot and that was imitated by a great number of romantics so that, for instance, Shelley's 'The Revolt of Islam' in its 12 books describing revolution in the East is a close imitation of 'Fallimar the Destroyer':

Man seeks for gold in mines, that he may weave
A lasting chain for his own slavery;—
In fear and restless care that he may live
He toils for others, who must ever be
The joyless thralls of like captivity;
He murders, for his chief's delight in ruin;
He builds the altar, that his idol's fee
May be his very blood; he is pursuing
O, blind and willing wretch! his own obscure undoing.

138 INTERNATIONAL SOCIALISM

That extract was from Shelley's 'The Revolt of Islam' which was at least published in Shelley's lifetime. Shelley's more direct political poetry, especially 'The Mask of Anarchy', 92 verses of ferocious invective against the bishops, lawyers, peers and spies who were in charge at the time, didn't see the light of day until long after Shelley died in 1822. 'Queen Mab' and 'Swellfoot the Tyrant', two long political poems were prosecuted by the Society for the Suppression of Vice. But the poems survived after Shelley's death. Like Byron's 'Don Juan', 'Queen Mab' was a favourite among the Chartists during their uprisings in the 1830s and 1840s. Many years later Karl Marx's daughter Eleanor, wrote to a friend:

> I have heard my father and Engels again and again speak of this and I have heard the same from many Chartists it has been my good fortune to know as a child and young girl. Only a very few months ago I heard Harney and Engels talking of the Chartist times, of the Byron and especially the Shelley worship of the Chartists. And on Sunday last Engels said, 'Oh, we all knew Shelley by heart then'.

Another allegedly romantic poet who was censored in his lifetime and patronised afterwards because of his politics was John Clare. Clare is described in the *Encyclopedia Britannica* as a 'great poet of the countryside'. John Lucas reveals that he was rather more than that.

The Society for the Suppression of Vice had, as one of its leading members, Lord Radstock. Lord Radstock was the patron of Clare and Clare's first volume had been published in 1820 and Radstock had made sure that certain poems and stanzas and lines were censored. He had particularly objected against some lines in a poem called 'Helpstone the Village' where Clare was born and brought up, which he called 'radical slang'. They are in fact a protest, a wonderful bitter protest against enclosure. Clare is a great radical voice in the early middle years of the 19th century but one who has been made almost invisible to us until at least very recently because of the way he has been handled by his first editors and then subsequent editors. There is a point here that I think does link into Blake. Different as they are, the fact is that they are artisan or working class, you might say, or peasant class, whatever, and they are treated uniformally with a mixture of condescension or scorn. You may say that can't possibly be true of Blake but actually it is. The critical history of Blake is one which demonstrated that until very recently most people who wrote about him at all wrote about him as though he was a kind of harmless madman or someone who got a bit above himself and who after all had not been to university, wasn't really all that skilled as a draughtsman and was rash and imprudent in certain ways. That is not said of Clare. What is said of Clare is that he shouldn't meddle in politics, and that he didn't really know enough about these things. But therefore he was okay when he kept to birds and mice, but when he started writing about the larger issues of the day, like enclosure above all, he really didn't know what he was talking about. Clare wrote a wonderful sonnet, 'England in 1830' which is a huge, bitter attack on the structures of English society at that time. It was never published in his lifetime and the reason it was not published in his lifetime is quite obvious—that it was not what a peasant poet should be doing.

> These vague allusions to a country's wrongs,
> Where one says 'Ay' and others answer 'No'
> In contradiction from a thousand tongues,
> Till like to prison-cells her freedoms grow
> Becobwebbed with these oft-repeated songs
> Of peace and plenty in the midst of woe—
> And is it thus they mock her year by year,
> Telling poor truth unto her face she lies,
> Declaiming of her wealth with gibe severe,
> So long as taxes drain their wished supplies?
> And will these jailers rivet every chain
> Anew, yet loudest in their mockery be,
> To damn her into madness with disdain,
> Forging new bonds and bidding her be free?

In Tom Paulin's recent anthology of political poetry, the poet with the most extracts is Arthur Hugh Clough. Clough was born in 1819. After a brilliant university career he resigned his fellowship in the Church of England and opted instead for a life of poverty and rebellion. Tom Paulin argues:

There is something wrong with the perceived history of Victorian poetry in Britain. Tennyson is given far too much attention, and Tennyson is basically an imperialist and conservative writer and has many admirers. But Clough is much the more interesting and neglected poet. There are hardly any critical studies of Clough. Nobody writes about him, nobody I'm sure practically teaches him. But Clough was energised by that great revolutionary European moment which spread over into Britain and Ireland in 1848. His great poem, 'Amours De Voyage', comes out of that revolutionary year. So that when you look at Clough, for example, Clough is describing a Highland burn, he is describing waterfalls, the momentum and the wet of the water falling. But actually what he is writing about is history, is politics, is the great movement of 1848 with revolutions right across Europe and attempted revolution in Britain led by the Chartists and a very botched uprising in Ireland. The result of that is a very classical, very nimble imagination using classical hexameters, addressing a moment of political popular uprising. There is a beautiful passage where he moves from imagery of the Atlantic Ocean to the then new expanding industrial city of Liverpool:

> *So in my soul of soul through its cells and secret recesses,*
> *Comes back, swelling and spreading, the old democratic fervour.*
> *But as the light of day enters some populous city.*
> *Shaming away, ere it come, by the chilly day-streak signal,*
> *High and low, the misusers of night, shaming out the gas lamps—*
> *All the great empty streets are flooded with broadening clearness,*
> *Which, withal, by inscrutable simultaneous access*
> *Permeates far and pierces to the very cellars lying in*
> *Narrow high back-lane, and court, and alley of alleys*

What he is writing about there is the idea of a democratic popular revolution and he harks back to what's known as the 'good old cause' to the English Revolution in the 1640s. What he is also trying to communicate, which is very very fascinating, is that when you have a revolution you have an expansion of consciousness. You feel everything can be re-written, everything can be re-read. There are new forms of consciousness, new ways of looking at reality. That reality itself is plastic and can be shaped, so he takes the idea of dawn in Liverpool and then he gives this wonderful line, 'all the great empty streets are flooded with broadening clearness'. Now that's not simply a literal description of sunlight coming through broad streets. It's an image of the enlightenment of revolution, of a whole new social order, because Clough is writing out of his committed sense, committed to the Chartist movement, that everybody has got to have the vote.

But they didn't even start to get the vote until a quarter of a century after the Chartists were defeated. What happened to English poetry in that period? Terry Eagleton:

By the mid-century, certainly by the time of, say, early Tennyson, politics is prosaic and boring and about social organisation and bureaucracy and poetry is delicate and intangible and ethereal and if the one touched the other, it simply did so to contaminate it. Our own present definition of poetry, what poetry means to the person in the street today, comes straight from that moment. The poetry is by definition, by the very texture of its langauge, by the very nature of its forms, nothing to do with, can't speak of, those wider political realities.

Perhaps the most striking example of the connection between poetry and those 'wider political realities' comes from the literature of 20th century Ireland. Marilyn Butler notes:

It's often very important that some of the best revolutionary poetry happens before revolutions. One of the great examples of this is the Irish nationalist literary revival. The literary revival in Ireland comes before the violence, although in a sense there has been violence in Ireland throughout, but the intense period of nationalist self consciousness that begins at the end of the 19th century and then builds up to what in effect is their war of independence, their achievement of independence at the end of First World War. All of that is partly re-created in literature, particularly by Yeats, the great figure of this movement. So that Yeats' early poetry, the Celtic revival poetry, creates a sort of mystical imagined Ireland first and then of course as the violence begins to build up with the great episode of the siege of the Post Office in Dublin, Yeats writes the most famous of his political poems, 'Easter 1916' in which he celebrates and laments what on the face of it was a defeat, the capture of the men and their execution, but he turns them into martyrs, into great heroes, through his eloquence:

> *Oh when may it suffice?*
> *That is Heaven's part, our part*
> *To murmur name upon name,*
> *As a mother names her child*
> *When sleep at last has come*
> *On limbs that had run wild.*
> *What is it but nightfall?*
> *No, no, not night but death;*
> *Was it needless death after all?*
> *For England may keep faith*
> *For all that is done and said.*
> *We know their dream, enough*
> *To know they dreamed on our dead;*
> *And what if excess of love*
> *Bewildered them until they died?*
> *I write it out in a verse—*
> *McDonna and McBride*
> *And Connolly and Pearse*

Now and in time to be,
Wherever green is worn,
Are changed, changed utterly:
A terrible beauty is born.

Tom Paulin adds:

Yeats actually kept very quiet about the poem because he was receiving
a civil list pension from the British government which he did not want
to lose. He also knew that the British government was spying on him
because they thought he was in contact with Germany during the First
World War. He held on to the poem and then he published it in the *New
Statesman* on the 23 October 1920. Why did he do that? Well actually
because what is known as the Anglo-Irish war, the war of independence
was going on at that time and there was a republican leader, Terrence
McSweeney, on hunger strike. It was a very, very long hunger strike, in
fact he died two days after Yeats' poem was published. Now what
Yeats was doing was aligning McSweeney and by extension the Irish
Republican Army, with the martyrs, as they are seen by republicans, of
the 1916 uprising.

**Marilyn Butler traces an intriguing development in Irish poetry for
the rest of this century:**

The strange thing about the Irish Catholic literary revival was that once
Ireland the republic had a revolution and it had succeeded and it had its
independence, from about 1922 the literary revival was more or less
over. The stimulus had gone. In modern 20th century Ireland it's the
tortuous past of the North and in the last two or three decades it's
clearly been Belfast and the North with Heaney and Muldoon and
Michael Longley that has given rise to a coherent movement. I mean
it's schismatic in a way. It is not the same people, they are not writing
in the same way, but as a group they reflect the schisms and the tensions in Northern Ireland. In the end that is what revolutionary poetry is
about. It isn't a poetry that is only backing one side. It can't be simple
nationalism, that would not be great poetry. Great poetry is made out of
is schisms, tensions and conflict.

**Michael Longley's poems are by no means obviously political. But
does he think there is a connection between what he writes and
what is going on in Northern Ireland?**

It seems to me that there is bound to have been some relationship between the recent poetic efflorescence in Ulster and the troubles. They

probably share the same roots in civil disturbances. At the level of ignorance and prejudice this disturbance expresses itself in street violence and murder and mayhem. At a higher level of information,
curiosity, imagination, perhaps it has resulted in the poetry you refer to.

**Do you think your poetry or your work does depend on politics in
some way or another?**

Well, there's a marvellous quotation from my dear friend Derek Mahon
who is one of the best Irish poets. He says something along the lines
that the act of writing is itself political but he goes on to suggest political in the fullest sense and then, and I'm quoting by heart a marvellous
prose statement he made about a good poem 'is a paradigm of good
politics, of people talking to each other with honest subtlety at a profound level'. At this moment in Ulster and Ireland it is revolutionary to
ask people to revise their sectarian beliefs and certainties. I would suggest that the revolutionary poem in Ulster now tends to be an elegy, it
resists any notions of selective mourning. Such a poem would still feed
off the fruitful paradox of Wilfred Owen's great and extraordinary line,
'I am the enemy you killed my friend'. That is from his poem 'The
Strange Meeting'. My poem 'Wounds' is trying to avoid taking sides
and I suppose the implication there is that it is not in this particular historical instance necessary to take sides:

> Here are two pictures from my father's head—
> I have kept them like secrets until now:
> First, the Ulster division at the Somme
> Going over the top with 'Fuck the Pope!'
> 'No Surrender!': a boy about to die,
> Screaming 'Give 'em one for the Shankhill!'
> 'Wilder than Gurkhas' were my father's words
> Of admiration and bewilderment.
> Next comes the London-Scottish padre
> Resettling kilts with his swagger-stick,
> With a stylish backhand and a prayer.
> Over landscape of dead buttocks
> My father followed him for fifty years.
> At last, a belated casualty,
> He said—lead traces flaring till they hurt—
> 'I am dying for King and Country, slowly.'
> I touched his hand, his thin head I touched.
>
> Now, with military honours of a kind,
> With his badges, his medals like rainbows,

His spinning compass, I bury beside him
Three teenage soldiers, bellies full of
Bullets and Irish beer, their flies undone.
A packet of Woodbines I throw in,
A lucifer, the Sacred Heart of Jesus
Paralysed as heavy guns put out
The night-light in a nursery for ever;
Also a bus conductor's uniform—
He collapsed beside his carpet-slippers
Without a murmur, shot through the head
By a shivering boy wandered in
Before they could turn the television down
Or tidy away the supper dishes.
To the children, to a bewildered wife,
I think 'Sorry Missus' was what he said.

'Wounds' by Michael Longley. So finally what should we make of the style of teaching and reading which separates poetry from its social and political background? Christopher Hill explains:

I think it deprives the poetry of a lot of its meaning and in particular of its contemporary relevance. This is a long story of course. Milton was deliberately sanitised in the early 18th century by Addison who wrote his famous essays on him which hushed up all this nasty side of Milton. This was kept up all through by the Victorians who made him the great Puritan poet, which he is in a sense but not in the sense that they meant Puritan. I mean he was a fighting Puritan. Of course the object of saying that this is not relevant to any political problems in the 17th century or anywhere else is that it is intended to de-gut and castrate the poetry and deprive it of the impact that it ought to have on readers who are faced with problems in their own day, not necessarily to be solved by revolution but to be resolved by political means which Milton thought of as an integral part of his poetry.

Tony Harrison adds:

It takes out all the vital organs of poetry. It creates a false spiritual nimbus around something which is earthed. The thing about poetry, especially poetry in the metre and rhyme is that it draws attention to its own physicality. It is air made physical. What happens in a great deal of teaching is to deny it even that kind of physicality and yearn for it to be pure air. Whereas its real energy comes from the way it is earthed, that is it's in the voice of the poet and the times of the poet.

Tony Harrison has a bust of Milton in his study, the real Milton, the fighting Milton. And in his poems today like 'Initial Illumination' Tony Harrison carries on that fighting, challenging Miltonic tradition.

Farne cormorants with catches in their beaks,
Showers fish scale confetti on the shining sea.
The first bright weather here for many weeks
for my Sunday G-day train bound for Dundee,
off to Saint Andrews to record a reading,
doubtful, in these dark days, what poems can do,
and watching the mists round Lindisfarne receding
my doubt extends to Dark Age Good Book too.
Eadfrith the Saxon scribe/illuminator
incorporated cormorants I'm seeing fly
round the same island thirteen centuries later
*into the **In principio's** initial I.*
Billfrith's begemmed and jewelled boards got looted
by raiders gung-ho for booty and berserk,
the sort of soldiery that's still recruited
to do toady's dictators' dirty work,
but the initials in St John and in St Mark
graced with local cormorants in ages,
we of a darker still keep calling Dark,
survive in those illuminated pages.
The word of God so beautifully scripted
by Eadfrith and Billfrith the anchorite
Pentagon conners have once again conscripted
to gloss the cross on the precision site.
Candlepower, steady hand, gold leaf, a brush
were all that Eadfrith had to beautify
the word of God much bandied by George Bush
whose word illuminated midnight sky
and confused the Baghdad cock who was betrayed
by bombs into believing day was dawning
and crowed his heart out at the deadly raid
and didn't live to greet the proper morning.
Now with noon day headlights in Kuwait
and the burial of the blackened in Baghdad
let them remember, all those who celebrate,
that their good news is someone else's bad
or the light will never dawn on poor Mankind.
Is it open-armed at all that victory V,
that insular initial intertwined

with slack-necked cormorants from black lacquered sea,
with trumpets bulled and bellicose and blowing
for what men claim as victories in their wars,
with the fire-hailing cock and all those crowing
who don't yet smell the dunghill at their claws?

Notes

'Poetry and Revolution' was originally broadcast on BBC Radio 3. *International Socialism* would like to thank the producer, Fiona McLean, and the contributors for the permission to print the transcript.

Rhetoric which cannot conceal a bankrupt theory: a reply to Ernest Mandel

ALEX CALLINICOS

Ernest Mandel took considerable space in the last issue of this journal to expose what he believes to be its theoretical and political errors. In part, the length of this article reflected the fact that Mandel chose to include among its targets not merely Chris Harman's piece responding to Mandel's earlier criticisms of the theory of state capitalism, but some other texts by members of the Socialist Workers Party, in particular an article by Derek Howl and my little book *Trotskyism*.[1] But the article's length was also a consequence of a method of argument long characteristic of Mandel's writing but taken to the point of caricature here, in which he attributes to others views which they do not hold and then proceeds exhaustively to attempt to refute these views. The result in this case is an elaborate rhetorical construction containing little of any substance. This reply will be briefer, but will, I hope, have rather more in the way of content.

Understanding modern capitalism

A good example of Mandel's method is provided by what he says about the central issue in the debate between the United Secretariat of the

Fourth International and the International Socialist Tendency, namely whether the orthodox Trotskyist degenerated workers' state theory or the theory of state capitalism provides the best interpretation of Stalinism. Mandel in his latest piece repeats his earlier claim that, in effect, acceptance of the theory of state capitalism leads us to conclude that 'general crises of overproduction do not exist in the imperialist countries.'[2] It is on this basis that he launches an assault on 'the Cliff-Harman-Callinicos school' for rejecting the general analysis of the laws of motion of the capitalist mode of production set out by Marx in *Capital*. We would have been proved right

> *if there had been no crises of overproduction for half a century; if there had been no serious unemployment in any imperialist country; nor any rising misery in Third World countries again for half a century or a century; nor any serious 'new poverty' in the West.*

The choice is clear enough, then: side either with 'Marx and his minor disciples like Mandel' in asserting that crises, unemployment, and poverty are endemic to capitalism, or with 'the Cliff-Harman-Callinicos school' in denying it. The only difficulty is that anyone familiar with, say, Chris Harman's book *Explaining the Crisis*, or indeed with *Socialist Worker*, the weekly paper which he edits, will find it hard to credit the idea that Harman doesn't regard crises of overproduction as an intrinsic feature of the capitalist mode of production. Yet Mandel imagines him telling the victims of the current recession in Britain that 'this is no "real" economic crisis of overproduction, but only "stagnation".' Let's turn to the offending text on which Mandel bases this interpretation of Harman's views. What do we find? First, the assertion that 'in looking at capitalism during the long boom of the 1940s, 1950s and 1960s it had not been good enough *simply* to talk in terms of "a crisis of overproduction" (as Mandel does). This was not the characteristic form of economic crisis in the West'. It is in this context, against the background of a discussion of the post-war *boom*, that Harman analyses the problems of stagnation and excess demand which afflicted Western capitalism in these years. But he, secondly, goes on to point how, as a result of the decline of the permanent arms economy and the internationalisation of capital, 'the state began to lose its ability to suppress symptoms of crisis, to stop overaccumulation of capital (the "crisis of underproduction") giving rise to a crisis of overproduction. Hence the generalised recessions of the mid-1970s and early 1980s'— to which we may now add that of the early 1990s.[3]

Harman, in other words, said the opposite of what he is alleged to have said. It was silly of Mandel to have attempted a distortion so easily exposed. It was doubly silly since the volume of his own writings is so great that it's quite easy to check up on Mandel's own views. In the early 1960s, at the height of the boom, he acknowledged that post-war capitalism 'has had no grave crisis and certainly nothing of the dimensions of 1929 or of 1938.' This 'reduction in cyclical fluctuations' reflected trends like the growth of monopoly capital and the development of state intervention. As a result, *'the whole system evolves not so much towards uninterrupted growth as towards long-term stagnation.'*[4] Mandel repeatedly taxes our tendency with being 'unable to foresee the recurrent crises of overproduction which have occurred since the early 1970s, while we were able to predict them'. Well, in 1961, at much the same time that Mandel was anticipating not a return of classical capitalist crises but *'long term stagnation'*, Mike Kidron wrote in this journal: 'Whatever the future holds, it is one of irreparable instability, of crises whose violence is such as to question the continued existence of capitalism as a world system at best, or at worst of civilisation itself.'[5] Hardly convincing evidence of our alleged tendency 'to *underestimate* the possibilities of capitalist crisis'.

The above should have established beyond dispute that Mandel is a dishonest debater. But it is important to understand the effect of this way of proceeding. It allows him to denounce at length his opponents for views which they don't hold: this acts as a kind of smokescreen through which it is hard to see the real issues. Thus, what's primarily at stake in this debate isn't whether or not Marx's general analysis of capitalist laws of motion is correct, but rather whether this analysis needs to be developed, and in certain respects modified, in order to take into account the evolution of 20th century capitalism.

This raises a question of method in a somewhat different sense from the way I have used it up to now. What method of scientific inquiry is to be used in developing a full understanding of capitalism? Marx advocates what he calls 'the method of rising from the abstract to the concrete'. In other words, he starts from the most general features of the capitalist mode of production—the nature of the commodity, and underlying this the dual nature of labour under capitalism as abstract social labour and concrete useful labour, the transformation of labour-power into a commodity, the extraction of surplus-value, the self-expansion and accumulation of capital—which allows him to establish the essential structure of capitalism. On this basis Marx then proceeds to develop, as he puts it, 'through a number of intermediary stages', a more concrete analysis of the actual dynamics of the capitalist system. The result is an understanding of capitalism that is not 'a chaotic conception of the whole' but 'a rich totality of many determinations and relations'.[6]

We can see this method at work in the three volumes of *Capital* where Marx moves from the highly abstract and formal analysis of the

commodity and money in the first part of Volume I to, at the climax of
Volume III, an explanation of capitalist crises which fully integrates the
concrete features deriving mainly from the division of the exploiting
class into competing 'many capitals'. But this movement 'rising from
the abstract to the concrete' does not halt with *Capital* itself. The decisive development of Marxist economic theory at the beginning of the
20th century, by Lenin, Luxemburg, Hilferding, Bukharin and others,
had as its objective the elaboration of Marx's analysis to take into account the effects of one of the main tendencies he explores, the concentration and centralisation of capital—the growing size of capitals, the
tendency for the fusion of banking and industrial capital, the integration
of private capital and the state. Whatever the undoubted flaws of this
body of work, it had the fundamental merit of identifying imperialism
as (in Lenin's words) a distinctive stage of capitalist development,
analysing some of whose features required a modification of Marx's
own concepts (see, for example, Hilferding's discussion of monopoly
profits in *Finance Capital*). It was in this context that Bukharin, during
the First World War, identified state capitalism and the associated tendency for military rivalry to supplant market competition as two of the
chief characteristics of imperialism.

Now Mandel seems—surprisingly for a writer so prone to parade his
Marxist 'orthodoxy'—simply to dismiss this entire tradition of analysis, even though it is, to my mind, one of the triumphs of classical
Marxism. This dismissal is implicit not only in Mandel's consistently
disparaging references to Hilferding and Bukharin, but also in his insistence that for an economy to be counted as capitalist it must directly
correspond in all its details to the model developed by Marx in *Capital*.
This insistence is typical of Mandel's formalistic approach: an economy is capitalist if it conforms to the checklist laid out in the approved
definition of capitalism. But it is also disabling, since it denies any possibility of understanding one of the main phases of modern capitalist
development.

Consider thus Mandel's lengthy discussion of the pathologies of the
Stalinist bureaucratic command economy—chronic shortages of consumer goods, large scale waste of productive resources, etc. 'All this',
he explains, 'is the result of *arbitrary* allocation of resources by the
nomenklatura' (emphasis added). These priorities are not, as Cliff and
Harman argue, those of capital accumulation dictated by the process of
military competition with Western capitalism. Rather, 'the privileges of
the bureaucracy in the field of consumer goods…motivate the bureaucracy's economic behaviour'. Although Mandel insists that the *nomenklatura* is not a ruling class, his argument suggests that the Stalinist
economy functioned in a manner analogous to pre-capitalist societies,
where the goal of production was ultimately the consumption of the ex-

ploiting class. The analogy has indeed been developed by Bob Brenner, a supporter of the Shachtmanite analysis of Stalinist societies as a form of 'bureaucratic collectivism', neither capitalist nor socialist.[7] But the USSR experienced, not the relatively slow growth of technique and output characteristic of pre-capitalist societies, but, as Mandel insists to the point of exaggeration, the massive development of the productive forces over 35 years. To explain this as a consequence of the 'arbitrary' priorities of a *nomenklatura* motivated chiefly by greed is pretty close to giving no explanation at all.

There is a far more illuminating analogy. All the features of the Stalinist economy on which Mandel dwells, involving excess demand and underproduction, are characteristic of the war economies constructed by the imperialist powers during the two world wars. These economies functioned on the basis of what Mandel calls '*a priori* allocation of resources' that is investment and consumer goods were to a large degree distributed on the basis of decisions by the state bureaucracy. The forms of behaviour he alleges to be peculiar to Stalinism— hoarding, deception of the central planners, for example, along with others which he doesn't mention such as the illegal circulation of scarce goods through the black market, reflected the concentration of productive resources on those industries directly required for the waging of war. This allocation was not, of course, 'arbitrarily' chosen; rather, it reflected the struggle for survival between the imperialist powers. Precisely the same could be said of the priorities of the Stalinist economy from its formation during the first Five Year Plan to its collapse at the end of the 1980s.[8]

Now what in any case would Mandel say about the imperialist war economies. Would he say that the prevalence of *a priori* allocation of resources implied a 'different socio-economic framework' from that prevailing under capitalism? Would he insist that the fact that the imperialist powers competed with each other militarily on the field of battle rather than economically through the exchange of commodities on the world market meant that 'the law of value...does not rule' in time of inter-imperialist war? Such a stance—the logical consequence of the reasons Mandel gives for denying that the USSR was state capitalist— would involve a peculiar kind of historical materialism, which (rather like Kautsky's version of internationalism) applied only in time of peace. Of course, he believes no such thing, and indeed has devoted a book to the Marxist interpretation of the Second World War (though one which, interestingly, has remarkably little to say about the nature and organisation of the war economies).[9] Mandel must thus confront the following dilemma: either the peculiar features of 20th century imperialist war economies must be seen as consequences of the extreme concentration and centralisation of capital within a national framework, in which case there is no reason to deny that the USSR was state capitalist, or a large sweep of modern history is unamenable to Marxist explanation and neo-Weberian sociologists like Tony Giddens and Michael Mann who see military competition as autonomous of capital accumulation are right.

This dilemma indicates that a lot more is at stake in this debate than the relative political virtues of the USFI and the IS Tendency. The first half of the 20th century was characterised by a pronounced and generalised tendency for state organisation of the economy, primarily for military purposes, to invade, and indeed to annex the domain of private capital. Thus the inauguration of the Four Year Plan in 1936-7 involved the Nazi regime, particularly in the person of Goering and his entourage, seeking to statise a large segment of productive capital. By the outbreak of war Goering's *Reichswerke* was the largest corporation in Europe; it continued to amass productive assets in conquered areas such as Alsace-Lorraine and Silesia, frequently in competition with German private capital.[10] It is simply implausible to treat the Nazi regime as a mere 'tool' of private capital. Bourgeois scholars conclude that the case of Nazi Germany demonstrates the 'primacy of politics' and the bankruptcy of Marxism. But the theory of state capitalism allows us to understand the statisation of productive capital that was a general feature of the bourgeois world in the 1930s and 1940s as the high-point of a longer term process central to which was the emergence of militarised state capitalisms. This process did not, as Bukharin, its main theorist, claimed, produce so high a level of 'organisation' as to overcome capitalism's tendency towards economic crises—the Great Depression of the 1930s was a consequence of a high organic composition of capital and low rate of profit.[11] But the depression precipitated a disintegration of the world market, thereby intensifying the tendency towards state capitalism whose extreme case was the construction of the Stalinist system during the first two Five Year Plans (1928-37).[12]

Mandel at one point is prepared to 'grant (tongue in cheek)' that Bukharin's analysis does accurately depict a 'given stage' of capitalist development, 'roughly 1890-1940'. 'The main new feature of "late capitalism"', however—that is, of the period since 1945—'is the growing internationalisation of the productive forces and, in function of that, the growing internationalisation of capital itself.' It is a bit rich for Mandel to announce this as if it were a piece of news—and indeed uncomfortable news—for the theorists of state capitalism. After all, central to Harman's interpretation of the fall of Stalinism in his seminal article 'The Storm Breaks', (*International Socialism* 46), is what he calls 'the shift from national capitalism to multinational capitalism'.[13] The Stalinist economies represented, as I have already said, the most extreme case of the national organisation of capitalism. This form of capitalism, what Cliff called bureaucratic state capitalism, was imposed by the acute pressures of mobilising resources for national accumulation in relatively backward societies. It involved the perpetuation for over half a century of features only fully realised in the West during time of war. By the 1980s this form of capitalism had been rendered obsolete by the growing internationalisation of capital. The political upheavals of 1989 and 1991 represented the point at which this fact was finally registered, with consequences we are still feeling. The theory of state capitalism is thus indispensable to understanding both the rise and the fall of Stalinism; it is also required for an understanding of 20th century capitalism.

An aside on permanent revolution

The linked questions of the nature of Stalinism and of modern capitalism provide the most important illustration of Mandel's peculiar way of conducting arguments. His article provides plenty of other examples. Rather than, however, trying readers' patience to breaking point by discussing these case by case, I shall concentrate on one other issue. This shouldn't be taken to imply that I accept those of Mandel's arguments which I do not discuss: on the contrary, most of what he says is either wrong or irrelevant. Those, for example, interested in the question of the law of value in the USSR should consult Derek Howl's excellent article, whose arguments Mandel, true to form, ignores or distorts.

The case I want to discuss is that of the post-war revolutions in the backward countries—Yugoslavia, China, Vietnam, Cuba, Nicaragua. Mandel takes me to task for defending Cliff's analysis of these upheavals as a particular kind of bourgeois revolution, in which imperialism was defeated typically by peasant movements led by urban intellectuals installing state capitalist regimes in power.[14] Mandel's line of attack involves an accusation and a dilemma. The accusation is that this position places me, and, I suppose, Cliff, who came up with the idea in the first place, alongside 'all those—Mensheviks and Stalinists —opponents of theory (better: the strategy) of permanent revolutions, all those advocates of a revolution by stages, who argue that it is possible to realise the central tasks of the national-democratic revolution (national independence and land reform) without destroying the class rule of the bourgeoisie-cum-landlords-cum-foreign capital, and without destroying the bourgeois state.'

I'll come to this accusation in a minute. Let's first consider the dilemma Mandel poses: surely by denying any 'qualitative difference' between the revolutionary nationalist regimes and those they replaced, I am adopting an abstentionist position whose logic is that 'revolutionists' should, for example, 'have been neutral in the civil war between Mihailovitch and the Ustashi on the one hand and Tito on the other hand'. The only alternative to this 'openly counter-revolutionary position' is to acknowledge, along with Mandel and his co-thinkers, that genuine 'social revolutions' took place in Yugoslavia and the other countries under discussion. This dilemma is entirely false. For it is a central theme of the classical Marxist tradition that revolutionary socialists should defend revolutionary nationalist movements which challenge imperialism despite these movements' bourgeois character. The famous passage cited by Mandel in which Lenin denounces 'Left Bolsheviks' for refusing to support the 1916 Easter Rising is part of an argument for this position, not an attempt to present the rising as anything but a bourgeois-revolutionary movement. It is on this basis that our comrades in the International Socialists of South Africa side with the African National Congress against the de Klerk regime while firmly criticising the ANC's strategy of negotiations with the same regime. On exactly the same basis we supported the Vietnamese and Nicaraguan regimes against US imperialism. Refusing to give what Lenin called 'communist coloration' to bourgeois-nationalist movements does not involve the slightest temptation to abstain when they fight imperialism.

As usual, Mandel's rhetoric serves to conceal the real issue which is whether or not these Third World revolutions amounted to social*ist* revolutions (he tries to befog matters further by using the more imprecise formulation of 'social revolutions') in which the working class broke the power of capital and conquered political domination for themselves. The accusation I cited above illustrates Mandel's peculiar method of resolving such issues. *If*, for example, the Chinese Revolution of 1949 wasn't a socialist revolution, then Trotsky's 'strategy' of permanent revolution has been invalidated. Since, however, it is inconceivable that Trotsky could have been wrong, the Chinese Revolution must have been socialist. There couldn't be a better example of Mandel's defence of orthodox Trotskyism at the price of ignoring or distorting facts. He takes great offence at my discussion of this in *Trotskyism*, invoking against me Goethe: 'Eternally green is life's golden tree'.[15] But it is precisely 'life'—to put it in more mundane terms, hard empirical evidence—which Mandel ignores here.

For surely the nature of the Third World revolutions should depend on the actual social processes at work in them rather than on the kind of scholastic logic used by Mandel. If these revolutions were socialist, then one would expect to see the working class playing the leading role, not in name, but in the shape of democratically structured organs of dual power—workers' councils, factory committees, popular militias. Is there a scrap of evidence that this occurred in any of the revolutions in question? None whatsoever. In the absence of this evidence, Mandel is forced to appeal to 'the key role of the subjective factor, and the undeniable merits of initiative and orientation' of the Stalinist parties in Yugoslavia, China, and Vietnam, and the revolutionary nationists in Cuba and Nicaragua. One is forced almost to admire his cheek in, only a few paragraphs earlier, attributing to me 'the preposterous sectarian conclusion that no "genuine" social revolution is possible without a conscious Marxist leadership'. On Mandel's, remarkably broadminded version of Marxism, you don't need the working class to overthrow capital, just a 'conscious' Stalinist leadership.

Recognising that the post-war colonial revolutions did not represent the conquest of power by the working class doesn't mean abandoning the theory of permanent revolution. It means, rather, recognising that Trotsky did not adequately consider the implications of a failure by the working class to assume the leadership of anti-imperialist struggles. This failure (to understand which we do need to consider the 'subjective factor': one of the chief lessons of the October Revolution is that, while workers certainly don't need a Marxist party to start a revolution, without one they cannot carry it through to a successful conclusion) does not mean anti-imperialist struggles cease to occur, but they take place under the leadership of social forces (usually a section of the intelligentsia) which, in Cliff's formulation, deflects these struggles in a particular direction, leading not to socialist revolution but to the triumph of a national capitalism untrammelled by outside control. To reject this analysis in the name of the letter of Trotsky's writing, as Mandel does, is not only to close off yet another portion of world history to Marxist theory, but is to transform socialist revolution from the self emancipation of the working class into a change of regime capable of being achieved by a variety of social forces.

The politics of shamefaced orthodoxy

Let us finally consider whether these disagreements, above all that concerning the nature of Stalinism, matter. Mandel has two views on this. His official position is that they don't, or at least not sufficiently to justify the existence of separate international tendencies based on the rival interpretations of Stalinism. The fact that the SWP and its sister groups in the IS Tendency insist on making the question of state capitalism a point of organisational differentiation is therefore a sign of the sterile sectarianism permeating our politics. Mandel appeals to us to see the light and adhere to the USFI. There's no doubt that this position corresponds to the official view of the USFI, several of whose leading mem-

bers have told me that differences over the assessment of Stalinism
belong to the past and should no longer divide revolutionaries.

It is hard to accept that Mandel really believes this. For one thing, if
the differences don't matter, why go to such inordinate length smiting
the theory of state capitalism hip and thigh? For another, the political
significance of the differences does surface several times in the text,
suggesting that Mandel's real view can't be equated with the official
line he loyally but half-heartedly defends. I'll give two examples.

Mandel argues that 'socialists in the USSR and Eastern Europe have
to fight on two fronts: against privatisation and for democratic rights'.
The latter struggle is directed against the old *nomenklatura*, the former
against what Mandel calls 'capitalist restoration'. He describes privatisation as 'a central issue of social and political struggles in the USSR
and in several East European countries', and denounces us for not
recognising this, and for being indifferent to the immense attacks on
jobs, living standards and services which have been launched as part of
the process of restructuring the Stalinist economies and integrating
them into the world market. Now of course we're not in fact in the
slightest bit indifferent to these attacks. But what we say is that, in resisting them, the key issue isn't preserving the legal property form of
state ownership, but the development by workers of organisations capable of defending jobs, wages, conditions, and services. In taking this
position we draw on the considerable experience of British workers'
struggles in state owned, or formerly state owned, firms such as British
Coal and British Steel. But for Mandel the defence of the property form
itself is the key issue. Thus he insists on the benefits Soviet workers derived from 'nationalised property' and declares: 'we are uncondition-
ally on the side of those workers who oppose privatisation, regardless
with what ideology and regardless of whether a section of the bureaucracy also supports them.'

For Mandel, then, defending workers' interests in the ex-USSR of
necessity takes the form of defending the old Stalinist command economy which, it is clear, despite all his equivocations, he regards as qualitatively superior to market capitalism. The practical implications of this
position are potentially disastrous. For the Thatcherite 'reforms' introduced by the Yeltsin-Gaidar government since the end of 1991 have
been opposed chiefly by what is known as the 'red-brown' coalition of
nostaglic Stalinists and open fascists, chiefly organised within the
framework of 'Labouring Russia' (*Trudorossia*). These forces are characterised precisely by the way in which they link virulent Russian nationalism with a pseudo-socialist defence of the old command
economy. Now, Mandel of course rejects the politics of the red-brown
alliance. Nevertheless, by making the key issue resisting 'capitalist
restoration', thereby conceding the superiority of the old regime, he de-

prives himself of any firm basis on which to oppose this politics. Indeed, he makes dangerous concessions to the idea, common in these circles, that the Yelstin-Gaidar programme amounts to the Western 'colonisation' of Russia, asserting: 'The decisive test of the restoration of capitalism today would be precisely such a restoration of the rule of the law of value through the world market, ie: large scale reversal of these countries to a semi-colonial pattern of output'. It is precisely this kind of perspective, emphasising, not the conflicts within Russian society between the working masses and the ruling class as a whole, but those between Russia and the West, which has led Boris Kagarlitsky and one wing of the old Socialist Party of the USSR effectively to tail the Stalinist-fascist coalition, even comparing the Trans-Dnester 're-public' in Moldova, one of the key instruments for the reassertion of Russian imperial power in the republics, to the Paris Commune.[16]

On a more mundane level Mandel drops a couple of interesting hints about the British Labour Party. He criticises the Militant Tendency for adopting tactics which 'brought [them]...into head on collision with parts of the working class and their own organisation's workers' basis'. The only illustration he gives is Militant's part in standing a left wing candidate against Labour in the 1991 Liverpool Walton by-election. He doesn't explain how this involved 'colliding' with organised workers, on the face of it a puzzling claim, since the by-election campaign conducted by Militant and other socialists in the Labour Party was conducted at the same time as, and in solidarity with, a bitter municipal workers' strike against the right wing Labour council. The nature of Militant's offence becomes clear when Mandel takes the SWP to task because 'it systematically counterposes itself to the Labour Party, in spite of the fact that that organisation still enjoys the loyalty of the overwhelming majority of the organised British working class.' This reproach is embellished by a tall story—'the SWP...make[s] recruit-ment to its organisation the main objective of its intervention in mass struggles like the anti poll tax movement', a slur which I'm sure will interest the thousands of activists who have worked with SWP mem-bers in anti poll tax groups, not to speak of those of our comrades im-prisoned for refusing to pay the tax.

The real issue, however, is that Mandel believes it to be a mistake for revolutionaries to organise independently of the Labour Party. And indeed the USFI's British section—aside from what appears in retro-spect as the interlude of the International Marxist Group between the late 1960s and the late 1970s—has consistently worked inside the Labour Party. The idea that to organise outside Labour is to cut oneself off from 'the overwhelming majority of the organised British working class' has lost whatever credibility it ever had with the enormous haem-orrhage of members—particularly those of a working class background—from Labour. The decision, by a majority of a group as dogmatically wedded to the idea of winning the Labour Party as a whole to revolutionary politics as Militant, to work independently is an indication this is now the only way in which socialists can effectively operate. The insistence to the contrary by Mandel and his small band of British co-thinkers is not merely a sign of their distance from reality. It is explicable only against the background of a worldview in which a self conscious working class is not a necessary condition of socialist revolution and therefore non-proletarian forces— Stalinists and nationalists in the Third World, reformist organisations in the advanced countries—can overthrow capital.

The differences between our two tendencies matter. They have direct implications for political practice. The official position of the USFI, which denies this, involves a devaluation of the role of Marxist theory as (in Engels's famous formulation) 'a guide to action'. Revolutionary leadership consequently becomes, not above all the clarification of ideas in order to identify the main tasks of the day, but a matter of pragmatic manipulation, with a few abstract theoretical formulas serving to conceal a multitude of concrete differences. Mandel's instincts are better than this, as is indicated by the vehemence with which he pursues his disagreements with us. The tragedy is that all this rhetorical skill and empirical knowledge are deployed in defence of an apologetic caricature of Marxism.

For our part, we continue to insist on the importance of the differences. This is not because we regard the theory of state capitalism as a fetish of political correctness. Rather it is because the theory is a condition of operating effectively as a revolutionary socialist today. Without a convincing, scientifically based explanation of the rise and fall of Stalinism, Marxism is a dead duck. Mandel's degenerated workers' state theory is incapable of playing this role, since it cannot explain how societies supposedly qualitatively superior to capitalism failed miserably to develop the productive forces on a scale comparable to the achievements of their Western rivals and were decisively rejected by the working classes in whose interest these societies were supposed (in however distorted a way) to be organised. The theory of state capitalism can, for reasons sketched out above and developed at much greater length by Chris Harman in earlier issues of this journal.

We consequently have a radically different assessment of the prospects for the revolutionary left. The outlook, according to Mandel, is grim. He has recently talked of a 'a deterioration of the balance of forces on a worldwide scale', in which 'the political initiative is in the hands of imperialism, the bourgeoisie and its agents.'[17] Although he dates this shift from the mid-1970s, it is clear that the 'restoration of capitalism' underway in the ex-USSR and in eastern Europe looms large in this diagnosis. This assessment follows logically enough from Mandel's overall analysis, since the collapse of Stalinism represents for him the elimination of societies transitional to socialism. For us, by contrast, the changes in the East represent (in Harman's formula) a 'move sideways', from state capitalism to market capitalism, and moreover a process involving the economic and political destabilisation, not merely of the ex-Stalinist states, but of West European capitalism, beginning at its very centre, Germany, but now, through the intermediary of financial disorder, spreading across to the European Community. These disruptions, closely linked to the war in the Balkans, and taking place against the background of a world recession suggest that this is hardly the moment either to bewail or to celebrate the triumph of Western imperialism.

We shall, on the basis of this perspective, continue to seek to build the forces of revolutionary socialism. We shall do so as part of an international tendency, and not, as Mandel alleges, as 'national communism'. When he first dredged up that slur in the 1970s, it did at least correspond to the SWP's relative international isolation. But this is no longer the case: we are certainly still the leading organisation in the IS Tendency, but nevertheless are part of a current whose supporters are beginning to implant themselves in many different parts of the world. It is probably kindest to put down Mandel's attempt to dismiss the IS organisations outside Britain as SWP 'clones' to his ignorance of, for example, the process through which our comrades in the Socialist Revolution Organisation (OSE) have come to have an increasing impact on the left of the Greek workers' movement. We refuse to proclaim the IS Tendency a new 'International' or to adhere to the USFI not out of parochialism, but from the understanding—confirmed above all by the sorry history of the various Fourth Internationals—that a real revolutionary International will emerge from mass workers' struggles, not from the resolutions of a few thousand revolutionaries. What we do now can, however, help lay the basis of such an International. The future will settle whether it is the politics of the IS Tendency or that of the USFI which can best promote genuine revolutionary internationalism. I have no doubt of the outcome.

Notes

1   E Mandel, 'The Impasse of Schematic Dogmatism', *International Socialism* 56 (1992). See also C Harman, 'From Trotsky to State Capitalism', *International Socialism* 49 (1990), E Mandel, 'A Theory Which Has Not Stood the Test of

Facts', C Harman, 'Criticism Which Does Not Withstand the Test of Logic', and D Howl, 'The Law of Value and the USSR', all in ibid.

2   E Mandel, ibid, p43

3   C Harman, 'Criticism...', pp77-78. See also ibid, p69-70.

4   E Mandel, *Marxist Economic Theory* (London, 1968), pp529, 531.

5   M Kidron, 'Rejoinder to Left Reformism, II', *International Socialism*, old series, 7 (1961), p20. See also, for example, *Western Capitalism Since the War* (Harmondsworth, 1970) p62, where, in a passage first published in 1968, Kidron discusses 'the freer play for recessionary tendencies' created by the decline in arms spending.

6   K Marx, *Grundrisse* (Harmondsworth, 1973), p100. See also K Marx, *Theories of Surplus Value* II (Moscow, 1963-72), p174. For (I hope) a relatively accessible discussion of Marx's method see A Callinicos, *The Revolutionary Ideas of Karl Marx* (London, 1983), chpts 4 and 6.

7   R Brenner, 'The Soviet Union and Eastern Europe', *Against the Current*, 30 and 31 (1991).

8   On the war economies see C Harman, *Explaining the Crisis* (London, 1984) pp70-74.

9   E Mandel, *The Meaning of the Second World War* (London, 1986).

10   See R J Overy, *Goering* (London, 1984) chpts 3 and 5.

11   A Callinicos, 'Imperialism, Capitalism and the State Today', *International Socialism* 35 (1987) pp84-88.

12   See C Harman, ibid, ch 2.

13   C Harman, 'The Storm Breaks', *International Socialism* 46 (1990) p45.

14   T Cliff, *Deflected Permanent Revolution* (London, 1983).

15   A Callinicos, *Trotskyism* (Milton Keynes, 1990), ch 3.

16   See L Sustar, 'After the USSR', *Socialist Worker* (Chicago) August 1992.

17   E Mandel, 'Socialism and the Future', *International Viewpoint* 234, 14 September 1992, p23.

Capitalism, cruelty and conquest

A review of Thomas Pakenham, **The Scramble for Africa** *(Weidenfeld and Nicholson, 1991) £22*

CHARLIE KIMBER

In 1880 most of the African continent was ruled by Africans. The European presence was restricted to a fringe of minute forts and trading posts around the coast except for the French conquest of Algeria and the Dutch-British presence at the Cape. Yet within 20 years five European powers had divided almost all of Africa between themselves. They created 30 new colonies and protectorates spanning 10 million square miles. They also became rulers over 110 million people.

The process of African conquest by Britain, Germany, France, Portugal and Italy, the 'scramble', was associated with fierce cruelty and blatant trickery. Africans were killed in their hundreds of thousands by foreign powers who treated them as mere impediments to their rule. Sometimes it was set piece military slaughter. At the Battle of Omdurman in 1898 the British commanders counted 10,000 Sudanese dead. They ignored the cries of 15,000 wounded who lay groaning in the desert. Often it was the casual butchery of treating black people as unimportant. The railway line from the Atlantic to Brazzaville cost the lives of 17,000 forced labourers. Sometimes butchery was designed to instil terror in those who resisted. When the Herero people revolted against German imperialism in south west Africa in 1904 General Lothar von Trotha issued an extermination order against them. The whole population were driven away from the wells to thirst in the Omaheke desert. About 20,000 people died.

The supposed slogan of African colonialism was Livingstone's motto of 'Commerce, Christianity and Civilisation'. In reality it was capitalism, cruelty and conquest. Where Africans were not bullied or murdered they were cheated. For example, Lobengula, king of the Ndebele, signed away the complete mineral rights in his Mashonaland territory (which became part of Rhodesia) on the understanding that not more than ten white men would come into the country and there would be no digging near towns. But the conditions were not included in the written agreement and were utterly ignored as mines sprouted everywhere. Within a few months his territory had been seized.

Thomas Pakenham's book sets out to understand the process of colonisation. He is very good at recording the characters who administered imperialism and pressed the scramble forward. In the process he demolishes some of the myths about the benevolence of European exploration. Stanley, the 'rescuer of Livingstone', is revealed as a cruel oppressor. Far from bartering gently with the local population on his travels, his expeditions sailed on a current of blood:

> To buy food of any kind was usually impossible. They had no cloth to spare for barter, and in any case the natives assumed the worst of them. Stanley's men had to fight them for food, raiding and burning villages along the way, and shooting the natives who tried to resist, as though they themselves were a gang of marauding slave traders. Indeed it was the Arab [slave] raiders they met who identified, as a matter of course, with Stanley's expedition, giving them food and looking after the sick.[1]

Carl Peters, a prominent German imperialist, openly confessed to the 'intoxication' of killing Africans:

> On 6 October 1889 he burst without warning into the kraal of some Galla tribesmen with whom he had previously signed a solemn treaty of peace and friendship. In the melee he killed a sultan and six of his leading men.[2]

A few months later Peters was in Kikuyu country. When 15 tribesman hired as carriers tried to run off with their advance payments Peters ordered them to be shot as a warning to others. As for the Masai he declared that 'the only thing that would make an impression on these wild sons of the steppe was a bullet from a repeater.'[3] The book also brings out the arbitrariness of the states into which Africans were forced by European conquest. Previously settled communities were either divided or (more usually) merged into units about which they knew nothing. 'Tribal loyalties' which had never existed were created or encouraged by powers anxious to provide new ways of dividing and ruling. Pakenham quotes from the novel by Harry Johnston, the vice-consul in the Niger delta, who was summonsed to the country house of British Foreign Secretary Lord Salisbury:

> *And now...that I am tolerably out of the hearing of my excellent tenantry...now let us settle the fate of the Niger. It is, I may observe, a curious anomaly that the future weal or woe of millions of black and brown people...is being determined in a Hertfordshire beech avenue in latitude 51 degrees something North.*[4]

In 1890 the Franco-British 'understanding' about future colonies gave almost a quarter of the continent to France without the slightest regard to the wishes of the local population.

Collecting together this material is useful and Pakenham has also done original research on episodes (such as the French seizure of Tunis in 1881) which are ignored in most histories. But Pakenham wants to do more than debunk a few heroes, defend others and fill a few gaps in our knowledge. He says that despite several attempts to understand the scramble there is 'no general explanation acceptable to historians—nor even agreement whether they should be expected to find one. And strange to say no one since Scott Keltie has attempted to write a one-volume narrative of the Scramble. In this book I have tried to fill the gap.'[5]

Pakenham is right to make the attempt—but he fails utterly, even in his own terms. In all the 738 large pages he makes almost no effort to analyse the motives for the colourful statesmen and traders who adorn his pages and whose deeds are catalogued. For example his 'explanation' of French imperialism is extremely superficial. 'Two opposing forces can be identified. One was hatred of Germany, dating from 1870-71; the other was envy and suspicion of Britain, dating from the Napoleonic wars and largely confined to members of the French navy.'[6]

This means the book is at best a vivid illustration of what happened without any general overview. At worse it is rather like those school history lessons which treat great men as the motor of history and divorce the battles of conquest from any wider economic and political context. Pakenham gives some of the material which is necessary to develop a real understanding of the scramble. He hints at an understanding based on changes in economic relations and, happily, uses the word imperialism. But he dismisses the work of Marxists like Lenin as 'Eurocentric'. Yet it is only by understanding what imperialism is and how it operates that we will really grasp the nature of the scramble.

Lenin and Bukharin's theory of imperialism held that at a certain point in the development of capitalism giant firms gobbled up all or most of the competitors inside their own nation states. They emerged as huge monopolies able to dominate their internal markets. Industrial capital also tended to merge with finance capital. The factory owners combined with the bankers to generate ever larger and more powerful trusts. Finally, the firms grew so large that the nation state itself became involved in protecting their interests.

Bolstering this tendency was the movement towards an internationalisation of productive forces. To continue expansion the giant firms required to go beyond simply economic competition and back it up with guns, ships and bayonets. So there was an integration between the big firms and the state. War and rivalry for territories were not an unfortunate aberration but a necessary consequence of a world divided between competing state-capital combinations.

Furthermore the division would never be frozen. Changes in economic and military might would tempt efforts to alter the division of the globe. The old parcelling up would be confronted and if new territories were available then they would be fought over. There would be wars between the imperialist states and further wars between those states and the weaker nations which they sought to exploit.

The scramble for Africa was one symptom that new state capitals had emerged to challenge British domination of the world both economically and militarily. Africa was the battleground of these new antagonisms, sometimes for immediate economic gain, sometimes for the hope of gain.

It is worth looking closely at the association between territorial seizure in Africa and developments in trade. Traffic between Europe and Africa existed long before the 1880s. Its major component was slaves. The Portuguese, who established trading stations in west and east Africa in the 16th century, were the first beneficiaries of the demand for slaves from the plantations of the New World. The slave trade, a trickle in the 16th century, reached flood tide in the 18th and deported tens of thousands of Africans every year. Around 12 million Africans were transported across the Atlantic.

In the front rank were British merchants who displaced the Portuguese. Behind them were the French and Dutch. In Africa coastal societies came to depend largely on the export of slaves and providing services for the traders. Local African states such as those of the Ibibio and the Ijo east of the Niger had completely changed their social and political systems to fit in with slave export. In areas such as the Sengambia, Gold Coast and Angola, where local Europeans were firmly established in towns or forts, the lives of neighbouring African people were dominated by slavery.

The end of slavery therefore required a profound change in the exploitation of Africa. In 1775 a British minister rejected pleas for banning the Atlantic slave trade on the grounds, he told the House of Commons, that no responsible British government could allow any check or discouragement to 'a trade so beneficial to the nation'.[7] Yet in 1807 the slave trade was declared illegal in British vessels and in 1834 the British parliament decreed an end to slavery throughout the empire. The reason for the change in policy was certainly not the humanitarian instincts of the British parliament. It was certainly not, as Pakenham suggests, that 'Europe became conscience-stricken'.[8]

Some Marxists have argued that slavery was rendered redundant by the rise of wage labour in the imperialist countries and the recognition that 'free' workers could produce bigger profits even in the colonies. Others, like Robin Blackburn, have put the emphasis on political factors. It was the great slave revolts in St Domingue which freed slaves from the French. Britain finally released its slaves after the great Jamaican rising of Christmas 1831 and the mass movement which forced the ruling class to concede parliamentary reform at home in 1832.

In any case the end of slavery forced a total reconstitution of African trade. Extracting wealth now depended on a diversification into exporting raw materials from Africa and selling back finished goods from the west. Some non-slave products were quickly established. Palm oil exports to Britain for example, used for soap and margarine, already ran at 10,000 tons a year by 1830. They grew to 40,000 tons by 1855 and rose fairly steadily throughout the century. But other products took longer to get a foothold. In the 1840s Senegalese producers were selling a few tons of peanuts to French companies. By the 1890s they were exporting an annual average of 68,000 tons and 30 years later 375,000 tons were sent out every year.

It was not until the 1860s that local missionaries discovered cocoa beans could do well in the Gold Coast. Local producers made skilful experiments but were able to export just 80lbs in 1891. But by 1905, after the industry was taken over by leading Western firms which used the local expertise, cocoa exports had risen to 5,093 tons. They grew to 13,000 tons by 1908 and 176,000 tons by 1918. Some imports kept pace. Between the early 1850s and 1900 the value of British trade with west Africa (Nigeria, Gold Coast, Sierra Leone and the Gambia) grew ninefold. In 1831 west African economies imported 2,384,000 yards of British cotton. By 1850 the figure was 17,000,000 yards.

There was an expansion of trade but it was not an immense flood. And even when there was expansion it did not mean an immediate rush to grab territory. The conventional wisdom at this period was that the British flag was a handicap to British trade. The British House of Commons select committee of 1865 recommended a 'non-expansive policy' in order not to burden the government with the costs of maintaining expensive outposts. Imperialism was seen as extremely costly. The Egyptian expedition in 1882 cost £2.3 million which required income tax to rise by 10 percent. After the defeat of the Zulus in 1879 the British government could have easily annexed the territory, but Disraeli refused, fearing that it would simply add massive cost without any corresponding reward.

Colonial office opinion held that most of Africa was economically worthless and therefore believed that occupation would be a liability. Instead of taking over colonies the British government tried to arrange lines of demarcation which set out areas of influence for its own traders and laid out those parts of Africa where it could carry out deals. Between 1875 and 1882 there were repeated efforts to settle trade areas with the French. The British government was prepared to concede Bathurst and the Gambia river possessions. Even in the 1890s the British were ready to allow French expansion in areas not considered vital.

If Britain had been the only great power it could have continued with its 'reluctant imperialism'. It could have expanded trade and developed new markets without any special need to devour new colonies. But by the late 19th century 'the world economy was notably more pluralist than before. Britain ceased to be the only fully industrialised, and indeed the only industrial economy.'[9] The new state-capitalist giants clashed with Britain and France in the latest site of potential expansion, Africa.

In the 1880s the German government launched moves to take territory where its companies were well established. The Baltic ports which had for decades stressed the merits of 'free trade' suddenly declared that the existence of rivals left no option but expansion of German control. The Hamburg Chamber of Commerce begged Bismarck to send a naval squadron to annex Cameroon in the name of the Kaiser. If Germany hesitated, they feared, others would not. In 1884 Bismarck authorised protectorates in areas where German traders were threatened by encroachment from foreign competition. He specifically mentioned Angra Pequena in south west Africa and the territory east of the Niger delta. Protectorates were declared in Togo and Cameroon.

The British reacted swiftly. Edward Hewett, the local British consul, concluded a series of agreements with rulers in the west of Cameroon. These formed the basis for the British Oil Rivers protectorate. In 1885 protectorates were formalised in the Niger districts and Bechuanaland. The previously spurned Zululand was taken in 1887. By the middle of the 1890s Kenya, Uganda and Zanzibar had fallen.

The French ruling class also sanctioned a massive expansion of territory. In 1882 a protectorate was declared in the Congo (Moyen)

area. By early 1885 the French officials had decided to resume their
advance into the western Sudan which had been temporarily halted. In
the same year gunboats were placed on the upper Niger and in 1886 the
French army began campaigns which ended in the annexation of Ivory
Coast and Guinea. In 1890 Madagascar was taken.

Many of the 'ground rules' for these appropriations were laid down
by the Congress of Berlin in 1884-5. It attempted to set up rough
guidelines by which European competitors could be secure from their
rivals. But it also speeded up the imperial process and thereby
increased the likelihood of conflict. A system where each state was out
to secure its interests at the expense of its fellows could not be policed
in the long term by gentlemen's agreements.

It is important to stress that much of the colony grabbing gave little
or no immediate economic benefit to the European powers. Some areas
were obviously exploitable—the mineral fields of South Africa, the tea
and coffee plantations of Uganda, the teeming markets of the Niger, the
cotton fields of Egypt and the Sudan. But other vast areas were
exchanged with almost no analysis of the likely benefits and were not
instantly developed. One British prime minister complained, 'We have
been engaged in drawing lines upon maps where no white man's foot
has ever trod; we have been giving away mountains and rivers and
lakes to each other, only hindered by the small impediment that we
never knew exactly where they were.'[10]

But expanding capitalist concerns, and the states which stood
alongside them, wanted control over areas which might turn out to be
as rich as the gold mines of the Transvaal (discovered in 1886) or the
diamond fields of Kimberley (discovered in 1867). Imperialism's inner
logic drove European powers to gain vast new territories. It opened up
the potential for cheap raw materials and huge markets. But it also
meant a 'New World Order' which was terrifying for some of those
who had become used to the old system. Queen Victoria wrote to her
prime minister that 'affairs are so different from what they used to
be'.[11]

Much of early imperialism was effectively 'privatised'. It was the
Royal Niger Company which acted as the agent for the British
government in west Africa, which was then challenged by the military
columns of the *Syndicat Francais du Haute-Benito* rather than the
French state. But behind these companies stood the national armies.
Imperialism and the carve up of the world laid the basis for the First
and Second World Wars. The nature of imperialism is the central
element in understanding the scramble. A second impetus was the
continuing (and in some places growing) resistance to European
colonialism. Of course, in the end, the Africans were usually defeated.
But it was often a tremendous and heroic struggle and the hostility of

local populations to European intervention forced the Western powers to do more than simply plant a flag and open the trading posts.

Pakenham recognises the strength of opposition in some cases, especially when there were great battles. He brilliantly describes the Battle of Isandlwana in 1879 where the British suffered their most humiliating defeat since the start of the century. Lord Chelmsford's army was shattered by the Zulu warriors. This victory, coming at a time when it was almost unthinkable that black African 'savages' could beat a white force, helped bring down Disraeli's government. He deals excellently with the Battle of Adowa in 1896 where Menelik's Ethiopian army faced a well armed Italian force of 18,000. He records the heroism of the Empress Taitu who led her bodyguard at the head of the force and broke the Italian line. At the end of the combat almost half the European army was either dead or missing. The news provoked rioting in most Italian cities and drove the prime minister from office.

But he misses out other examples. There is no mention of, for example, the Angolan resistance to Portuguese colonisation by people like Ngola Liluange, Nzinga Mbandi, Ngola Kanini, Mandume and others. You would not know that in Angola there were three decades of military campaigns before the colony was 'pacified' in the 1920s. There is no sense of the intransigent resistance put up by people like the Somali nationalist leader Mohammed Abdile Hassan. He fought the British for 20 years, defeating them four times despite the overwhelming difference in weaponry, and was finally beaten only by an air war.

This is not to say that all Africans fought the imperialists. Some leaders revelled in the chance to carry out a more systematic exploitation of their subjects backed by a stronger power which had fearsome weaponry. Often they delivered soldiers to fight for Europeans against Africans. The earliest French black troops were formed early in the 19th century by agreement with local chiefs. The British invasion of the Asante in 1896 employed 1,000 Hausa soldiers recruited from northern Nigeria and about 800 from the coastal peoples of the Gold Coast colony. In the next campaign against the Asante in 1900 it was possible to dispense with British troops altogether.

But the refusal of most Africans to bend the knee meant that at various points in the 1880s the European governments decided they had to annex territory or risk losing control of possible raw materials and markets. Even worse, they feared, victories against imperialism could provoke revolt elsewhere in colonies which were definitely very profitable.

In 1885, after the death of Gordon in Khartoum, Gladstone was persuaded to launch a fearfully costly punitive expedition because of the effect on other colonies. He said that the stakes were high and involved the very survival of Britain's empire in India. 'The Cabinet's decision, the PM told Hamilton (in what would today be called the domino theory) had "been determined by the regard which they felt bound to have for the effect which the triumph of the Mahdi would have on our Mahometan subjects".'[12]

Another obvious example of resistance leading to territorial shifts was the antagonism of an earlier group of white settlers to wider imperial control. But in South Africa the imperial power did not take outright control. The Boers clashed frequently with the British imperialists. They fought two major wars and inflicted terrible defeats. The second war (1899-1902) cost the British government 20,000 lives and £200 million, the equivalent today of at least £7,000 million. At the end of it there was an uneasy compromise between Boer leaders and the British government which led eventually to the Union of South Africa in 1910 controlled by Boers and Afrikaners.

Strategic reasons also played some part in the scramble, particularly for the British ruling class. Almost immediately after it was opened in 1869 the Suez Canal became a major factor in British diplomacy. It commanded both trade and military routes and proved hugely profitable for the Western shareholders who owned it. The British occupation of Egypt in 1882 was largely conditioned by the belief that France would become dominant and threaten the canal.

Later fears of another state controlling any portion of the middle and upper Nile helped the Salisbury government decide to occupy the Sudan and Uganda. At the other end of the continent, Simonstown on the Cape was Britain's most important naval base and coaling station in the world. In 1877, despite the opening of the Suez Canal, two thirds of Britain's trade with India and the East still went by the Cape route. To guard it Britain needed not only a fortress—like Gibraltar—but a fortress colony whose loyalty could be counted on. But these strategic reasons were intimately tied to the development of imperialism's military logic and cannot be divorced from it.

Another point which Pakenham ignores is resistance to imperialism in the European countries. Most of the socialist parties which came together to make up the Second International in 1889 initially opposed colonialism. It was only the drift of those parties towards open reformism that meant by 1907 the International would sanction colonial freedom only when the 'natives have achieved a sufficient cultural level'. Despite this the best of the socialists maintained a consistent and principled opposition to imperialism. Even in Britain there was resistance. In 1885 William Morris and Eleanor Marx were among the Socialist League's signatories to a denunciation of the Sudan war:

A wicked and unjust war is now being waged by the ruling and propertied classes of this country, with all the resources of civilisation at their back, against an ill-armed and semi-barbarous people whose only crime is that they have risen against a foreign oppression.[13]

For all its paternalism the manifesto is the authentic voice of protest which it is always important to remember. Imperialism was based on ruling class interests, not the interests of all of the 'British nation'. Because Pakenham's book does not begin with an understanding of imperialism, his ability to describe people and events vividly is wasted. To understand the process you would do better to look at books by people like Victor Kiernan and Basil Davidson. To grasp the economics Eric Hobsbawm's work is useful.

Notes

1   T Pakenham, *The Scramble for Africa* (Weidenfeld and Nicholson, 1991) p323.
2   Ibid, p352.
3   Ibid, p353.
4   Ibid, p337.
5   Ibid, pxvi.
6   Ibid, p111.
7   B Davidson, *Africa in Modern History* (Harmondsworth, 1978) p62.
8   T Pakenham, op cit, p18.
9   E Hobsbawm, *Age of Empire* (Harmondsworth, 1981) p51.
10   B Davidson, op cit, p81.
11   T Pakenham, op cit, p504.
12   Ibid, p263.
13   'A Manifesto against Colonial War', reprinted in *Labour Monthly*, July 1952.

Comments on Colin Barker's review of Thompson's *Customs in Common*

DAVE McNULTY

Edward Thompson is an exhilarating writer. Readers are swept along by the wit and verve of his prose. This is precisely why we need to be careful about where he is taking us. Colin Barker's review of *Customs in Common* in *International Socialism* 55 uncritically repeats Thompson's comparison of 18th century England with a Latin American junta or banana republic ruled by a gang of predatory parasites. As Perry Anderson pointed out 12 years ago this isn't very helpful. England wasn't a semi-colonial dependency, it was on the way to becoming the world's major imperialist power. Whigs weren't simply enriching themselves, mere gangsters outside of class interests. Rather they developed a state machine which served capitalist interests remarkably well.[1]

Further, when Thompson describes them as 'parasites' it is not merely abuse. He has a concept of 'parasitism' whereby a particular group can latch onto the state and use it for self enrichment without altering the wider social process on which it is parasitic. He has used this, citing 18th century England as an analogy, to explain what happened in the Soviet Union. He has speculated that the Soviet Union is arguably a more classless society than those of the West, that if it could shake loose its 'parasitism' it could unleash the socialist potential inherent in its state ownership.[2]

All historians write about the present when they examine the past even if they aren't aware of it. Thompson does so explicitly. We shouldn't go along with wrong political arguments through lack of attention.

Colin argues that 'custom was necessarily the property of the people; law was not', that custom was a system of popular justice which, despite its blemishes, prefigures socialism whereas law replaces popular control with state control. I think both law and custom are more complicated than this and so is the interaction between them.

Colin should have retained Thompson's caution and ambivalence which he urges us to ignore. When crowds referred to 'regraters' and 'forestallers' they were referring to specific legal offences. This wasn't to put human need before market forces but to set limits to the operation of the market: to keep profits reasonable and not excessive by preventing prices being raised 'artificially', say, through hoarding. Workers didn't just invoke old laws to legitimise their actions. They campaigned and with some success to introduce legislation in their favour. Campaigning for these laws in the 18th century and to defend them in the early 19th century was crucial to the building of workers' organisations and the development of class consciousness. When groups of workers organise to present detailed programmes for laws to regulate their trade, is this less of an anticipation of socialist society than the sale of wives?

'Custom of the trade' on the other hand assumed a common interest between masters and men. This had obvious implications for the type of actions which workers would take and could be a barrier to the development of class consciousness. When they felt under threat workers would invent or develop 'customary practices' which they argued were a property right which like any other should have the protection of law. If the rule of law is so uncomplicatedly a weapon of state repression why was it necessary to abandon it so frequently between 1793 and 1820? Why couldn't the state get convictions against radicals? Why did an 1830s jury return a verdict of justifiable homicide when a policeman was killed during a demonstration?

The straightforward point is that the 'rule of law' is an advance on totally arbitrary government. It does put some checks on power otherwise exercised unrestrictedly. We can accept this without having any liberal illusions in the class nature of law and the state.

Notes

1   P Anderson, *Arguments within English Marxism* (London, 1980), pp88-92.
2   E P Thompson, *The Poverty of Theory* (London, 1978), pp162-172.

The Socialist Workers Party is one of an international grouping of socialist organisations:

AUSTRALIA: International Socialists, GPO Box 1473N, Melbourne 3001

BELGIUM: Socialisme International, Rue Lovinfosse 60, 4030 Grivengée, Belgium

BRITAIN: Socialist Workers Party, PO Box 82, London E3

CANADA: International Socialists, PO Box 339, Station E, Toronto, Ontario M6H 4E3

CYPRUS: Ergatiki Dimokratria, PO Box 7280, Nicosia

DENMARK: Internationale Socialister, Ryesgade 813, 8000 Arhus C, Denmark

FRANCE: Socialisme International, BP 189, 75926 Paris Cedex 19

GERMANY: Sozialistische Arbeitergruppe, Wolfsgangstrasse 81, W-6000 Frankfurt 1

GREECE: Organosi Sosialisliki Epanastasi, c/o Workers Solidarity, PO Box 8161, Athens 100 10, Greece

HOLLAND: International Socialists, PO Box 9720, 3506 GR Utrecht

IRELAND: Socialist Workers Movement, PO Box 1648, Dublin 8

NORWAY: Internasjonale Socialisterr, Postboks 5370, Majorstua, 0304 Oslo 3

POLAND: Solidarność Socjalistyczna, PO Box 12, 01-900 Warszawa 118

SOUTH AFRICA: International Socialists of South Africa, PO Box 18530, Hillbrow 2038, Johannesberg

UNITED STATES: International Socialist Organisation, PO Box 16085, Chicago, Illinois 60616

The following issues of *International Socialism* (second series) are available price £2.50 (including postage) from IS Journal , PO Box 82, London E3 3LH.

International Socialism 2:56 Autumn 1992
Chris Harman: The Return of the National Question ★ Dave Treece: Why the Earth Summit failed ★ Mike Gonzalez: Can Castro survive? ★ Lee Humber and John Rees: The good old cause—an interview with Christopher Hill ★ Ernest Mandel: The Impasse of Schematic Dogmatism ★

International Socialism 2:55 Summer 1992
Alex Callinicos: Race and class ★ Lee Sustar: Racism and class struggle in the American Civil War era ★ Lindsey German and Peter Morgan: Prospects for socialists—an interview with Tony Cliff ★ Robert Service: Did Lenin lead to Stalin? ★ Samuel Farber: In defence of democratic revolutionary socialism ★ David Finkel: Defending 'October' or sectarian dogmatism? ★ Robin Blackburn: Reply to John Rees ★ John Rees: Dedicated followers of fashion ★ Colin Barker: In praise of custom ★ Sheila McGregor: Revolutionary witness ★

International Socialism 2:54 Spring 1992
Sharon Smith: Twilight of the American dream ★ Mike Haynes: Class and crisis—the transition in eastern Europe ★ Costas Kossis: A miracle without end? Japanese capitalism and the world economy ★ Alex Callinicos: Capitalism and the state system: A reply to Nigel Harris ★ Steven Rose: Do animals have rights? ★ John Charlton: Crime and class in the 18th century ★ John Rees: Revolution, reform and working class culture ★ Chris Harman: Blood simple ★

International Socialism 2:52 Autumn 1991
John Rees: In defence of October ★ Ian Taylor and Julie Waterson: The political crisis in Greece—an interview with Maria Styllou and Panos Garganas ★ Paul McGarr: Mozart, overture to revolution ★ Lee Humber: Class, class consciousness and the English Revolution ★ Derek Howl: The legacy of Hal Draper ★

International Socialism 2:51 Summer 1991
Chris Harman: The state and capitalism today ★ Alex Callinicos: The end of nationalism? ★ Sharon Smith: Feminists for a strong state? ★ Colin Sparks and Sue Cockerill: Goodbye to the Swedish miracle ★ Simon Phillips: The South African Communist Party and the South African working class ★ John Brown: Class conflict and the crisis of feudalism ★

International Socialism 2:49 Winter 1990
Chris Bambery: The decline of the Western Communist Parties ★ Ernest Mandel: A theory which has not withstood the test of time ★ Chris Harman: Criticism which does not withstand the test of logic ★ Derek Howl: The law of value In the USSR ★ Terry Eagleton: Shakespeare and the class struggle ★ Lionel Sims: Rape and pre-state societies ★ Sheila McGregor: A reply to Lionel Sims ★

International Socialism 2:48 Autumn 1990
Lindsey German: The last days of Thatcher ★ John Rees: The new imperialism ★ Neil Davidson and Donny Gluckstein: Nationalism and the class struggle in Scotland ★ Paul McGarr: Order out of chaos ★

International Socialism 2:47 Summer 1990
Ahmed Shawki: Black liberation and socialism in the United States ★ Fifty years since Trotsky's death ★ John Rees: Trotsky and the dialectic ★ Chris Harman: From Trotsky to state capitalism ★ Steve Wright: Hal Draper's' Marxism ★

International Socialism 2:46 Winter 1989
Chris Harman: The storm breaks ★ Alex Callinicos: Can South Africa be reformed? ★ John Saville: Britain, the Marshall Plan and the Cold War ★ Sue Clegg: Against the stream ★ John Rees: The rising bourgeoisie ★

International Socialism 2:45 Autumn 1989
Sheila McGregor: Rape, pornography and capitalism ★ Boris Kagarlitsky: The market instead of democracy? ★ Chris Harman: From feudalism to capitalism ★ plus Mike Gonzalez and Sabby Sagall discuss Central America ★

International Socialism 2:18 Winter 1983
Donny Gluckstein: Workers' councils in Western Europe ★ Jane Ure Smith: The early Communist press in Britain ★ John Newsinger: The Bolivian Revolution ★ Andy Durgan: Largo Caballero and Spanish socialism ★ M Barker and A Beezer: Scarman and the language of racism ★

International Socialism 2:14 Winter 1981
Chris Harman: The riots of 1981 ★ Dave Beecham: Class struggle under the Tories ★ Tony Cliff: Alexandra Kollontai ★ L James and A Paczuska: Socialism needs feminism ★ reply to Cliff on Zetkin ★ Feminists In the labour movement ★

International Socialism 2:13 Summer 1981
Chris Harman: The crisis last time ★ Tony Cliff: Clara Zetkin ★ Ian Birchall: Left Social Democracy In the French Popular Front ★ Pete Green: Alternative Economic Strategy ★ Tim Potter: The death of Eurocommunism ★

International Socialism 2:12 Spring 1981
Jonathan Neale: The Afghan tragedy ★ Lindsey German: Theories of patriarchy ★ Ray Challinor: McDouall and Physical Force Chartism ★ S Freeman & B Vandesteeg: Unproductive labour ★ Alex Callinicos: Wage labour and capitalism ★ Italian fascism ★ Marx's theory of history ★ Cabral ★

International Socialism 2:11 Winter 1980
Rip Bulkeley et al: CND In the 50s ★ Marx's theory of crisis and its critics ★ Andy Durgan: Revolutionary anarchism in Spain ★ Alex Callinicos: Politics or abstract thought ★ Fascism in Europe ★ Marilyn Monroe ★

International Socialism 2:10 Autumn 1980
Steve Jeffreys: The CP and the rank and file ★ Ian Birchall: A short history of *NLR* ★ Nigel Harris: Crisis and the core of the system ★ Cuba ★ English Civil War ★

International Socialism 2:9 Summer 1980
Callinicos/Rogers: Southern Africa after Mugabe ★ Chris Harman: Theories of the crisis ★ Pete Goodwin: *Beyond the Fragments* ★ Debate on Cuba ★ Raymond Williams & Co ★